IMAGES
of America

SUFFIELD'S OLD BRIDGE NEIGHBORHOOD

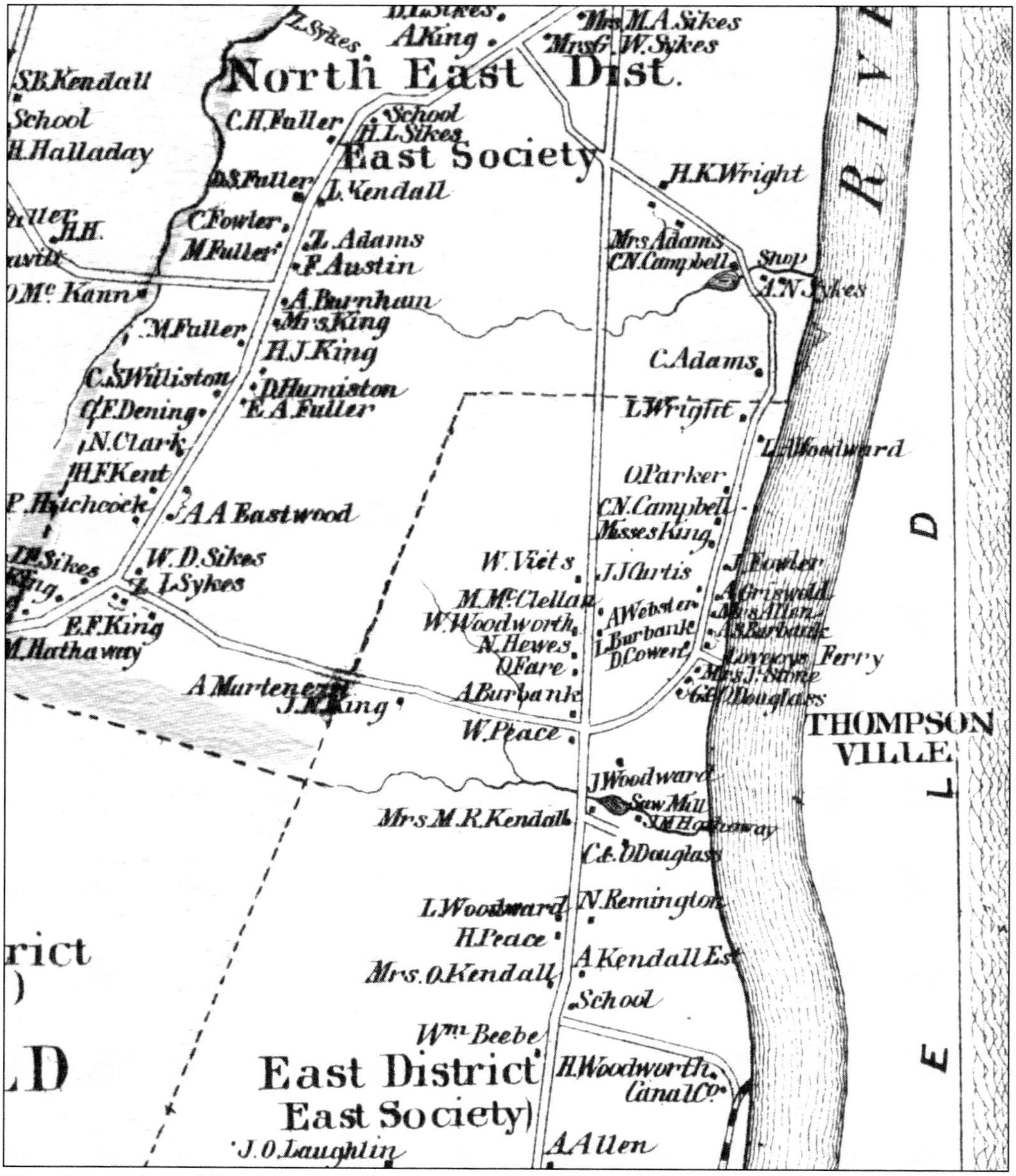

This detail of a Suffield map from the 1869 Baker and Tilden Atlas of Hartford City and County depicts parts of Suffield's East and North East school districts. Near Lovejoy's Ferry (center right), on the Connecticut River, is where the Thompsonville-Suffield Bridge would later be situated. (Courtesy Art Sikes.)

On the cover: See page 49. (Courtesy Tavino family.)

IMAGES
of America

Suffield's Old Bridge Neighborhood

Laurie Tavino

ARCADIA
PUBLISHING

ISBN 978-0-7385-6582-8

Published by Arcadia Publishing
Charleston, South Carolina

Printed in the United States of America

Library of Congress Control Number: 2009921276

For all general information contact Arcadia Publishing at:
Telephone 843-853-2070
Fax 843-853-0044
E-mail sales@arcadiapublishing.com
For customer service and orders:
Toll-Free 1-888-313-2665

Visit us on the Internet at www.arcadiapublishing.com

To all the loved ones,
some long since passed,
who took the precious time
to tell me a story.

Contents

ACKNOWLEDGMENTS

I consider myself fortunate to come from a family that collected and saved everything. The Tavino family, including Uncle Pat Lamagna, took an unusual number of photographs and loved to share the stories and folklore of their youth and the old country. I spent over two years researching, interviewing, and gathering images to add to this collection. A portion of the source material was derived from genealogies and family documents. The anglicizing of names, multiplicity of languages, plus variances in spellings made this a challenge.

I thank all my current and former neighbors and their descendants, far too many to list here, who took the time to dig through closets and attics for this project—it could not have been accomplished without their help.

Special thanks to my mother, Louise Tavino, for her support and to Alice Dudek Czyz, Stanley Dynia, Patricia McHugh Roehl, and the Caramazza, Sullivan, Taylor, and Underwood families for sharing their large collections of images and writings with me. Former Suffield AA football team members Lenny Krogh and Everett Brown; journalist Heather Lockwood; Mary Anne Zak, author of *Sacred Heart Church, 1882–2004*; Adrienne Saint-Pierre, curator of the Fairfield Museum; Jen Thermes, author of *Sam Bennett's New Shoes*; and former Sea Scout commodore Roger Crossland, retired U.S. Navy captain, all volunteered their expertise. Images of Leslie Adams from the *Sunday Republican* (from September 9, 1951) are copyright of the Republican Company, all rights reserved, and reprinted with permission.

The staffs at the Ashfield Historical Society, Connecticut State Library, Enfield Central and Middle Libraries, Enfield Historical Society (EHS), Suffield Historical Society (SHS), Suffield's Kent Memorial Library (KML), Suffield Town Hall, and the Springfield Public Library were very helpful and generous.

Special recognition goes to the late Delphina H. Clark, former Suffield historian, who I never met but whose documentation I relied on for so much.

A most grateful, heartfelt thanks goes to my editor-historian contributors: Rich Matyskiela, Mike Miller, Art Sikes, Lester Smith, and Mary Anne Zak. Finally, I could not have produced the exhibits or this book without the countless hours of photographic and editorial help from my husband, Ray Pioggia.

Introduction

In 2007, a photo-documentary titled "Tales from the East Side" debuted at Suffield's Kent Memorial Library. It was a compilation of the author's numerous family photographs, along with collected bits of local history about her East Suffield neighborhood, its farms and businesses, and its connection to the town of Thompsonville in the early 20th century. Research for the exhibit yielded a substantial collection of images and history from surviving older neighbors and family members. The surprising success and public interest in the show led to even more images and to this book, *Suffield's Old Bridge Neighborhood.*

The north-central Connecticut towns of Suffield and Enfield, located between Springfield, Massachusetts, and Hartford, Connecticut, face each other across the Connecticut River. This area had been home to indigenous Native Americans for centuries. In the late 1600s, early English settlers, attracted to the fertile valley of "Ye Greate River," set their homes in farming communities. In 1691, the first of a series of ferry crossings connected the two towns. In 1808, a bridge was constructed here, the first to span the river for its entire length in Connecticut.

In 1828, Orrin Thompson of Suffield established a carpet mill in Enfield. Over the next century, this industry grew into a huge complex of buildings with thousands of employees. The village that sprang up around the mill became known as Thompsonville. Also known as the "Carpet City," this mill town called across the Atlantic Ocean to thousands of people hungry for new opportunities. Qualified weavers from Scotland were the first to arrive. Irish laborers and French Canadian masons expanded the mill in the 1800s. The early 20th century witnessed a burgeoning population of predominantly Polish, Italian, Greek, Lithuanian, and English immigrants. Initially many new arrivals moved into homes provided by the carpet company. Some of these neighborhoods still bear names such as Frenchtown and Cottage Green.

In 1893, an iron bridge was opened, connecting Main Street in Thompsonville with the east side of Suffield at the convergence of what is now River Boulevard, Burbank Avenue, and Thompsonville Road. The spillover of Thompsonville's immigrant workforce created a neighborhood of great diversity. This area of East Suffield, already home to established Yankee families, was culturally becoming more a part of Thompsonville than Suffield.

What occurred here reflected America's changing landscape. Even though each newly arrived group of immigrants suffered discrimination, ethnicities were woven together as the next generation came up, speaking a common language and bringing a unique American culture into the homes of their old country parents.

Chapter 3, titled "Suffield's East Side," features some of the neighborhood schools and social clubs that people living in the vicinity of the bridge had contact with. Although for many there were more social and economic ties to Thompsonville, the old bridge neighbors intermingled within the two towns' established communities. These photographs give a hint of the lifestyle of an era. Images of teams, clubhouses, and quaint educational facilities capture a glimpse of the fashions and leisurely pursuits of the time, which helped to provide respite from farm and factory.

Comprising nearly half of this book, the fourth chapter, titled "Families, Farms, and Businesses," demonstrates how, within a few square miles, an entire cross-section of newly established Americans lived and worked closely together, cultivated their dreams, and either passed on their ethnic heritage or chose to shed it. Shared experiences run through this chapter. Besides Thompsonville's industry and immigration, the economic force of the tobacco industry dominated. Disruptive events such as two world wars and the heart-breaking devastation of tuberculosis changed the future for many.

This neighborhood had the flavor of ancient recipes and the sounds of old country dialects and accents. Several generations of a family often lived with or near each other. Most everyone had gardens; even steep riverbanks were tilled. Today not many remember "the Patch," located between Douglas and Woodworth Streets, where residents from both sides of the river gardened. Some photographs depict how open this part of the neighborhood once was.

By 1971, the carpet industry relocated to the American south, and the aged Thompsonville-Suffield Bridge was demolished. This was truly the end of an era. The loss of traffic and businesses changed this part of East Suffield into a quiet neighborhood. At the same time, Thompsonville's glory days faded, along with its aging, abandoned mill buildings. However, by the 1990s, the site of the Bigelow-Hartford Carpet Mills was listed in the National Register of Historic Places, and the restored waters of the Connecticut River earned its designation as an American Heritage River.

While researching one subject, oftentimes another may fall into your lap. Historical tidbits and little-known treasures such as lone graves, hidden shoes, and lost letters are like time capsules. These items lend color and intrigue to the history of a home or neighborhood. Found in the wall of a house was an especially moving letter from an ailing Civil War soldier to his parents. Far from home, he writes of his anguish and homesickness. Old landmarks and natural land formations, aptly named by earlier residents, have fortunately been represented in paintings and photographs. Other cultural gems such as herbal remedies or superstitious beliefs can only be documented and retold. Such "curiosities" have come to light in the research for *Suffield's Old Bridge Neighborhood* and are gathered together in chapter 5.

Too seldom are pictures available of the artists, street peddlers, and palm-reading gypsies who used to "ply their wares." Fortunately an eccentric genius can be remembered in the photographs in the last chapter. Though he chose to live the life of a recluse, he did allow a newspaper interview.

Unlike the grand architectural landmarks pictured in other Images of America books, the pages that follow tell about a small locality, its people, and their process of becoming American. Sometimes simple family photographs are all that remain as evidence. Not every ethnic group, family, or business is equally represented here, as not everyone took photographs or even owned a camera.

History, past and present, is a living thing. It grows, goes through changes, and lives in our minds. Books, photographs, and films help memories stay alive. It is the author's hope that this book will not only provide something of interest to everyone but perhaps inspire others to collect and conserve similar material. Like carving one's initials in a tree, it proclaims and acknowledges that "we were here."

One

The Connecticut River

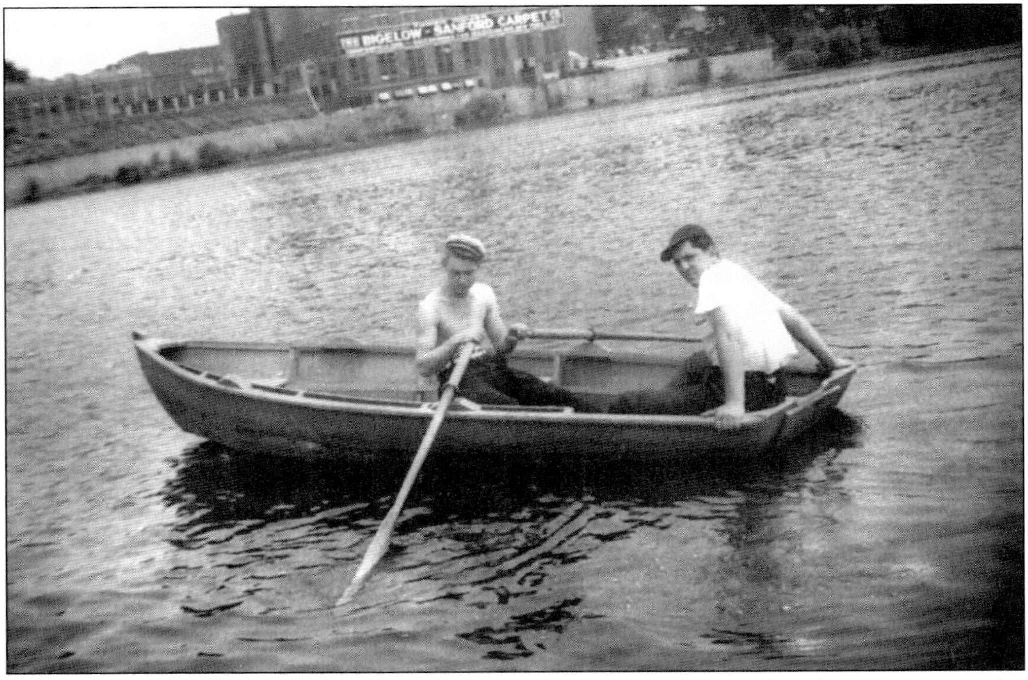

Charlie Albert (left) and an unidentified companion enjoy fair-weather boating on a calm day, just upriver from the Thompsonville-Suffield Bridge in north-central Connecticut. In the centuries going back to Colonial times, this particular stretch of river saw ferries, then bridges. It is a curious mix of conditions and circumstances that determine a specific geographical location where a river will be crossed. (Courtesy Underwood family.)

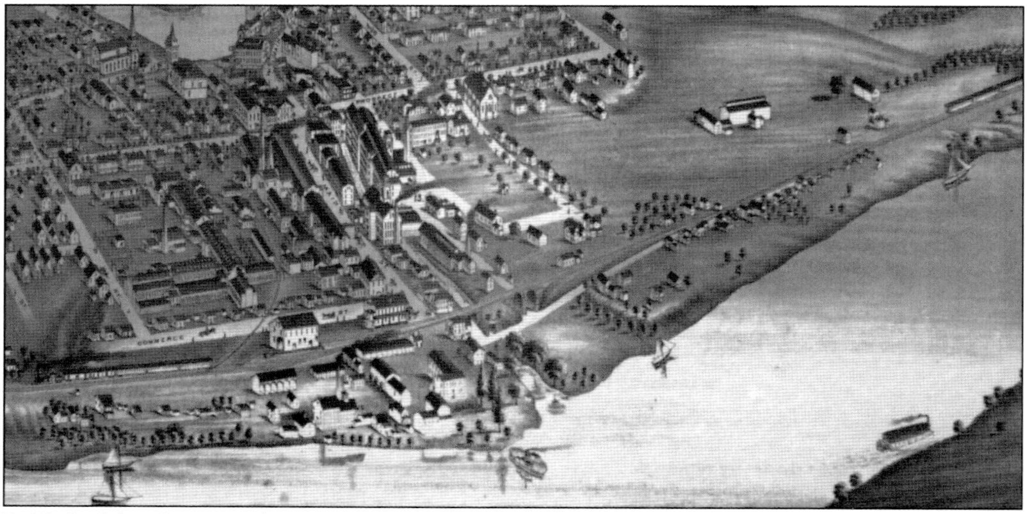

Published by O. H. Bailey and Company in Boston, an 1878 map shows a bird's-eye view of Thompsonville's commercial district, the Connecticut River, and a wedge of the Suffield shoreline at the bottom right. Predating the iron bridge that connected the two towns, ferry services provided transportation. Not visible in this image, downstream to the right, are the Enfield Falls, the Windsor Locks Canal, and the old covered bridge that connected Enfield and Suffield. (Courtesy EHS.)

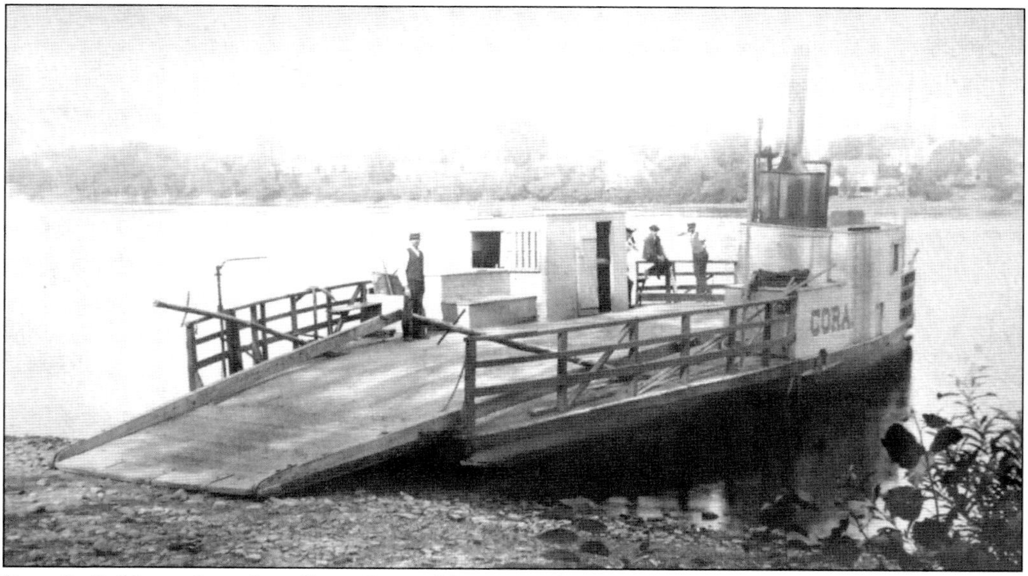

East Suffield resident Servillius Griswold operated *Cora*, the steam-powered ferry, until the Thompsonville-Suffield Bridge opened in 1893. Vague records show that there were several ferry services along River Road (later called River Boulevard) dating back to 1691. Over the centuries, owners changed hands often. Some of the names mentioned in town records are Pengilley, Lovejoy, Sikes, Kibbe, Abbe, Trumble, and Adams. (Courtesy EHS.)

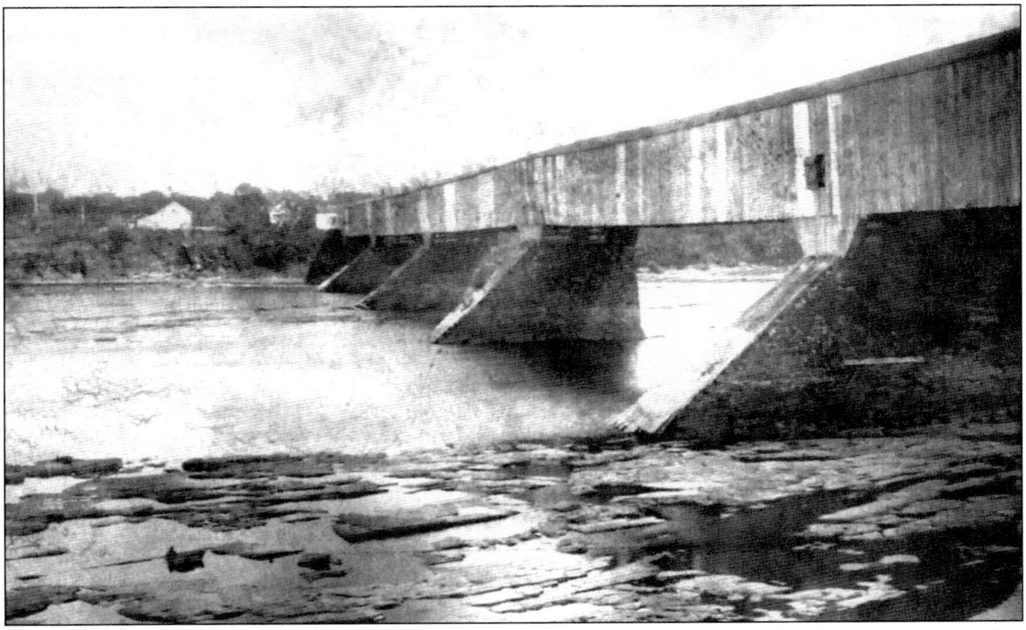

"The bridge was opened in 1809, a marvelous new convenience. It was the first span across the Connecticut River for its entire length" states Suffield records. After collapsing in 1821, it was rebuilt this time as a covered bridge and opened again in 1832. This connection between Suffield and Enfield lasted until February 1900, when an ice jam carried away part of the bridge along with its attendant, who survived. Scant remnants of its piers are still visible. (Courtesy KML.)

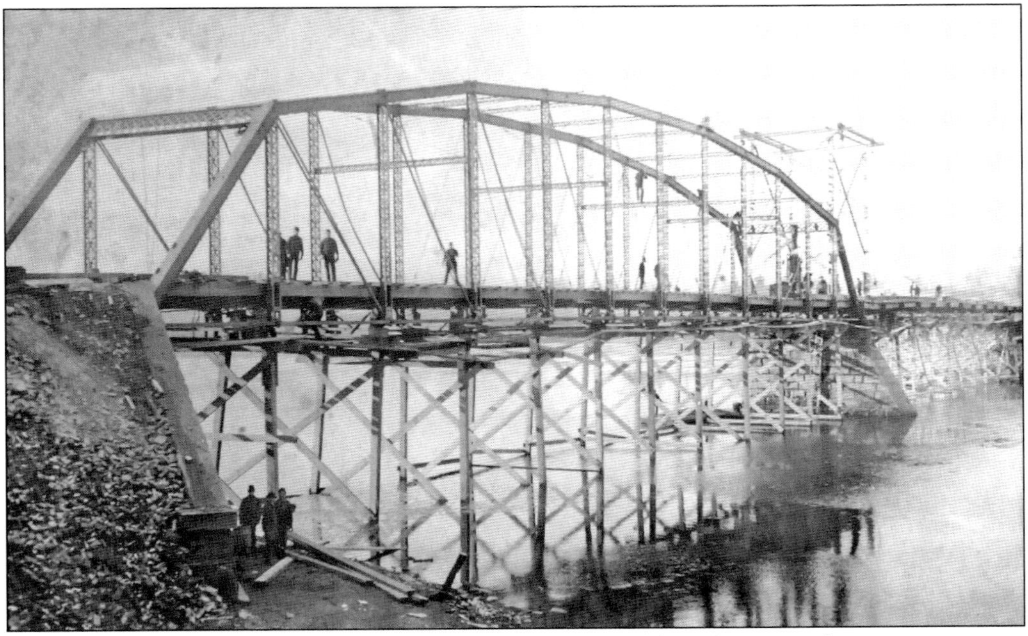

A mile and a half to the north, the Thompsonville-Suffield Bridge was a five-span iron-truss structure. This photograph shows it under construction, which began in August 1892. The opening date was February 20, 1893. The bridge crossed over the Connecticut River and connected Main Street in downtown Thompsonville to Suffield's eastern shore at the convergence of Burbank Avenue, River Boulevard, and Thompsonville Road. (Courtesy EHS.)

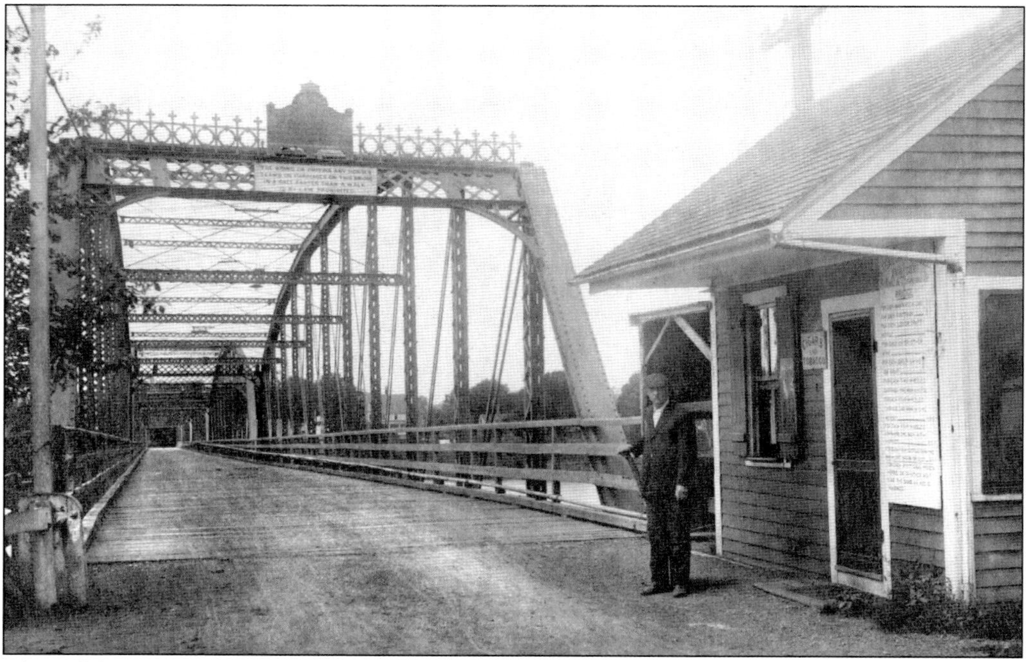

The toll keeper stands ready at the eastern entrance of the Thompsonville-Suffield Bridge. The sign at the right lists the crossing fees for everything from goats to draft horses and wheeled carriages. Bridge traffic was heavy, as Thompsonville was a major business and shopping area, much closer and more convenient to East Suffield residents than their own town's center. (Courtesy Bob Sullivan.)

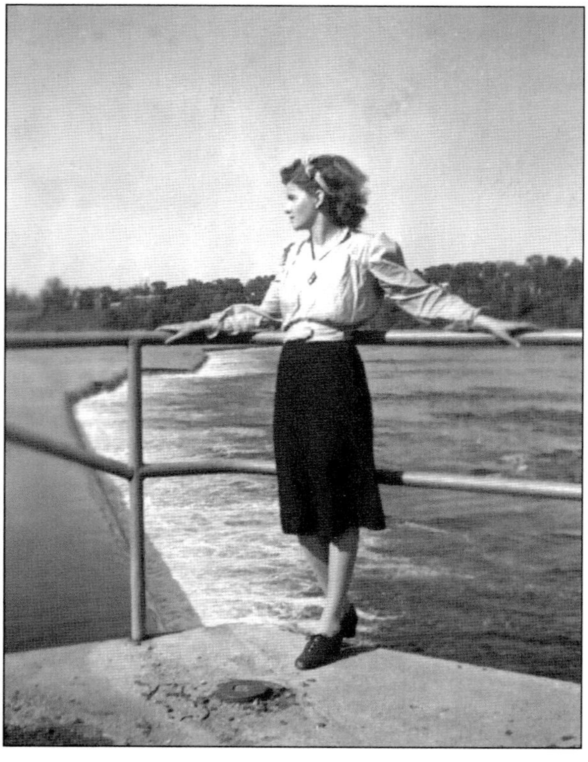

In Colonial times, southbound boats carrying commodities could get better prices if they sold their goods in Warehouse Point or better yet, Hartford. But to reach those destinations, watermen risked the danger of shooting the rapids at Enfield. The Windsor Locks Canal and the Enfield Dam were built to bypass the Enfield rapids as the dam maintained navigable water upstream of the canal. Lucy Czyz stands near the northern lock overlooking the dam in this 1940s photograph. (Courtesy Alice Dudek Czyz.)

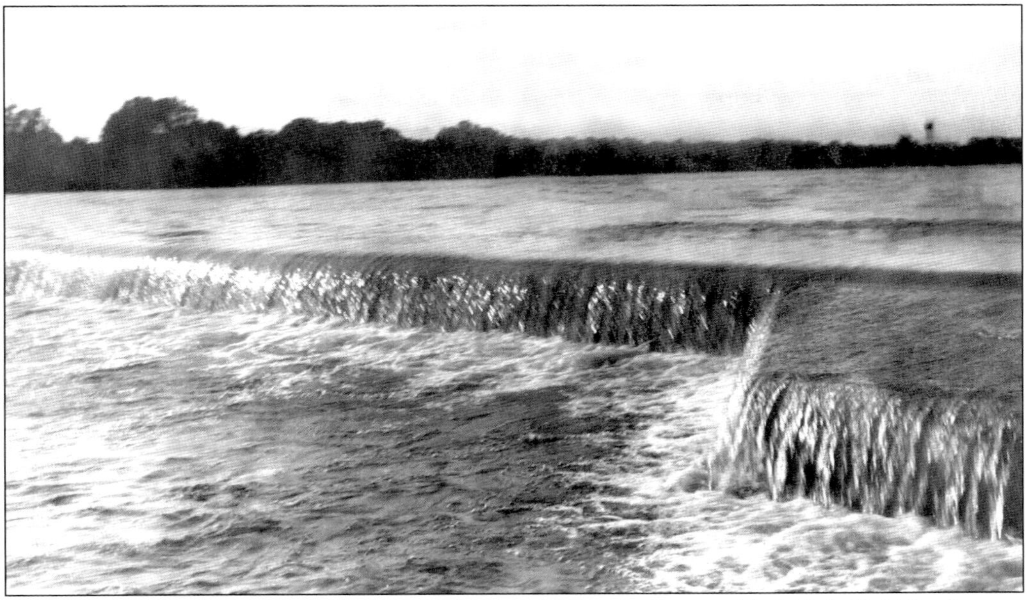

Both of these photographs show the Enfield Dam before the current Enfield-Suffield Bridge was built. In the late 1920s, Luisa Tavino once again warned her children not to go in the river. In spite of this, when the river was running high, her daughters decided to go out with a friend in a rowboat. They were teenage girls and tried to row against the current, but it was too strong for them. Fear of the approaching falls started a panic. Frantic prayers and screams got the attention of people on the Enfield shore. Finally they managed to get to land on the Suffield side just before reaching the dam. Even though a local newspaper reported the event the next day, it took 30 years for the girls to tell their mothers. (Above, courtesy Robert Underwood; below, courtesy EHS.)

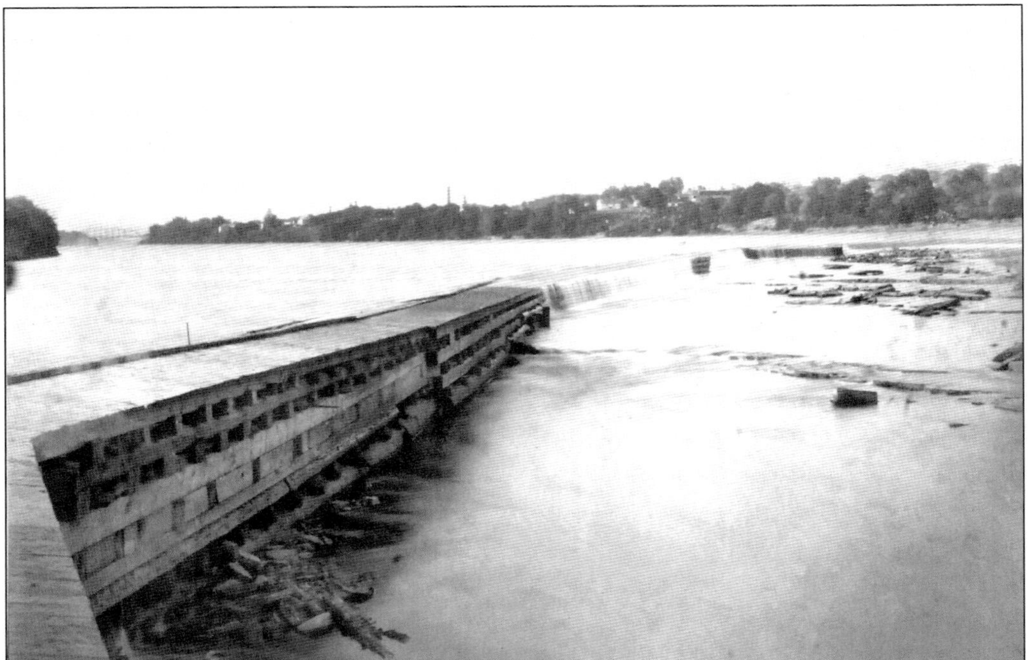

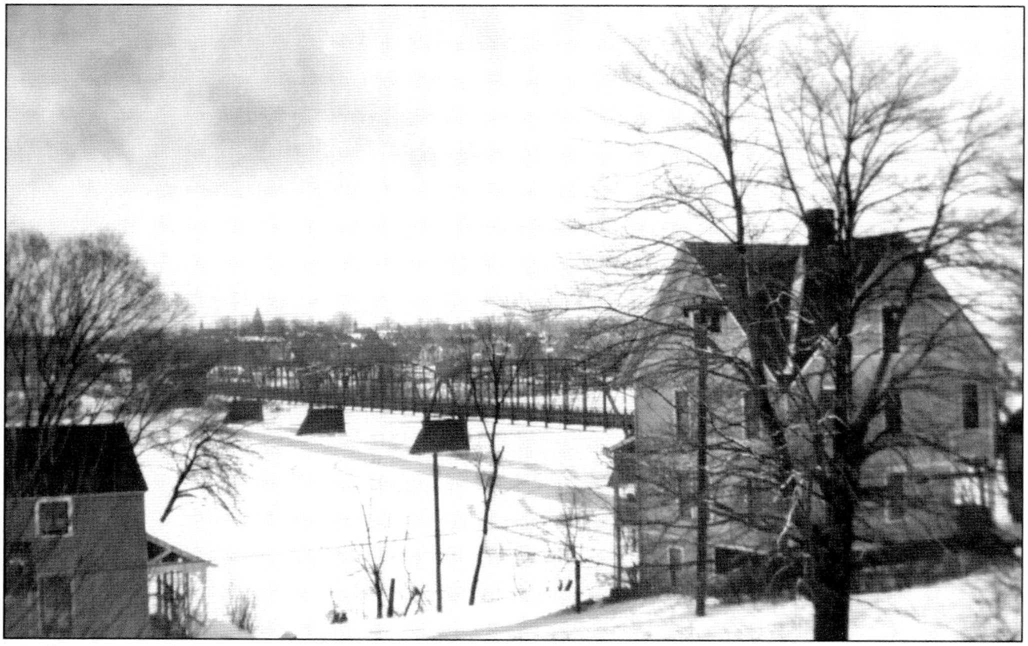

Chilly scenes of the Thompsonville-Suffield Bridge spanning the snow-covered river were taken from attic windows on Suffield's east side. Years ago, it was common for the river to freeze over, which people took advantage of in many ways. People skated upriver for miles, and some held horse-and-sleigh races. Pedestrians often took shortcuts across the solid ice to get from one town to the other, bypassing the toll bridge. Ice harvesting in the Connecticut Valley was a thriving business. It was difficult and dangerous seasonal work affected by weather conditions and the thickness of the ice. Ice-harvesting jobs were available during the coldest part of the year, and there were usually many unemployed farmers and carpenters available to fill the positions. The industry thrived until refrigerators replaced the icebox in the late 1930s. (Courtesy Tavino family.)

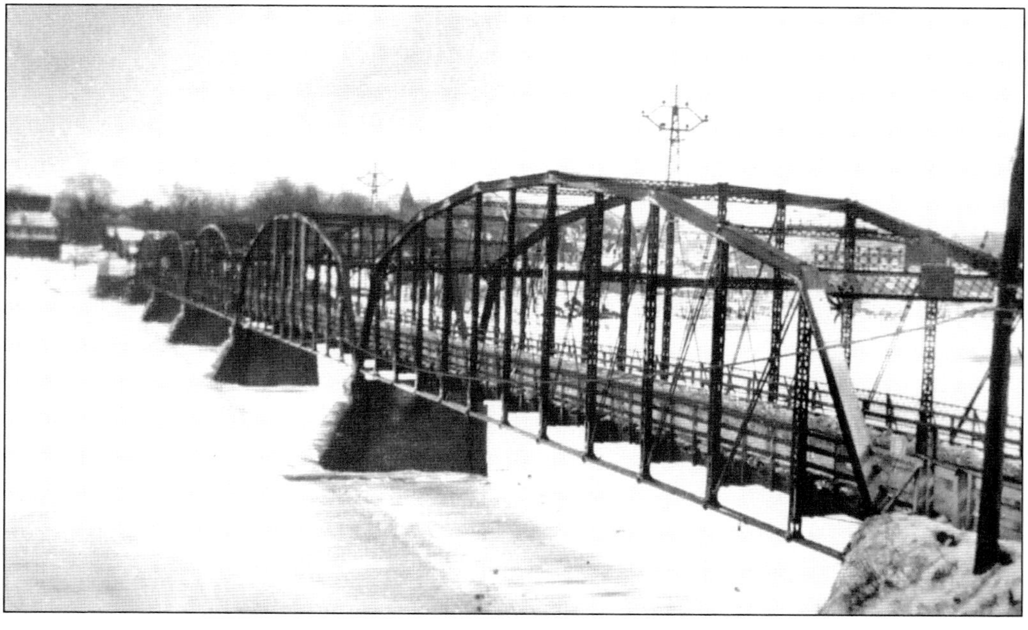

Jo Tavino stands across the street from a barnlike structure on the riverbank in East Suffield. Blocks of ice were stored in buildings like this along the river's edge, well-insulated with hay or sawdust. The Griswold family; farmers, boatmen and residents of River Road for over a century, had this barn built in the 1850s and converted it into a house around 1937. It was later home to the Alexopoulos family for 53 years. (Courtesy Tavino family.)

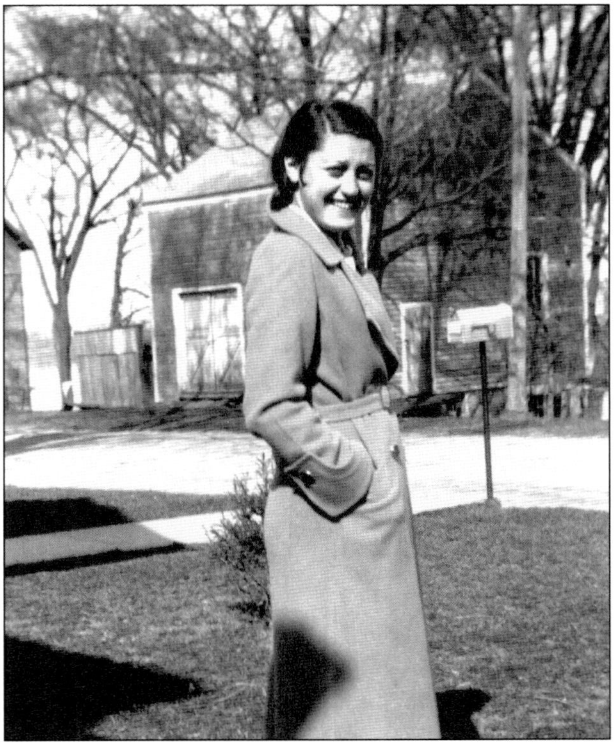

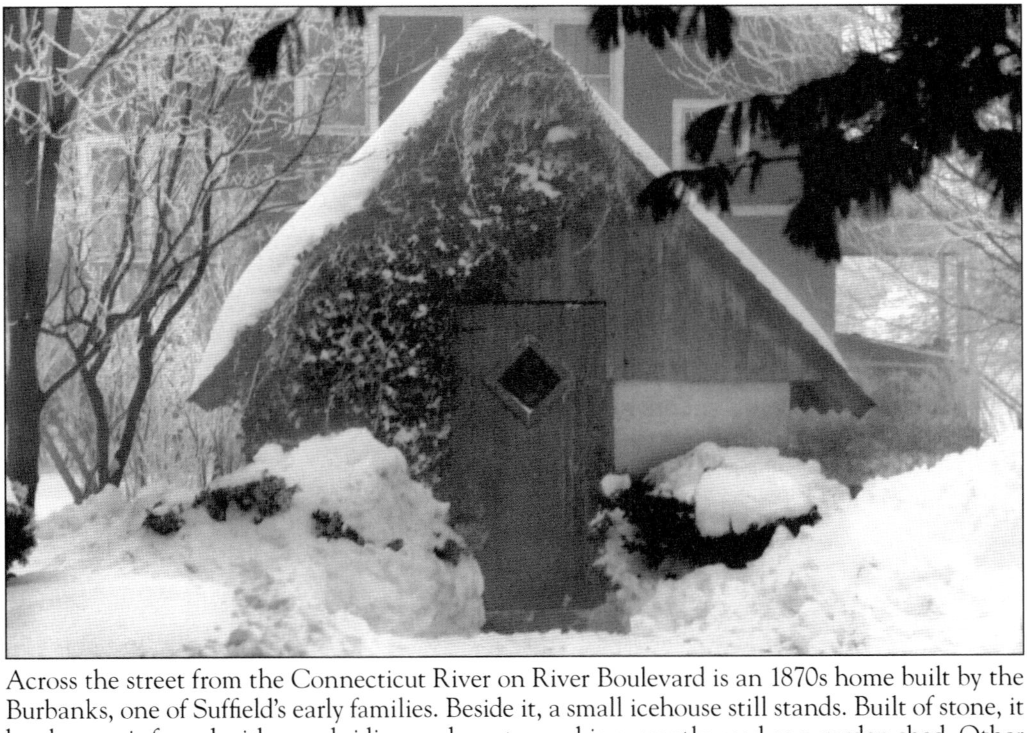

Across the street from the Connecticut River on River Boulevard is an 1870s home built by the Burbanks, one of Suffield's early families. Beside it, a small icehouse still stands. Built of stone, it has been reinforced with wood siding and mortar and is currently used as a garden shed. Other homes along the river had dugouts in the riverbanks for that same purpose. (Photograph by Laurie Tavino.)

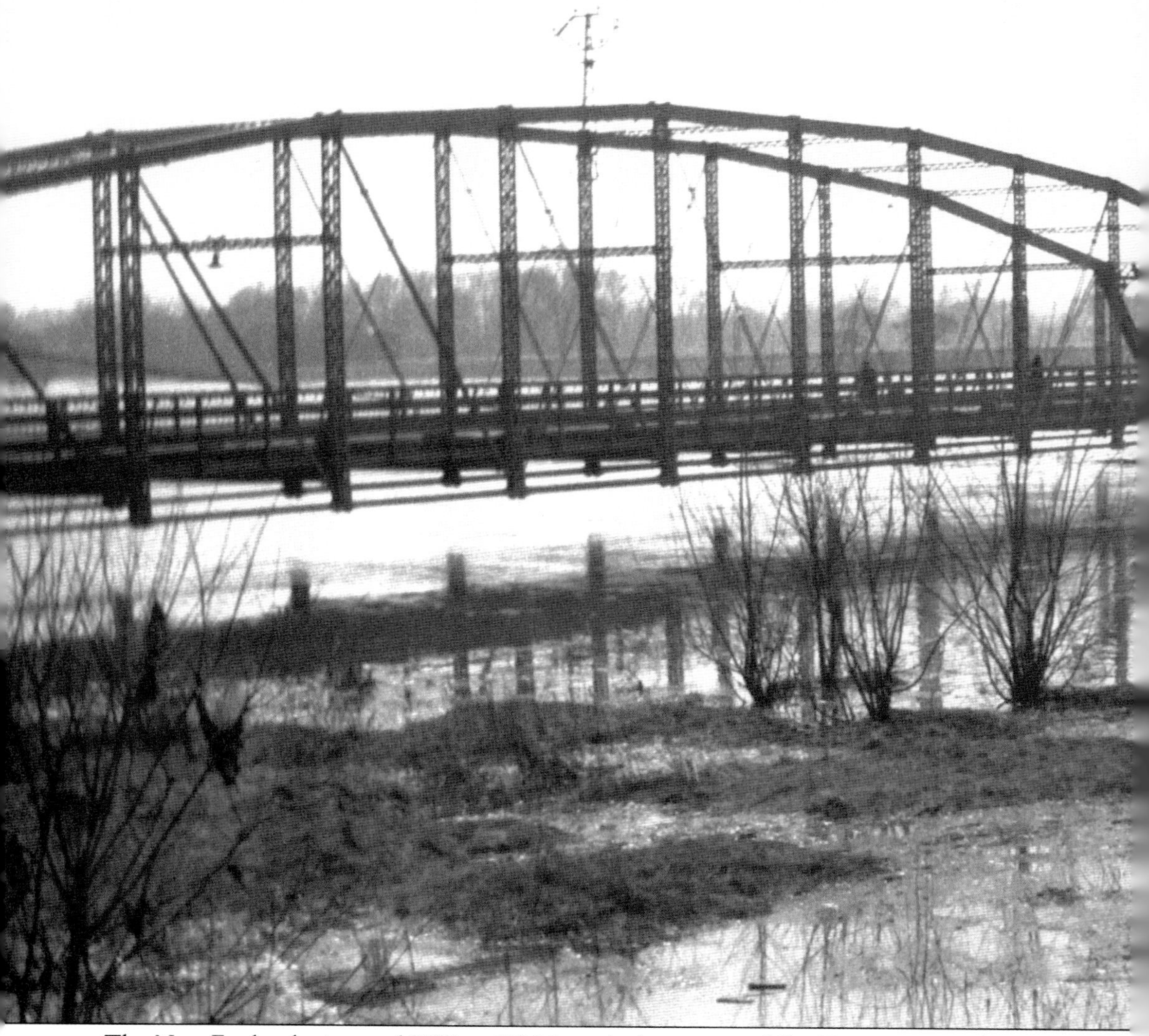

The New England winter of 1935 to 1936 brought heavy snowfalls. Temperatures plunged and turned the rivers and their tributaries into ice. Spring came early, breaking the ice into enormous chunks and setting them loose downstream. Next came torrential rains and melting snow. Ice blocks battered dams and bridges. Devastating flooding took place throughout New England and as far south as Virginia. It was called the great flood of 1936. This photograph of the swollen

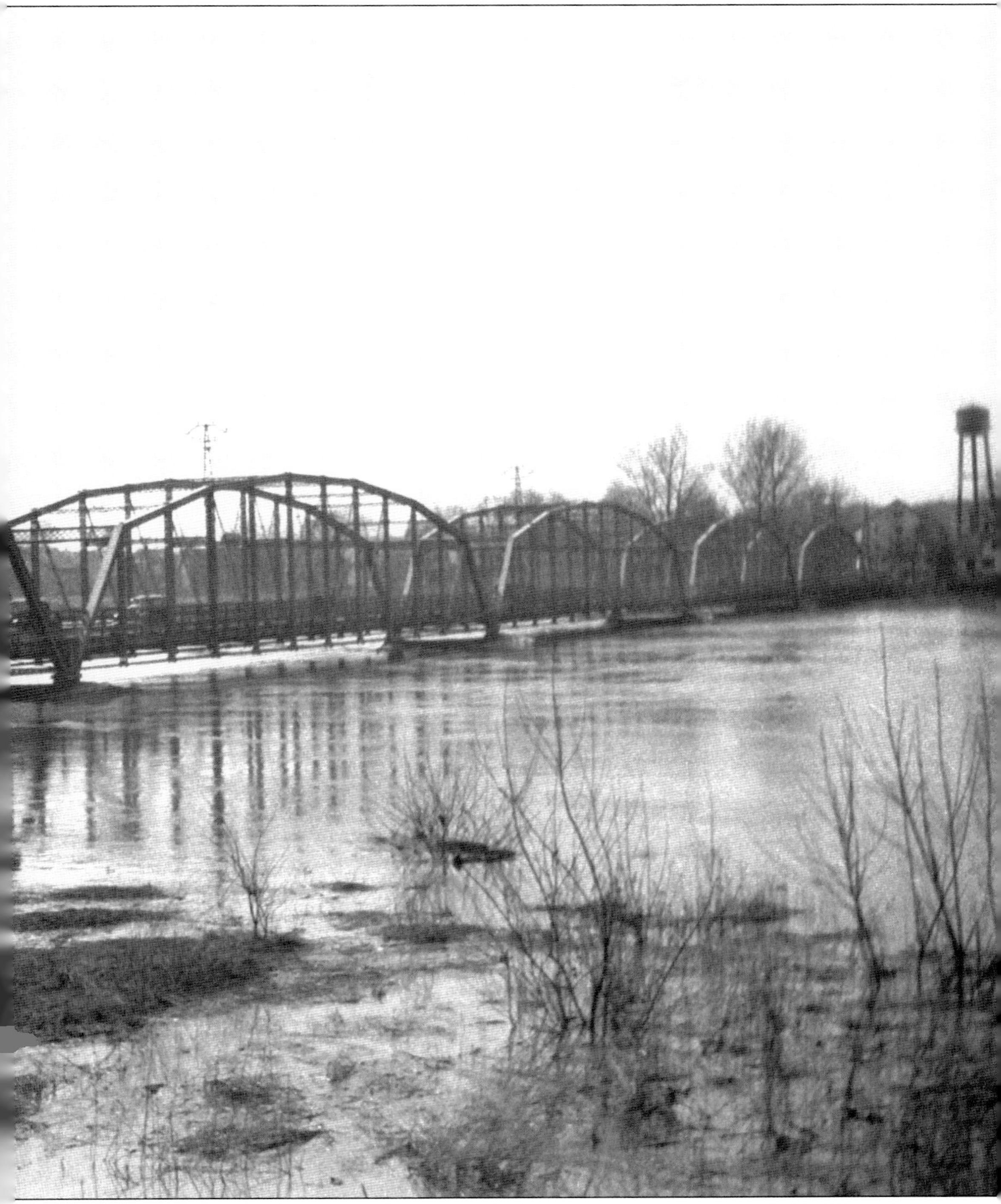

Connecticut River was taken from Thompsonville facing southwest toward Suffield. When the river reached dangerously high levels, carpet mill employees in Thompsonville were notified that the bridge would be closing soon. Suffield resident May Merrill left work, running as fast as she could across the bridge to get home. She recalled feeling the bridge vibrating from the force of the raging current. (Courtesy Tavino family.)

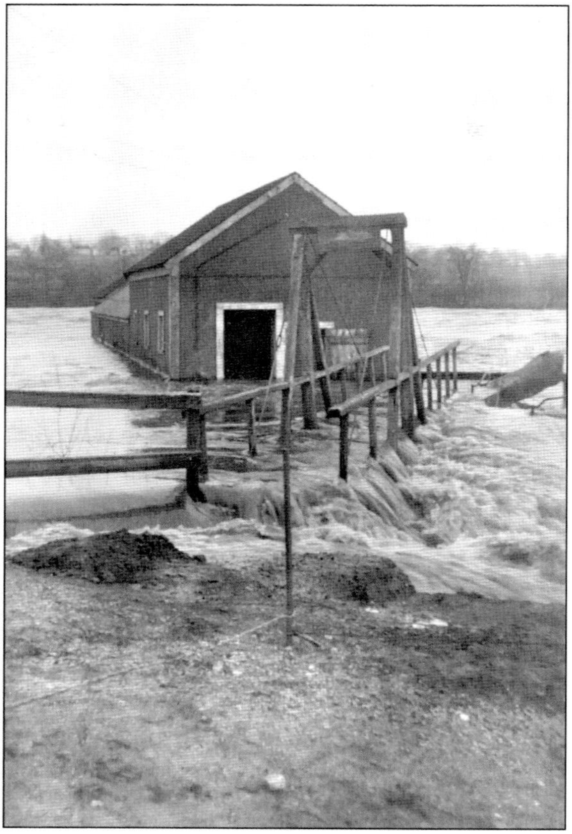

May Merrill's 1936 photograph shows floodwaters rising up the sides of the canal gatehouse and overflowing its drawbridge. The purpose of the Enfield Rapids Canal was to make a bypass for boating traffic around the Enfield Falls. Some 400 Irish contract workers came to Pine Meadows (now Windsor Locks) in the 1820s and built the canal by hand, taking five years to complete. Its northern section ends in Suffield. It was later renamed the Windsor Locks Canal. (Courtesy Sullivan family.)

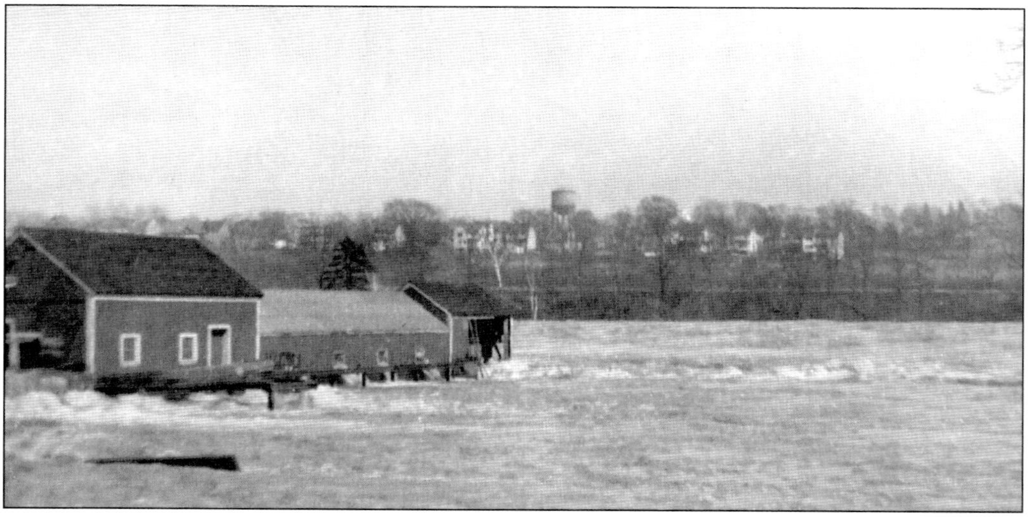

High floodwaters obliterate the canal bank in this view. The barnlike gatehouse doubled as a stable for the horses and mules that pulled the boats. In 1978, the canal ceased to function. Currently a group called the Friends of the Canal maintains the five-mile-long path from Suffield to Windsor Locks for wildlife and recreational use. Below the Enfield Dam is also a popular fishing spot. (Courtesy Sullivan family.)

East Suffield did not suffer the flood damage that Thompsonville did. On the north side of the Suffield approach to the bridge is this 19th-century home built by Alva Allen. Most of the large backyard and the steep riverbanks are submerged. Within a two-week period, the combination of snowmelt and rainfall totaled over 10 inches. (Courtesy Tavino family.)

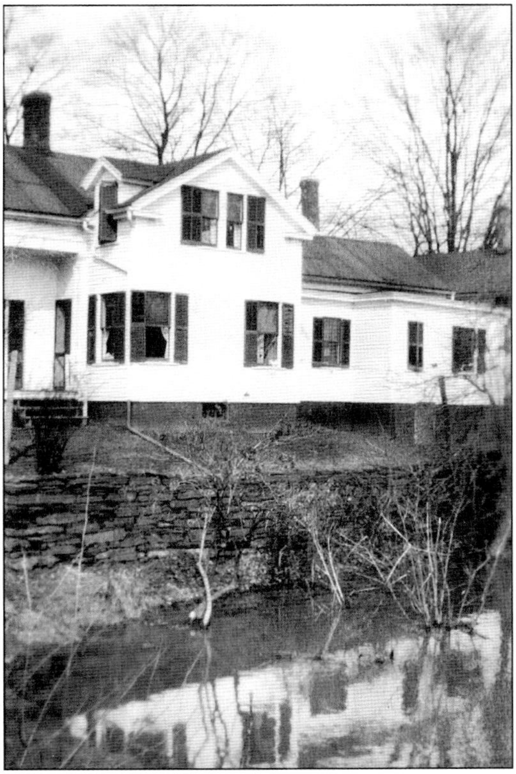

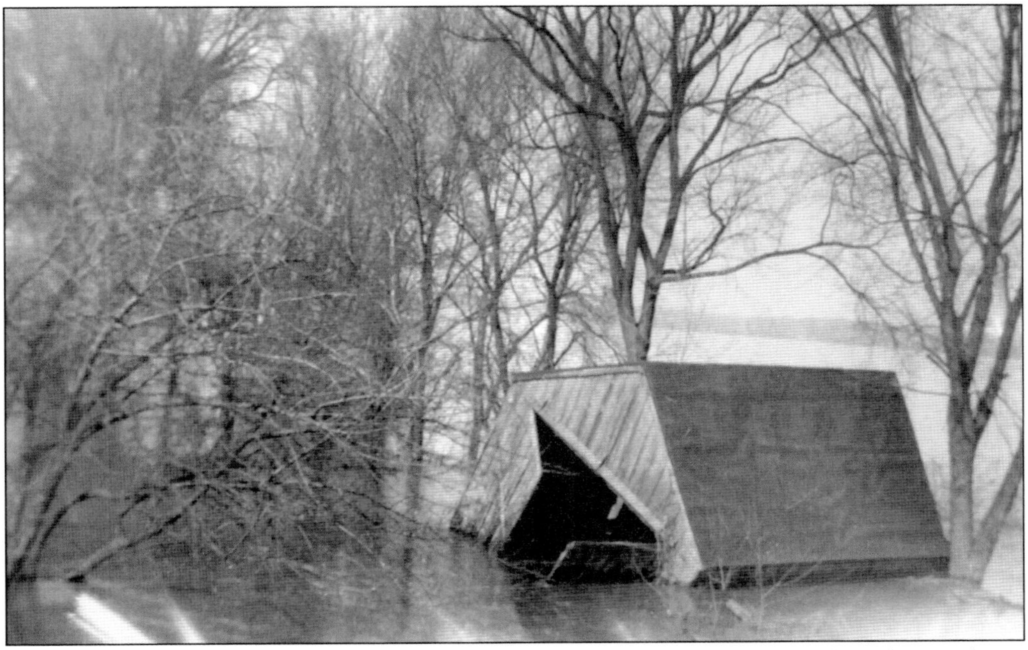

Unable to withstand the river's current, this barn, located in the backyard of the house above, was washed away along with many others during the great flood of 1936. At one point, the river level was rising at the rate of two inches an hour. The flood level records of 1936 remain unbroken after 70 years. (Courtesy Sullivan family.)

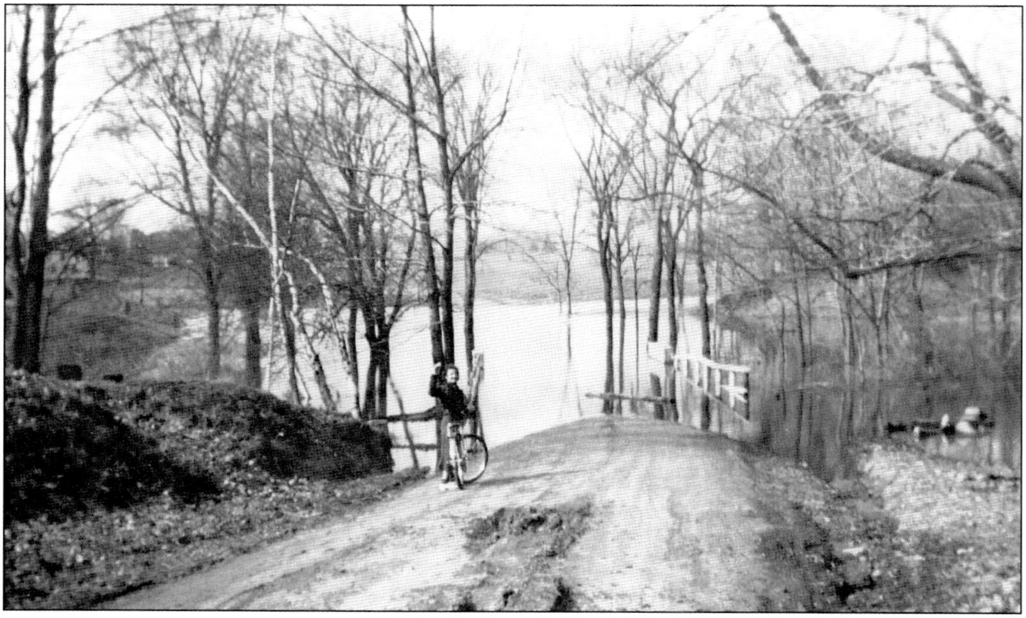

A cyclist pauses on her bike ride near the small wooden bridge over Deep Brook on River Boulevard. What appears to be a lake behind her are the floodwaters of what is normally the small brook feeding into the Connecticut River. Meanwhile in the photograph below, Freshwater Pond overflows and sends a torrent of water into Thompsonville's Main Street and downtown area. The carpet mill closed with eight feet of water in the engine room of its power plant. Mail and train services came to a halt. (Above, courtesy Tavino family; below, courtesy Harry F. Hilditch Collection.)

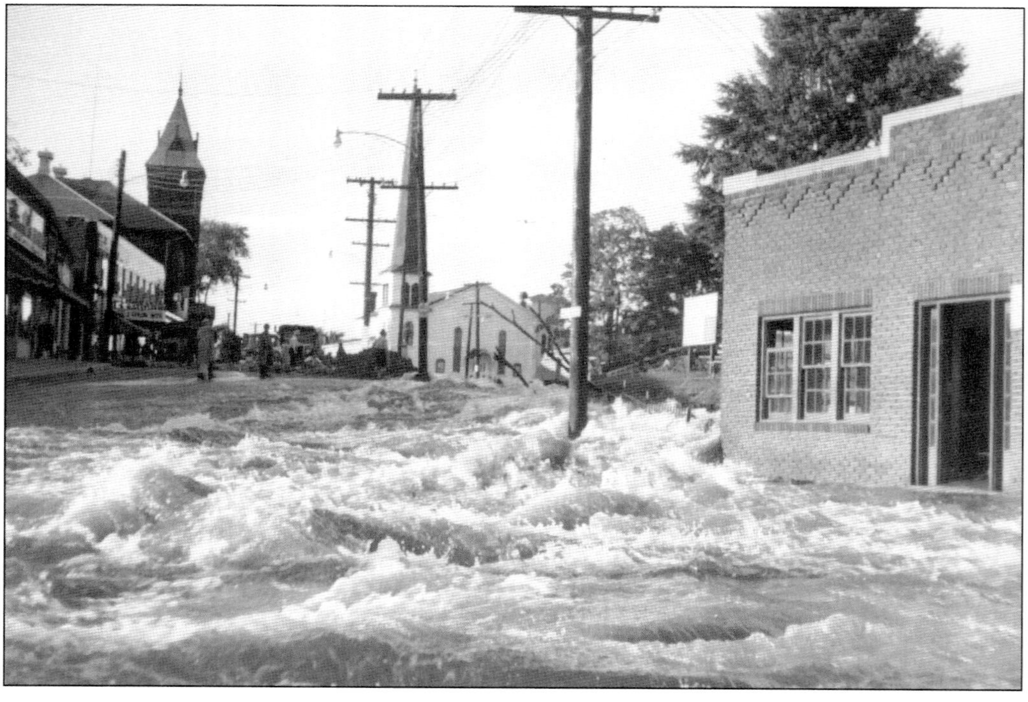

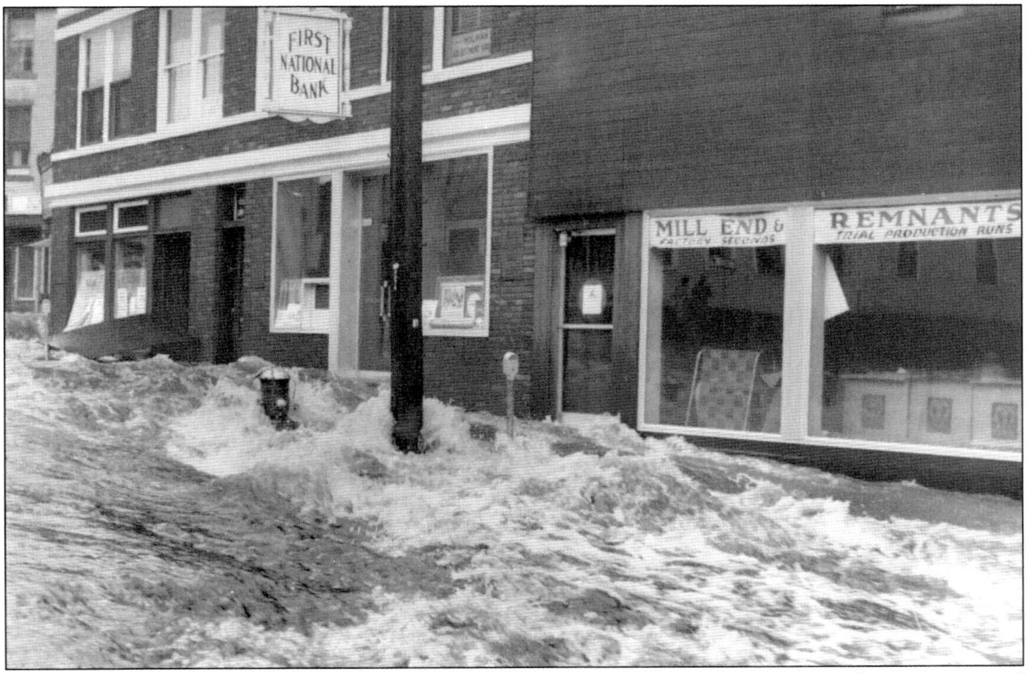

The flood of 1955 was caused by unusual circumstances. In August, after a high volume of summer rainfall, back-to-back hurricanes, Connie and Diane, passed over southern New England leaving behind record levels of flooding. This was a flood that caused more destruction from raging tributaries than from the swollen Connecticut River. Thompsonville's Main Street, in the above photograph, was devastated after Freshwater Pond overflowed its banks. (Courtesy Stanley Dynia.)

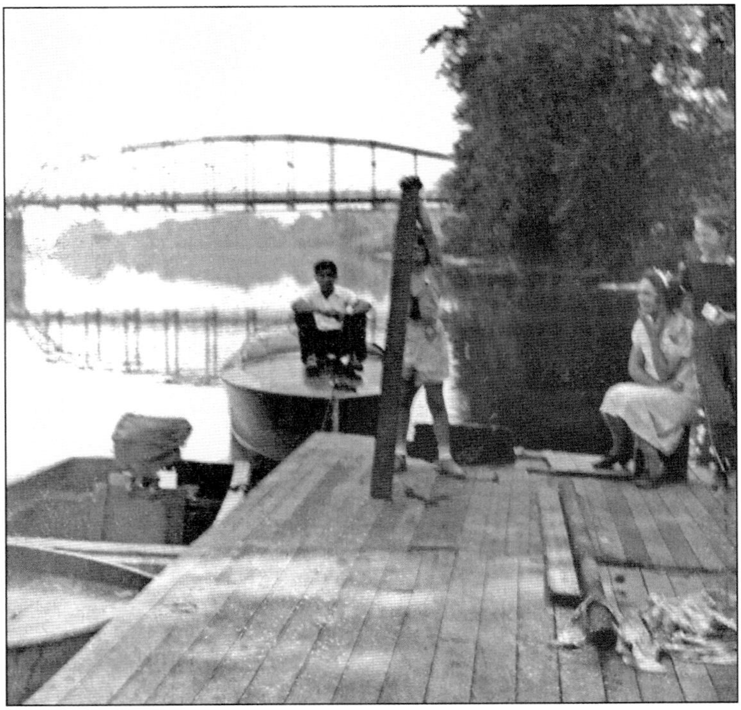

Just north of the Thompsonville-Suffield Bridge, neighborhood kids in East Suffield enjoy a summer day on one of the many boat docks that peppered the river shoreline. In spite of water pollution and the active carpet mill, fishing and boating were still some of the favorite summer pastimes. (Courtesy Underwood family.)

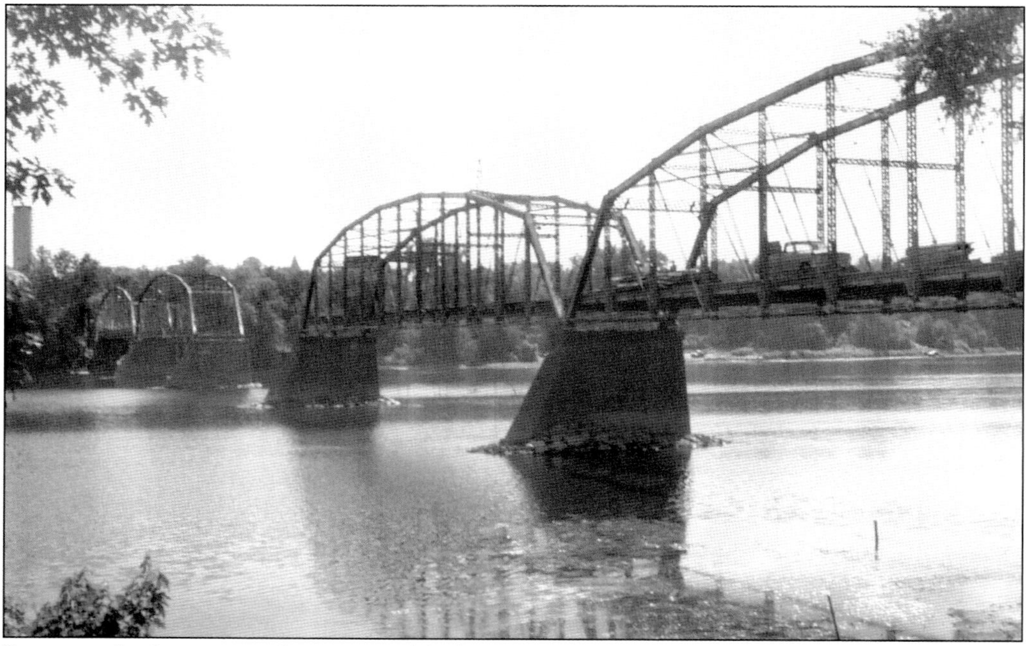

Because of safety issues, the 74-year-old Thompsonville-Suffield Bridge was closed to traffic in 1967. This followed the opening of the new bridge at Route 190, approximately a half mile to the south. It was the summer of 1971 when the iron-truss bridge met its end. In this series of photographs, dynamite charges are set to explode and demolish another of the five sections of the old landmark. Save-the-Bridge (a small group of citizens composed of social, civic, and veterans' organizations from both sides of the river) opposed the bridge's destruction. After the demolition actually occurred, the focus then became support for a new structure at the same site. (Courtesy Romie Hathaway.)

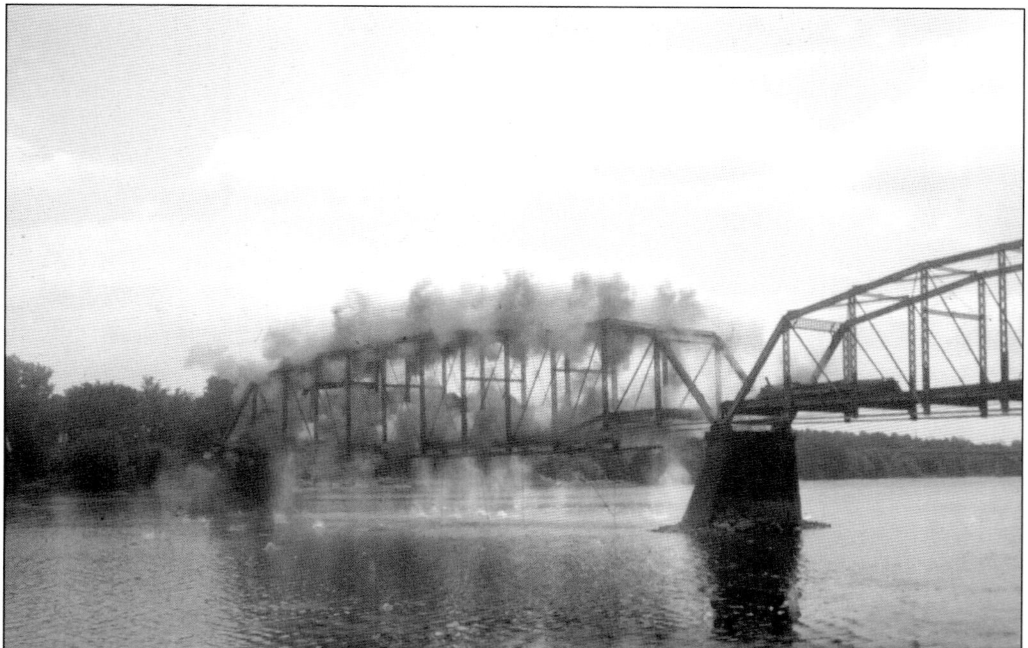

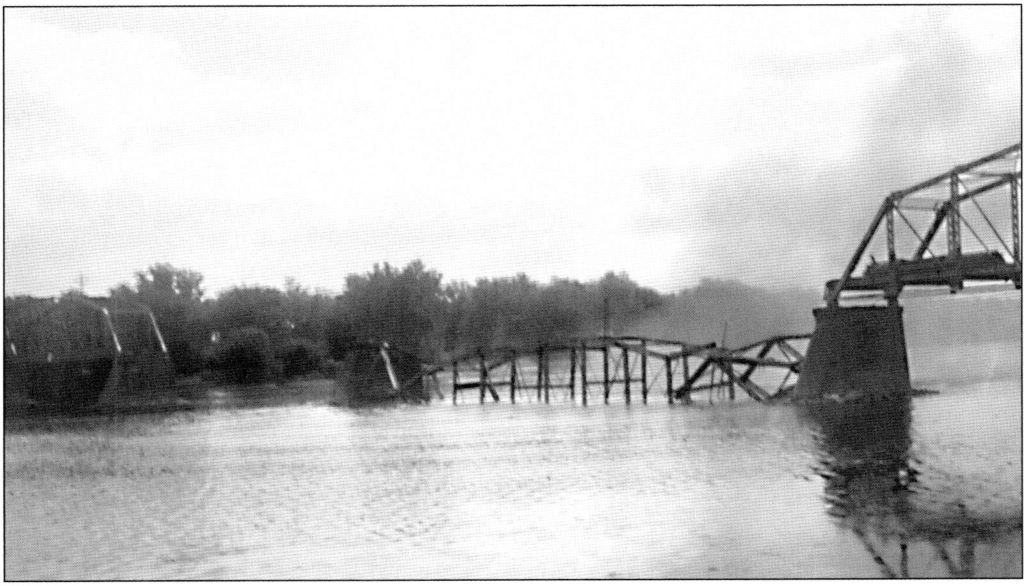

Thompsonville appeared deserted after the closing of the Bigelow-Sanford Carpet Company with its 35 acres of old buildings. Many of the town's mom-and-pop businesses closed or moved away. East Suffield's residents who walked to Thompsonville to work, shop, or worship were now isolated and dependent on rides. The photograph above shows a dynamited section of the bridge dropping into the river. Below is a 1990s photograph of the brownstone piers that are all that remains of the iron bridge that connected the two towns. Thompsonville still waits for the long-delayed urban renewal and revitalization projects that were planned. (Above, courtesy Romie Hathaway; below, courtesy Laurie Tavino.)

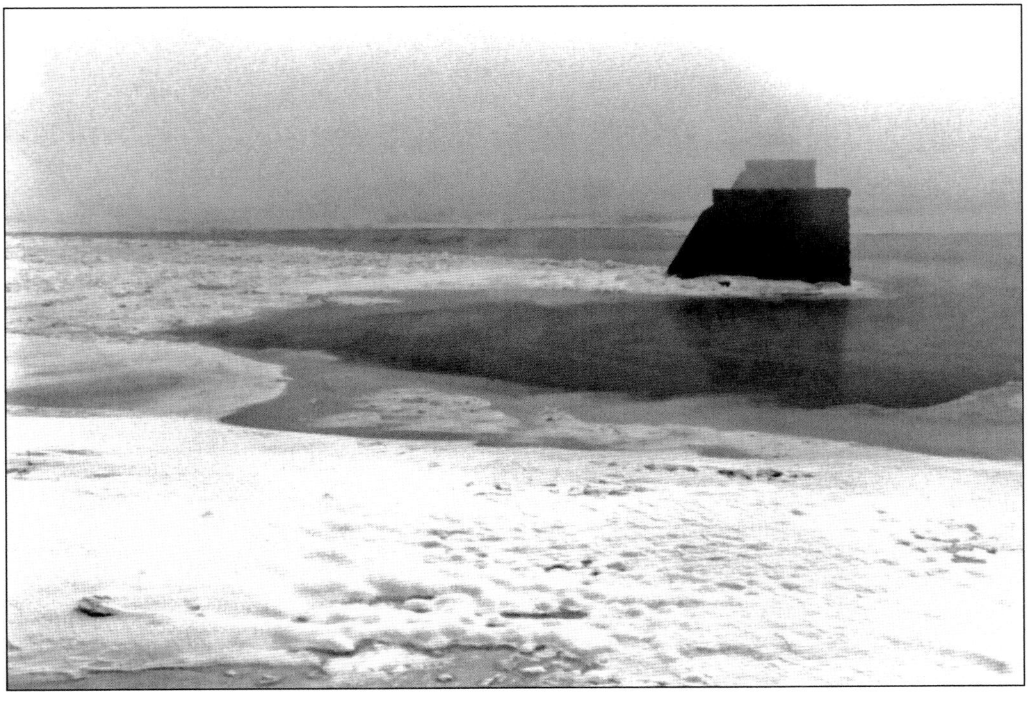

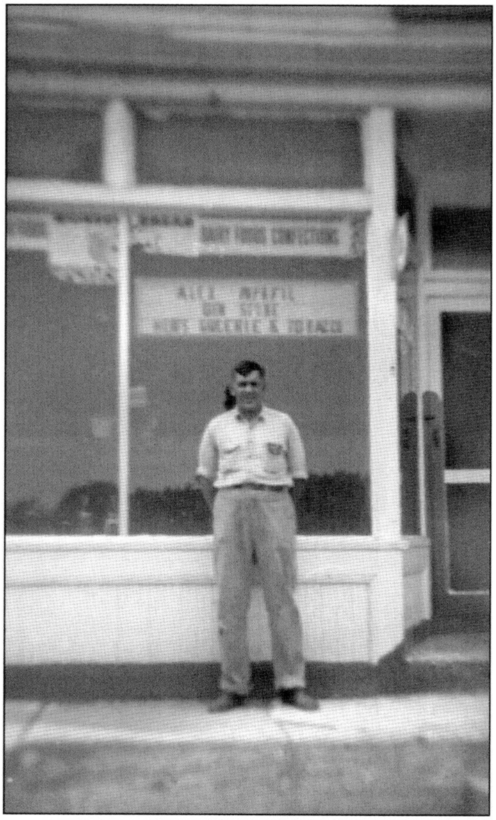

No one fought harder to save the old bridge than Alex Papafil. The proprietor of Papafil's General Store on Thompsonville Road, Alex believed the destruction of the old bridge caused him to go out of business and also brought on the deterioration of Thompsonville. Alex's father, Theodore, built the store in 1914. With the bridge's destruction, Thompsonville Road, which was maintained by the state when it led to the bridge, became a town road. (Courtesy Rookey family.)

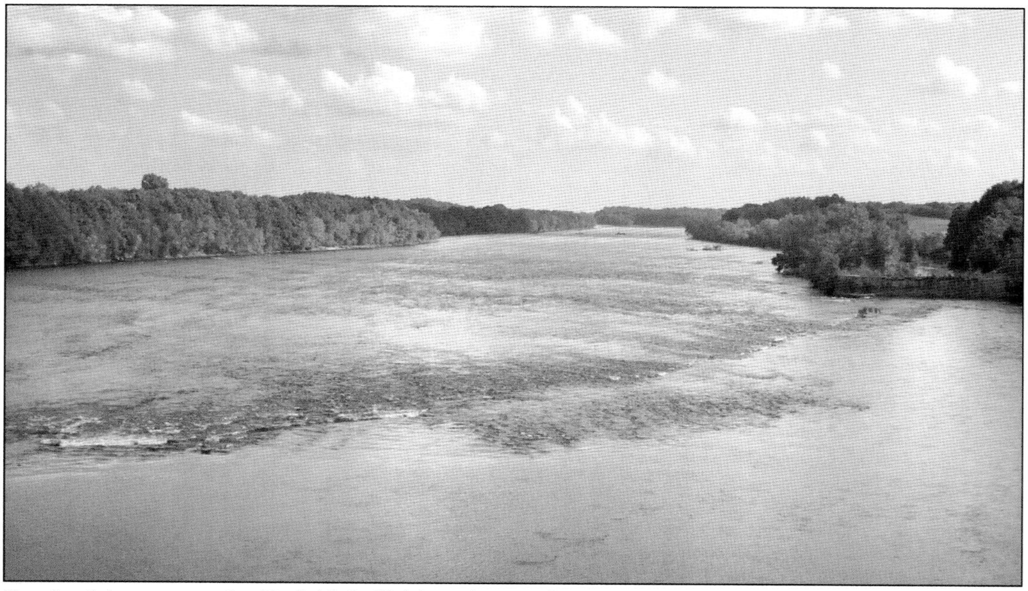

South of the present-day Enfield-Suffield Bridge are the Enfield Dam and Rapids. Erosion has worn away much of the dam. At the far right is the Windsor Locks Canal. Piers from the old covered bridge are barely visible in the far distance. Before regulation, the Connecticut River was polluted by industrial waste and sewage. Now vibrant with the return of fish, wildlife, and recreation, the 410-mile waterway has been designated an American Heritage River. (Courtesy Ray Pioggia.)

Two

THE THOMPSONVILLE CONNECTION

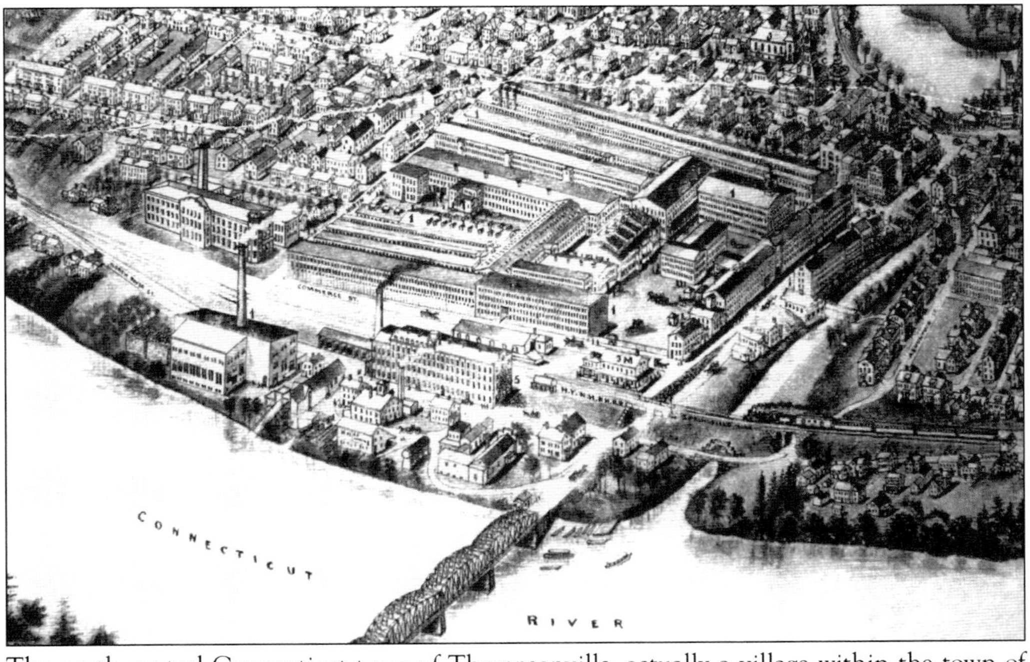

The north-central Connecticut town of Thompsonville, actually a village within the town of Enfield, was home to a vibrant carpet industry beginning in the early 1800s. This 1908 bird's-eye view, published by Hughes and Bailey, shows the expanse of the carpet mill. From this vantage point, one can see how the village developed in rows around the industrial center to accommodate housing, schools, churches, and commerce for the burgeoning workforce. (Courtesy EHS.)

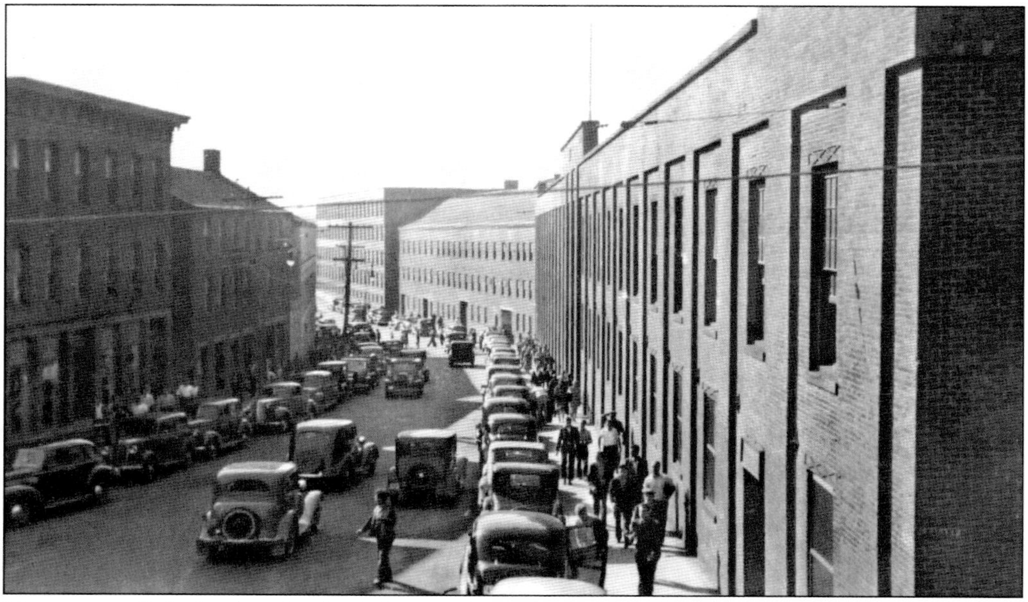

Thompsonville's Bigelow-Sanford Carpet Company was one of the oldest and largest carpet manufacturers in North America and employed thousands of people. The above photograph is a view looking down Main Street in the heart of the mill complex. The mill was hit hard during the Great Depression but never shut down; it rebounded during the 1940s and then finally closed in 1971. The aerial image below was made by photographer Edward J. Malley Jr. in the 1950s. An iron-truss bridge reaches across the Connecticut River from the concentrated industrial area of Thompsonville to the patchwork of East Suffield's farms. The cluster of buildings at center right is Cottage Green, a neighborhood of homes built for Scottish weavers, the first mill employees in 1829. (Above, courtesy Tavino family; below, courtesy James M. Malley.)

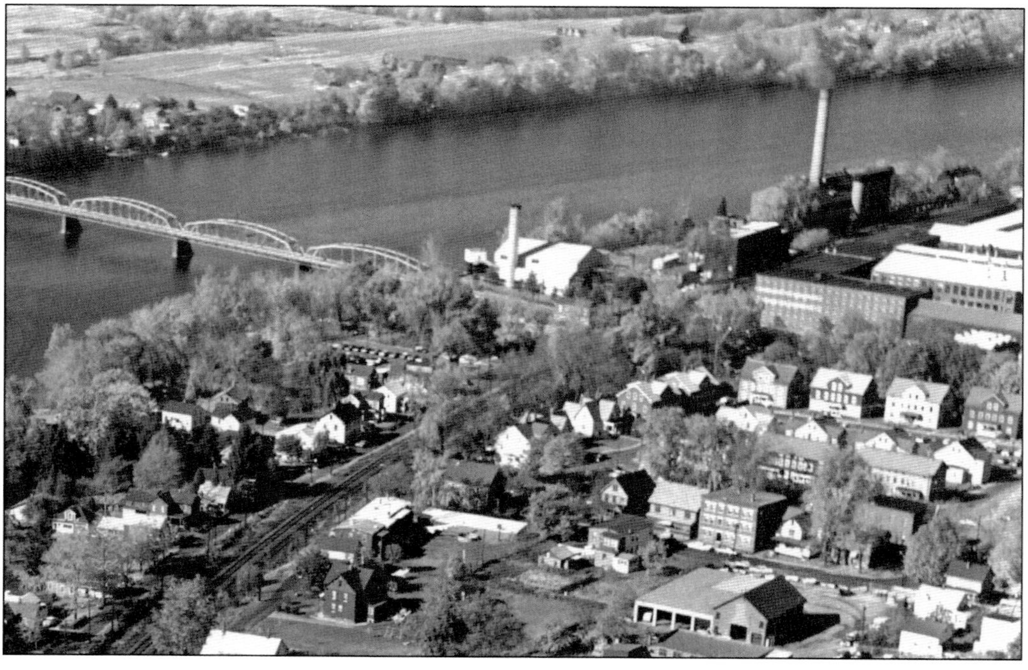

Suffield resident Robert F. Underwood, an avid amateur photographer, is pictured in front of the Freshwater Pond dam. The old First Presbyterian Church is in the background. A recent Enfield Historical Society newsletter states "Enfield's earliest remaining mill dam was built in 1828 by Orrin Thompson to power his first carpet mill. Had it not been built there would not have been a Thompsonville Carpet company. And, of course, there would have been no Thompsonville." (Courtesy Underwood family.)

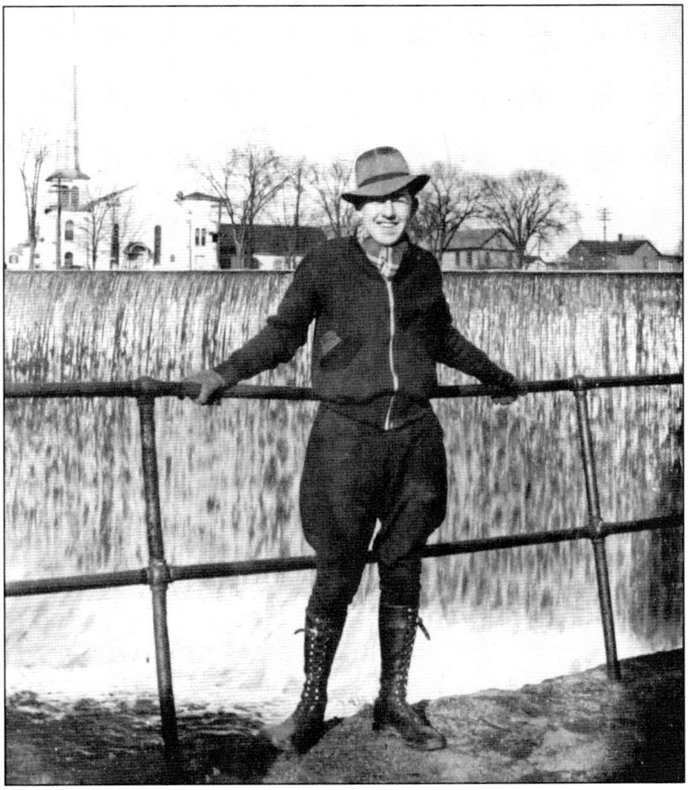

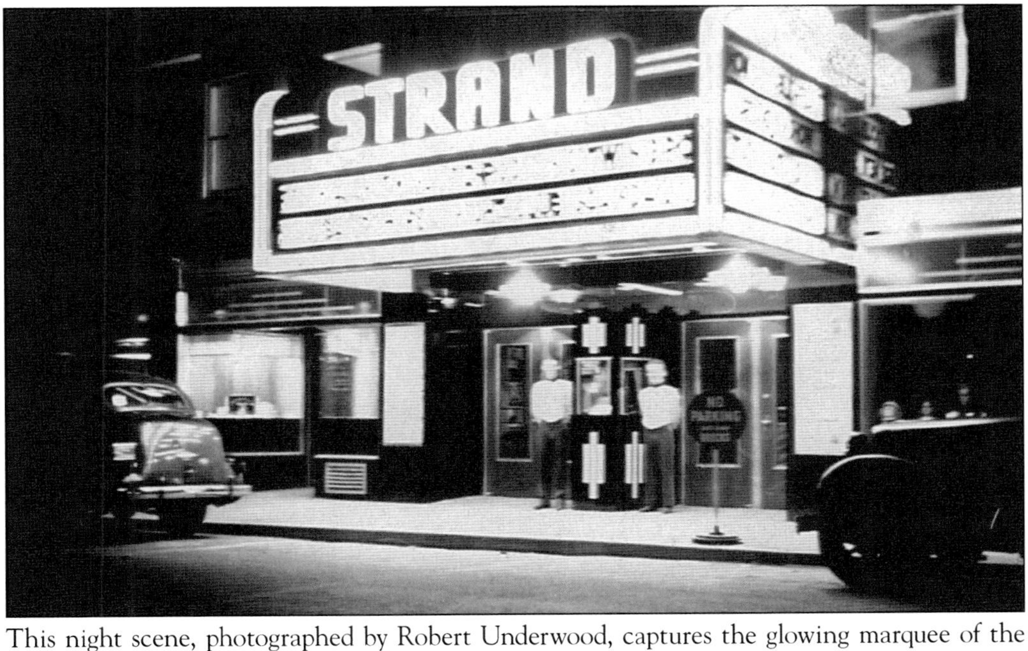

This night scene, photographed by Robert Underwood, captures the glowing marquee of the Strand Theater and the welcoming appearance of its smartly dressed ushers. Built in 1937, it was one of three theaters in the area. A simple walk across the bridge and a stroll up North Main Street led East Suffield moviegoers to great entertainment. The building still stands but has been closed for over 20 years. (Courtesy Underwood family.)

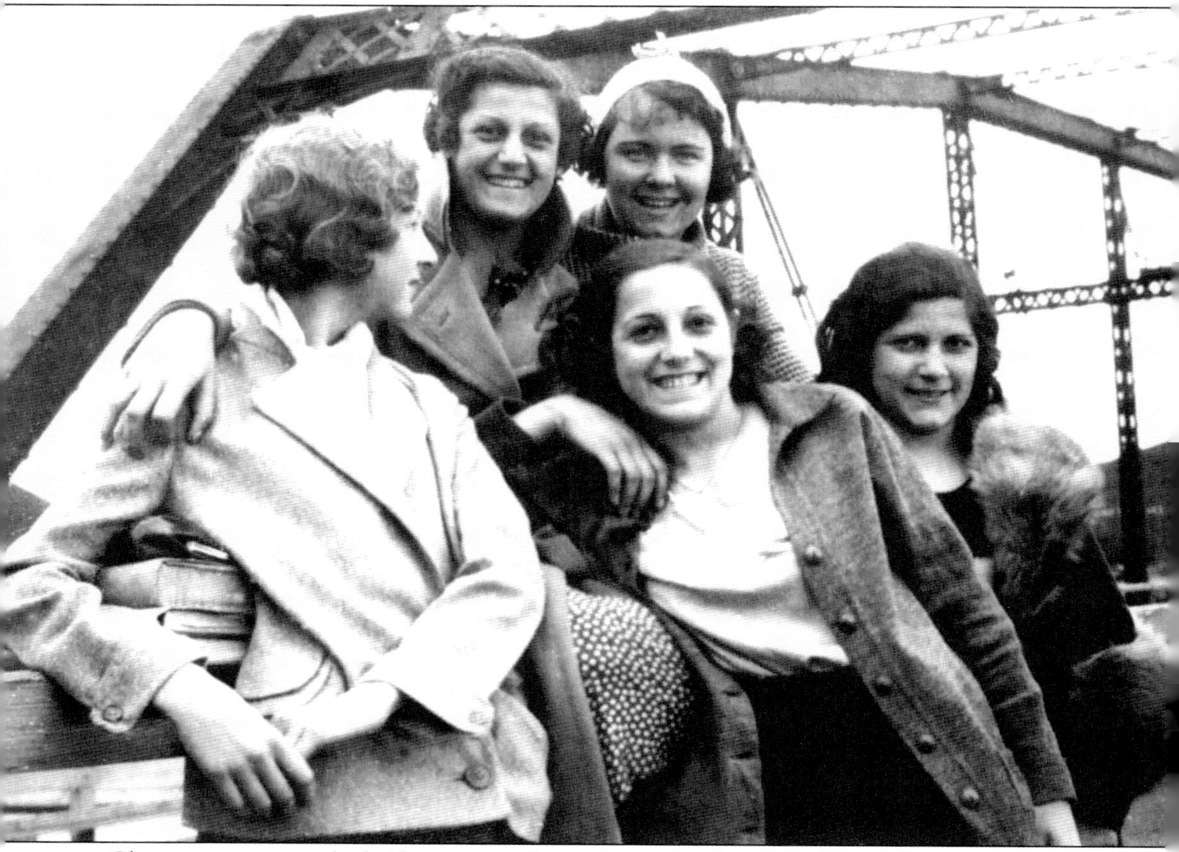

Classmates pose on the bridge en route home from school in 1932. From left to right are Martha Malinoski, Romie Tavino, Shirley Walker, Kay Petrakis, and Lillie Frasino. As Suffield did not provide a public high school until 1939, many East Suffield students attended Thompsonville's more accessible public and parochial schools. Although neighborhood youths had farm and domestic responsibilities, there were plenty of fun activities available just over the bridge. A winter favorite was ice-skating on Freshwater Pond followed by a sundae at the Midnight Spa soda fountain on North Main Street, a popular teenage hangout in the 1930s and 1940s. The Bigelow-Sanford Carpet Company offered organized teams and clubs to join such as bowling and tennis. Marching bands, fife and drum corps, and sports teams abounded, all sponsored by businesses, churches, and the ethnic communities in town. Teenagers driving their own cars were unheard of. For transportation one would walk, ride a bicycle, or if going some distance, catch the trolley or train. (Courtesy Tavino family.)

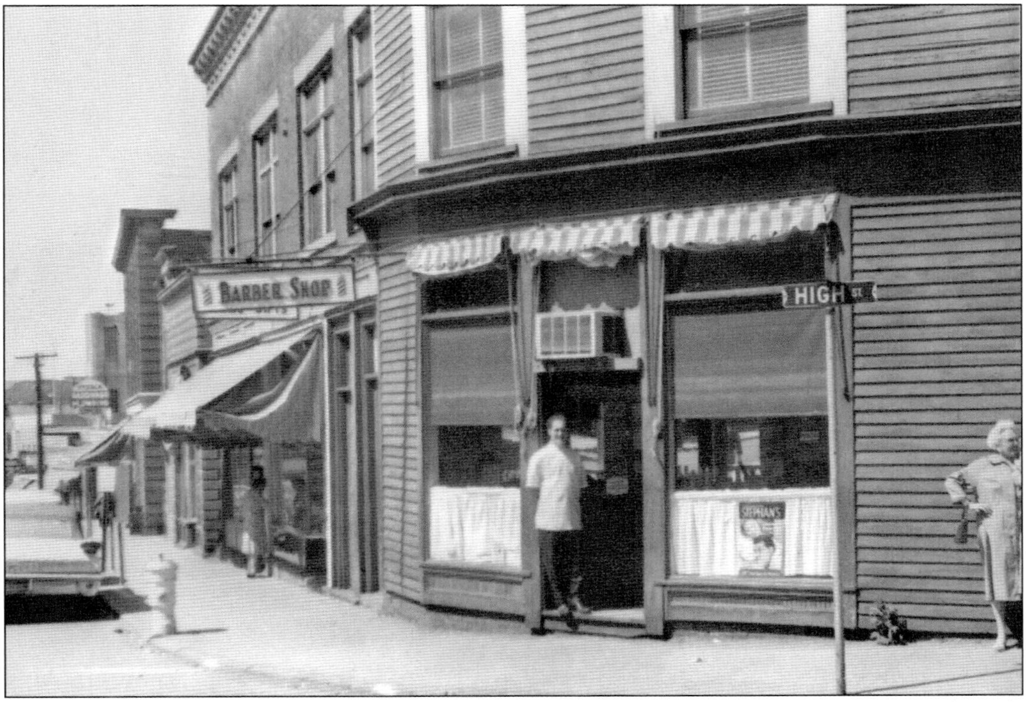

Charles Rinaldi stands in front of his barbershop (above) at the corner of Pearl and High Streets around 1960. Thompsonville's multicultural neighborhood businesses and markets were plentiful; national chain stores and retail franchises were the minority. DiLeo's store and the Maniscalchi Market are pictured below on Whitworth Street around 1949. East Suffield resident Ann Maniscalchi Padegimas grew up working at her family's neighborhood market and recalled the success of the mom-and-pop stores that thrived during the years the carpet mill operated. (Above, courtesy Florence Rinaldi Falkowski; below, courtesy Stanley Dynia.)

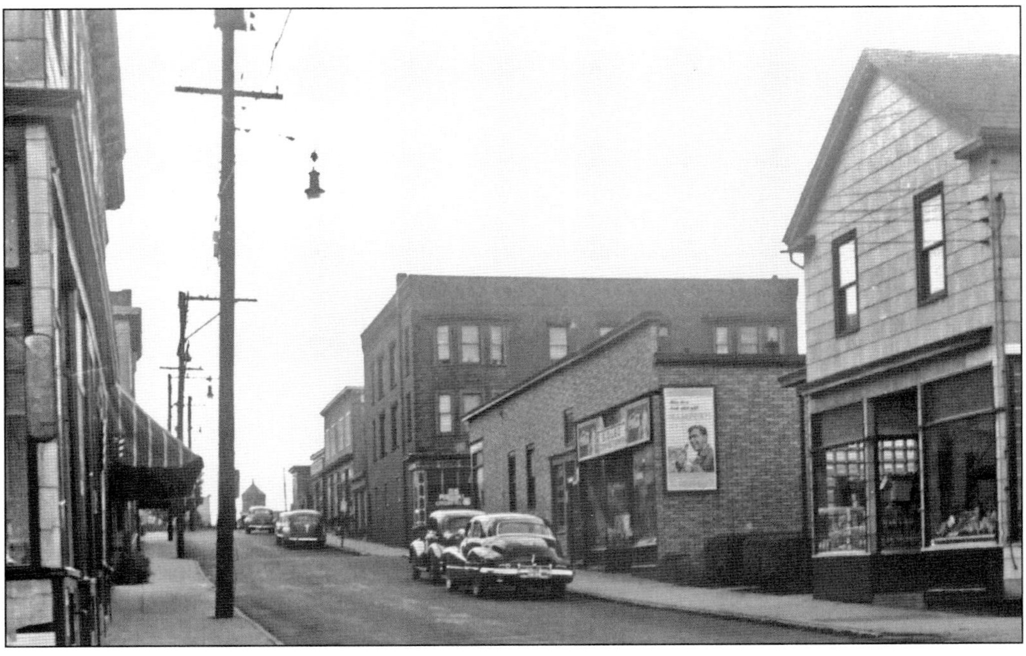

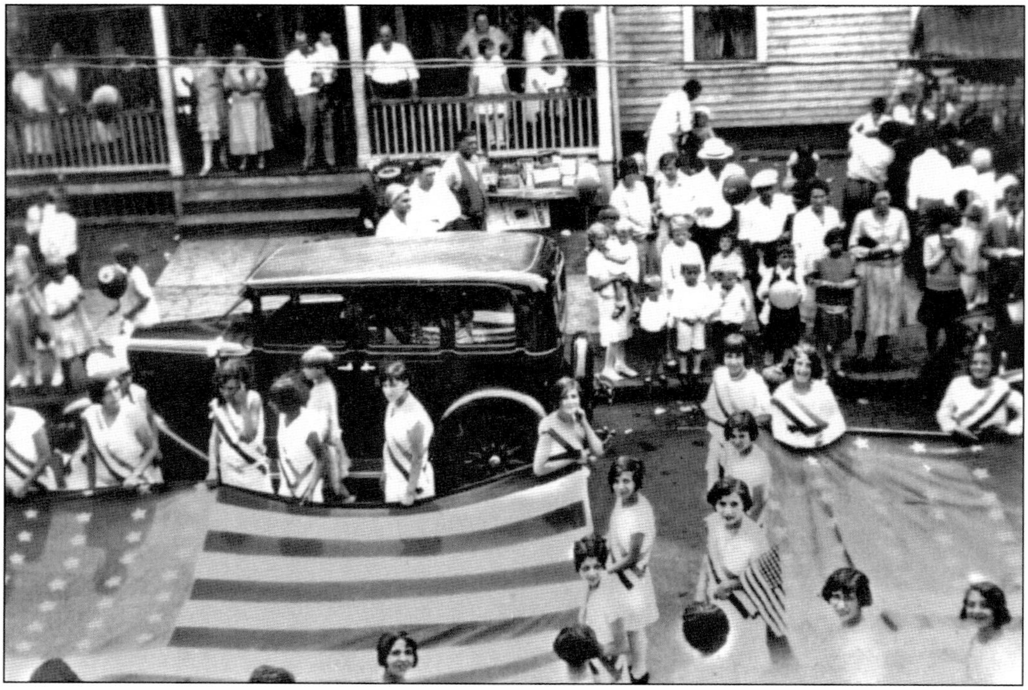

Thompsonville hosted numerous parades for holidays, political events, and ethnic celebrations. As the population of each ethnic community increased, it organized social groups, such as the Italian community's San Calogero Society (above) and later the Mount Carmel Society. Large parades with bands for celebrations, like the one pictured below in front of St. Patrick's Catholic Church, were open to the public and enjoyed by all. There were also smaller, informal gatherings, such as St. Joseph's Day Feast, put on by local working people in their neighborhoods. The Mount Carmel Society, founded in 1925, has continued for 80 years, hosting its Italian Festival (commemorating the miraculous end of a terrible drought in southern Italy in 1882) the first weekend of August. (Above, courtesy Stanley Dynia; below, courtesy James Caramazza.)

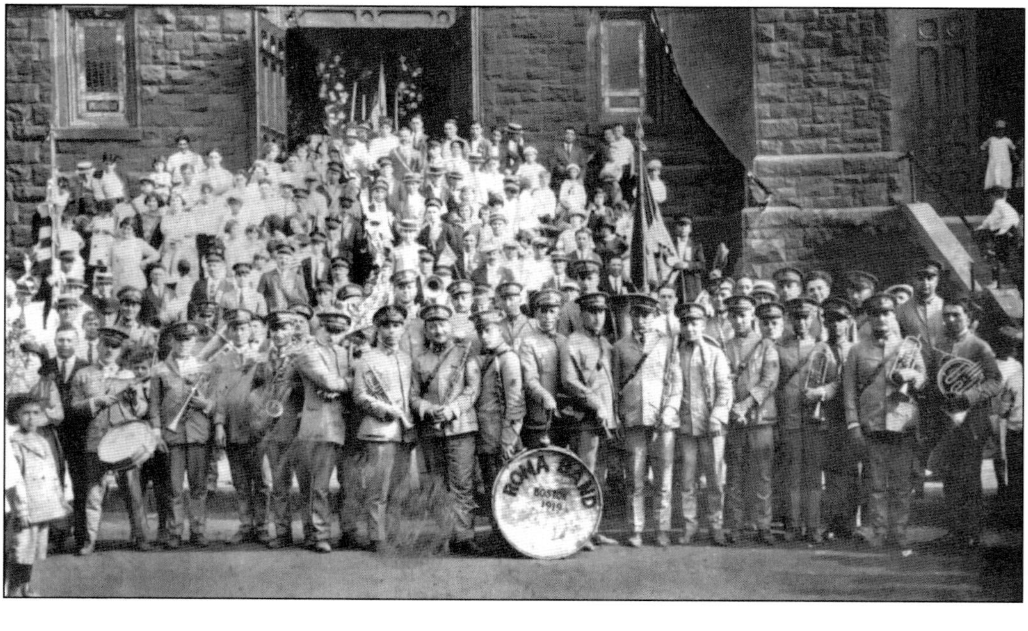

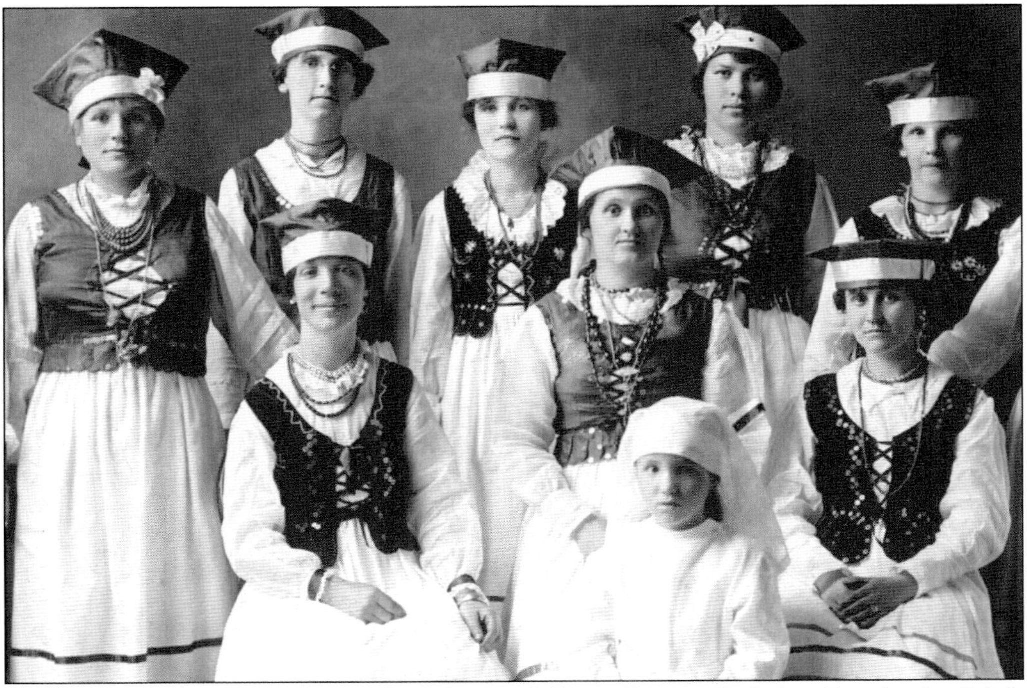

The thriving Polish community founded St. Adalbert's Roman Catholic Church, the Polish National Catholic Church, and the Polish National Home, along with smaller organizations. Numerous businesses and clubs supported their culture and heritage. Justyna Sitarz (above, front row left), was born in Poland, lived in Thompsonville, then later moved to Hartford and worked with the Polish Red Cross. In old country fashion, she clung to traditional customs and values throughout life. The Polish Krakusy Society (below) celebrates the July 3, 1923, opening of the Polish National Home. Located on Alden Avenue, it served as a bustling cultural center. (Above, courtesy Grigitis family; below, courtesy Stanley Dynia.)

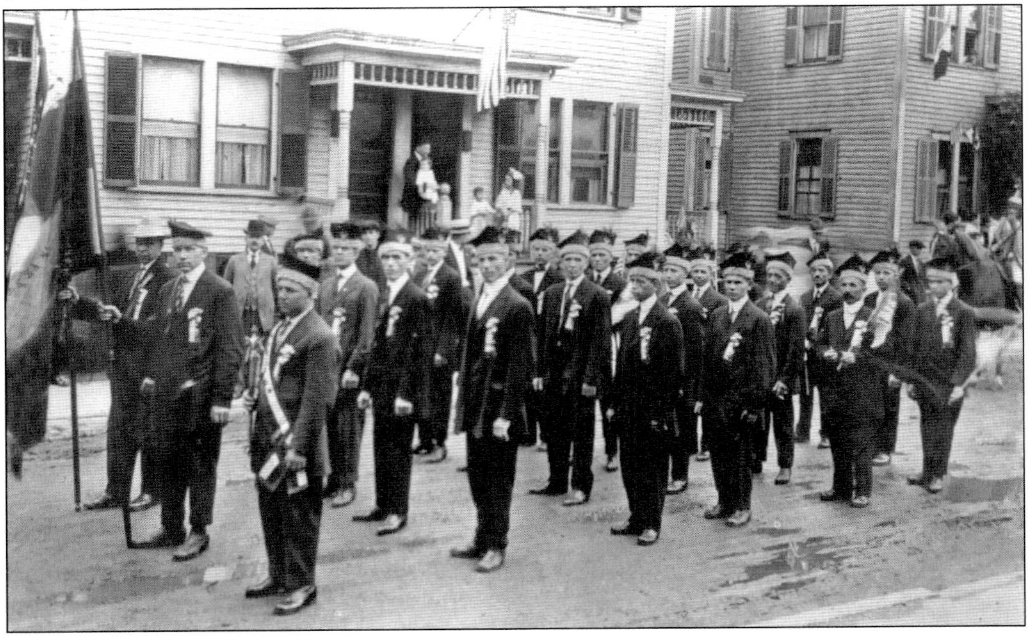

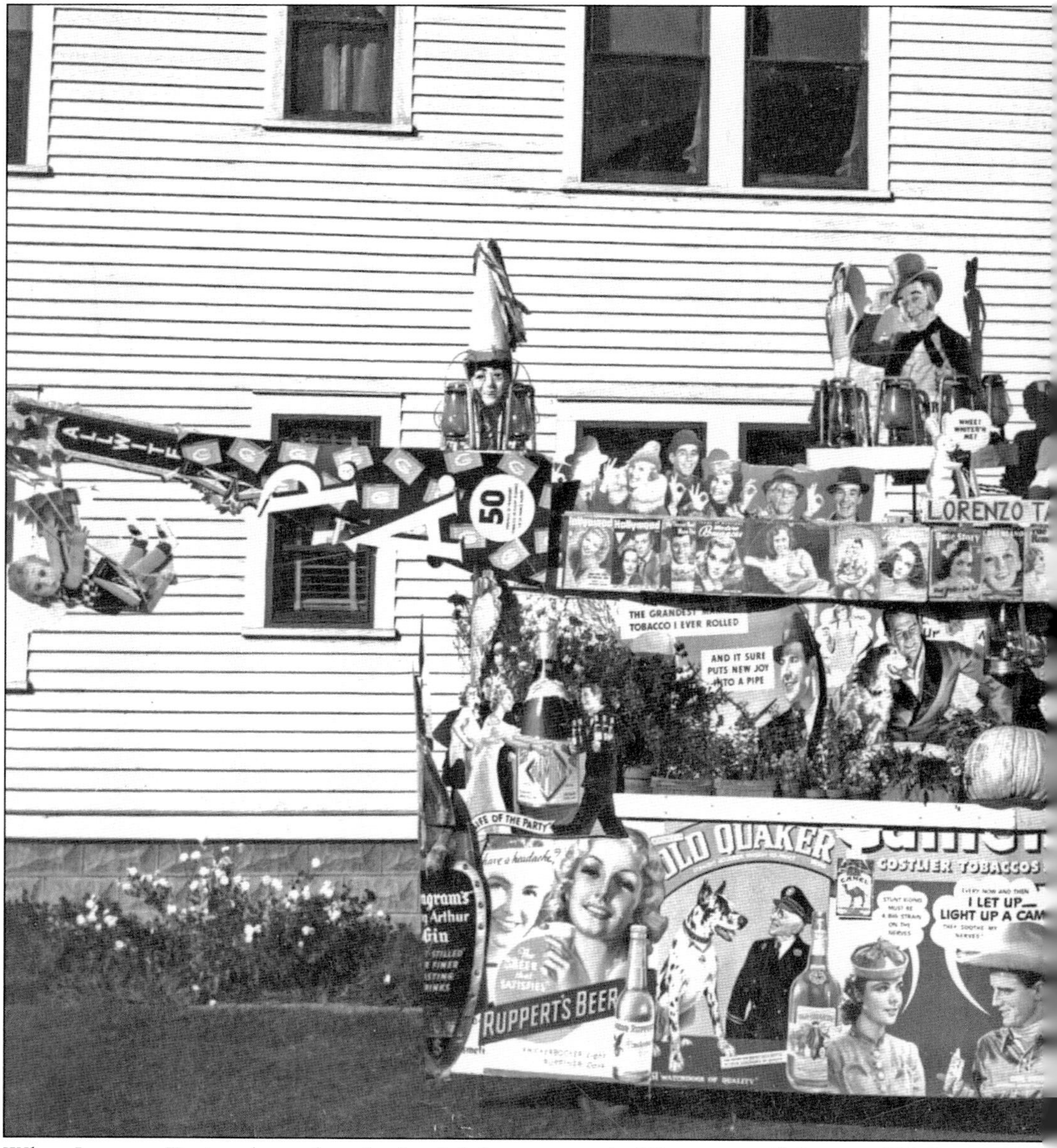

When Lorenzo Tavino dressed up the family's farm wagon for Thompsonville's annual Halloween parade in the late 1930s, the horse-drawn vehicle turned into an elaborate float. It was covered with posters of Hollywood movie stars, advertisement billboards, and a mix of seasonal flowers and vegetables. Rotating platforms with circles of lanterns adorned the top. Swinging at far left is a cutout of a little girl, operated with rope and pulley by an assistant inside the float. Neighbor Charlie Galetta, who was a young boy at the time, described the interior as having three cranks

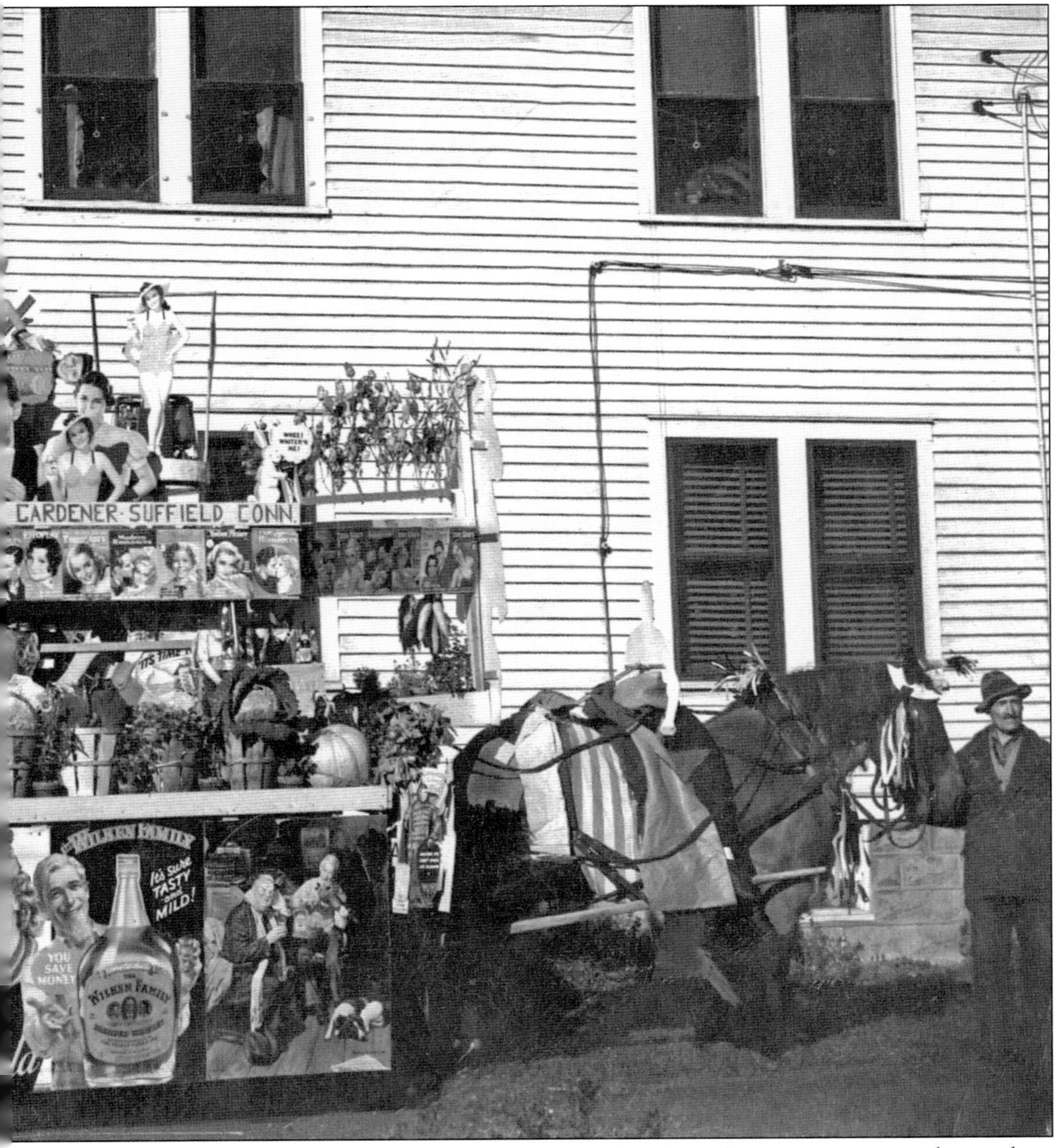

that turned the decorated lanterns. Lorenzo planned to have his teenage son and a nephew operate the moving parts, but they had other ideas. They gave Charlie a quarter to do all the work himself. As soon as the wagon crossed the bridge, the older boys jumped out, leaving poor Charlie alone. He recalled that "even though things got a little hectic, I really didn't mind the job." (Courtesy Tavino family.)

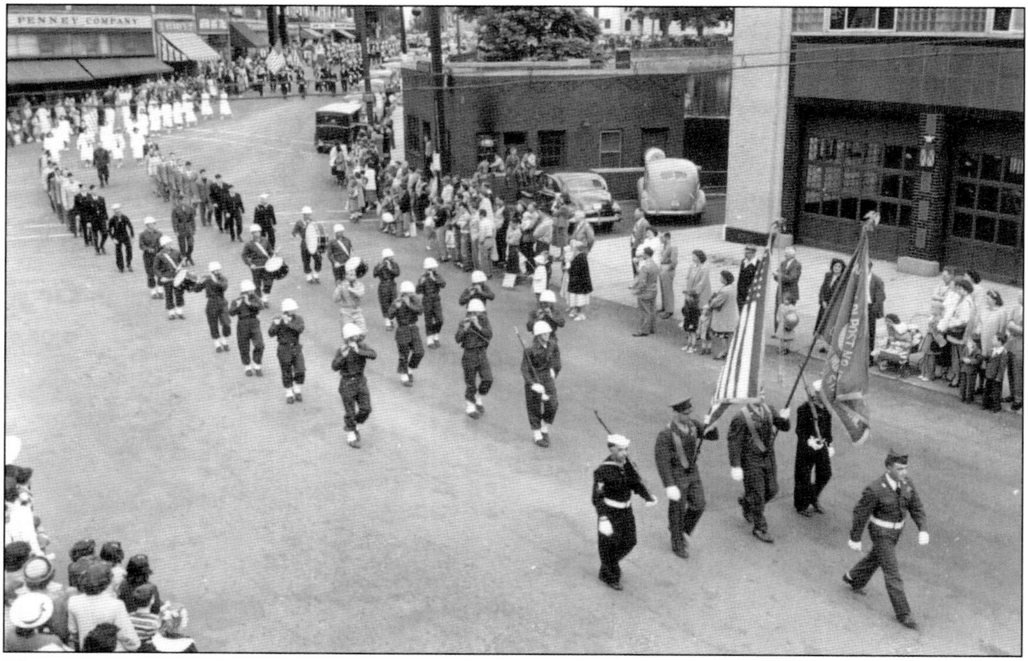

The 1949 Memorial Day parade marches down North Main Street in Thompsonville. This mill village had high rates of draftees and enlistment because of its industry and concentrated population. In July 1943, the *Thompsonville Press* wrote, "Over 1500 local persons now in fighting forces." Approximately 12 percent of the population was serving in World War II, one of the proudest records in the state. The carpet mill retooled for the war effort, producing blankets, nylon, rayon for tires, and parts for submarines, planes, and radar. In the image below, (from left to right) Ralph D'Amato, Charley Iacolina, unidentified, and Matty Bonk help each other with chores in a lot behind Tariff and New Streets in Thompsonville in the mid-1930s. It was young men like these who helped to fill the service ranks. (Above, courtesy Rose Vella Shelanskas; below, courtesy Stanley Dynia.)

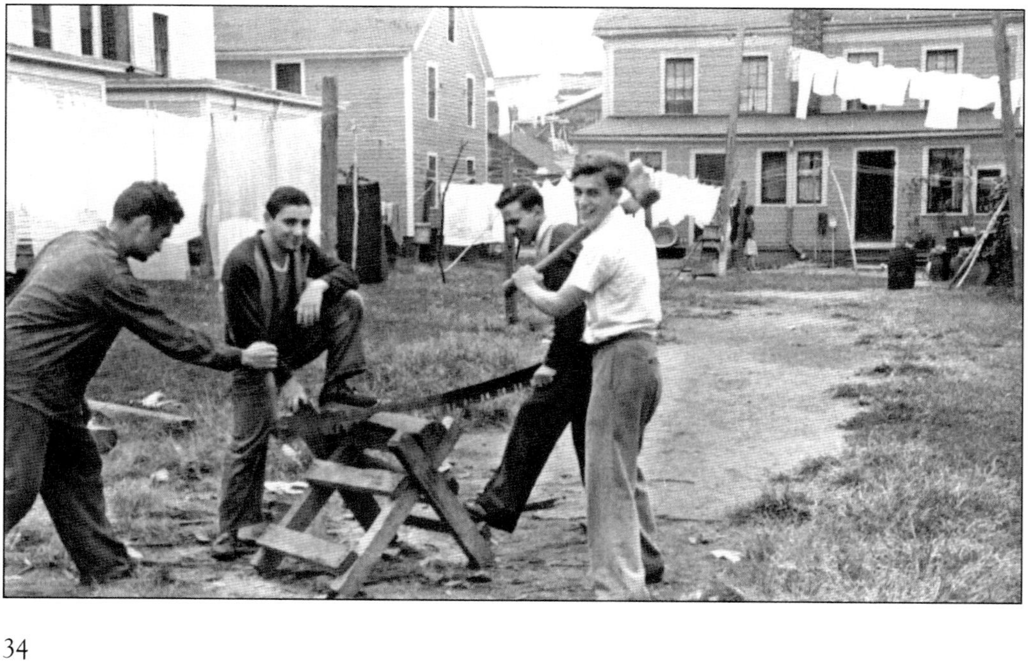

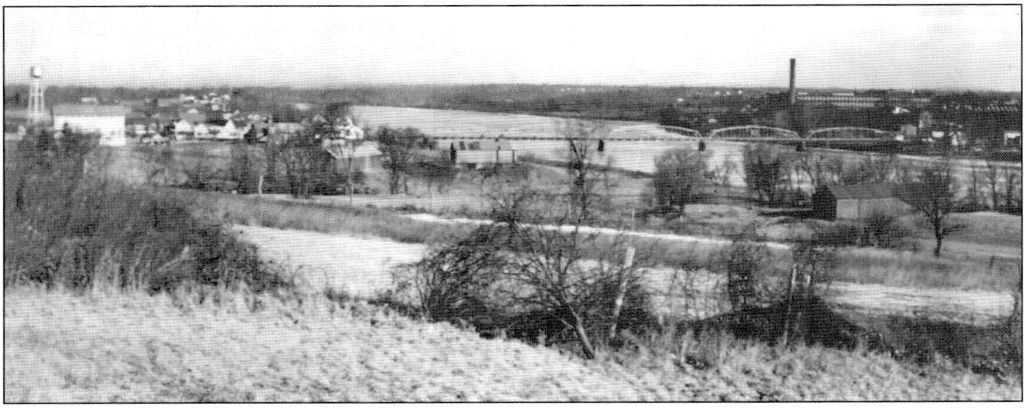

This panorama, looking northeast, best depicts how the communities of East Suffield and Thompsonville were linked. May Merrill photographed the scene from her home atop Mile Hill on East Street in 1939. At far left are her grandfather John L. Sullivan's water tower and warehouse on Burbank Avenue amid the cluster of homes and businesses near the bridge's entrance. (Courtesy May Sullivan Merrill.)

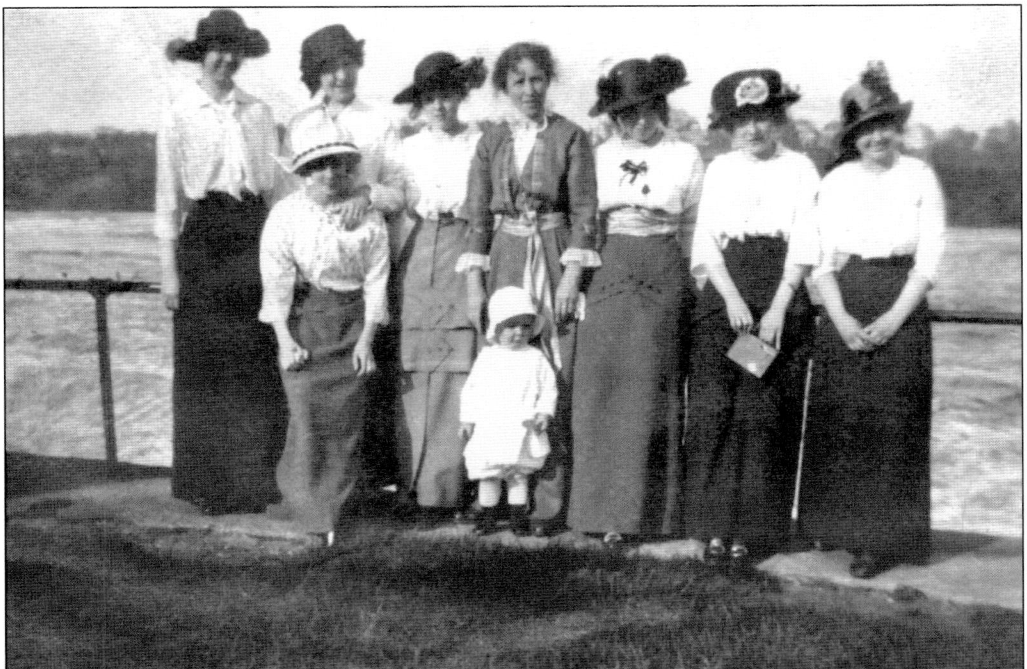

These well-dressed ladies walked a good distance from Thompsonville, across the bridge, then up the hill on East Street to visit their friend Clara Sullivan (center) and her toddler son John. In this 1914 image, the group posed at a spot overlooking the Enfield Falls. Young John eventually took over the Sullivan family's tobacco business. (Courtesy May Sullivan Merrill.)

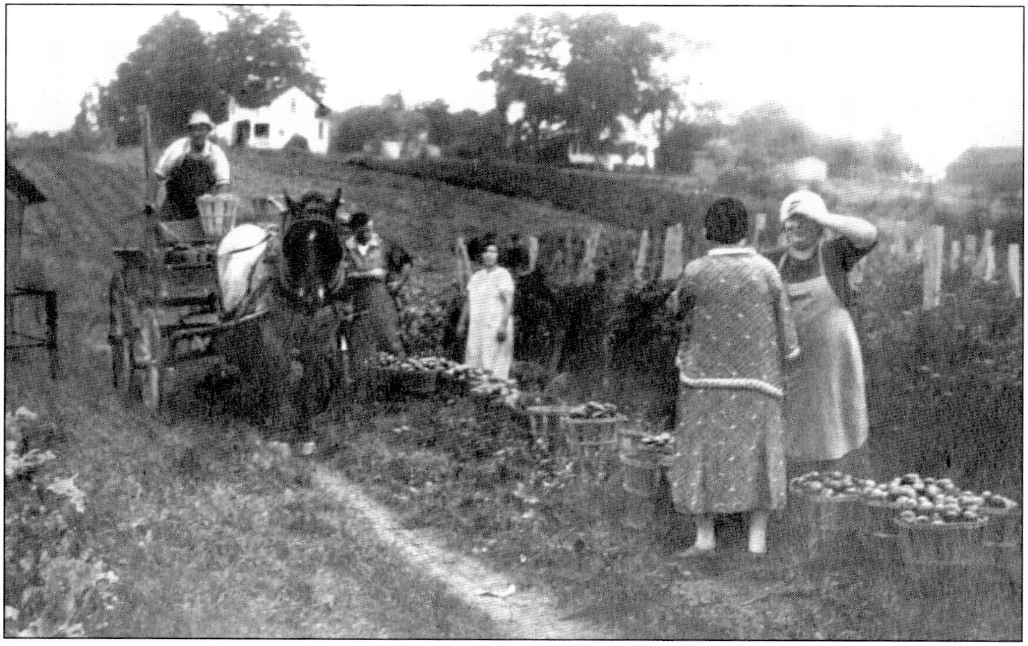

Compatriots from both sides of the river, family, and friends maintained close ties helping each other. Working together was also visiting time. Tony and Nicolina DeMaso (center), from Thompsonville, help with the tomato harvest on Tavino Farm, reaping the food that kept many a family going during the Great Depression. The homes in the background are located along East Street. (Courtesy Tavino family.)

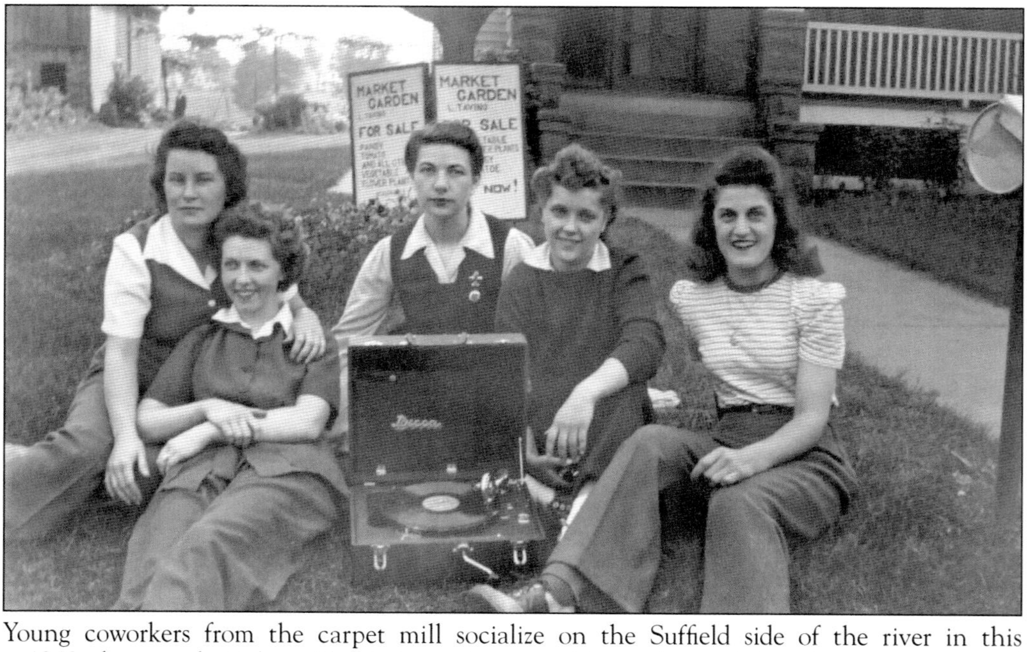

Young coworkers from the carpet mill socialize on the Suffield side of the river in this c. 1940 photograph. Valeria Bladek (center), Romie Tavino (far right), and three unidentified Thompsonville friends worked together in the "picking room" mending flaws in the carpets. In Valeria's opinion, it was one of the best places in the mill to work—they could dress nice and earn decent wages. (Courtesy Tavino family.)

Three

SUFFIELD'S EAST SIDE

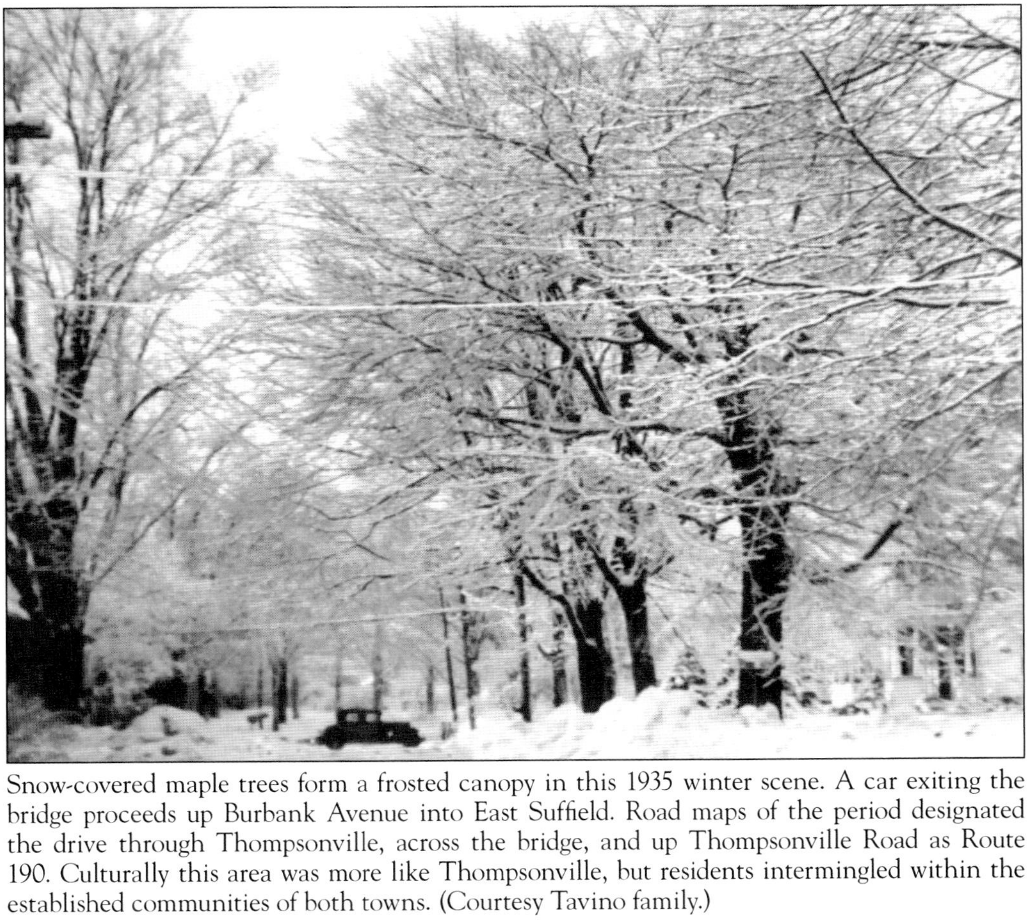

Snow-covered maple trees form a frosted canopy in this 1935 winter scene. A car exiting the bridge proceeds up Burbank Avenue into East Suffield. Road maps of the period designated the drive through Thompsonville, across the bridge, and up Thompsonville Road as Route 190. Culturally this area was more like Thompsonville, but residents intermingled within the established communities of both towns. (Courtesy Tavino family.)

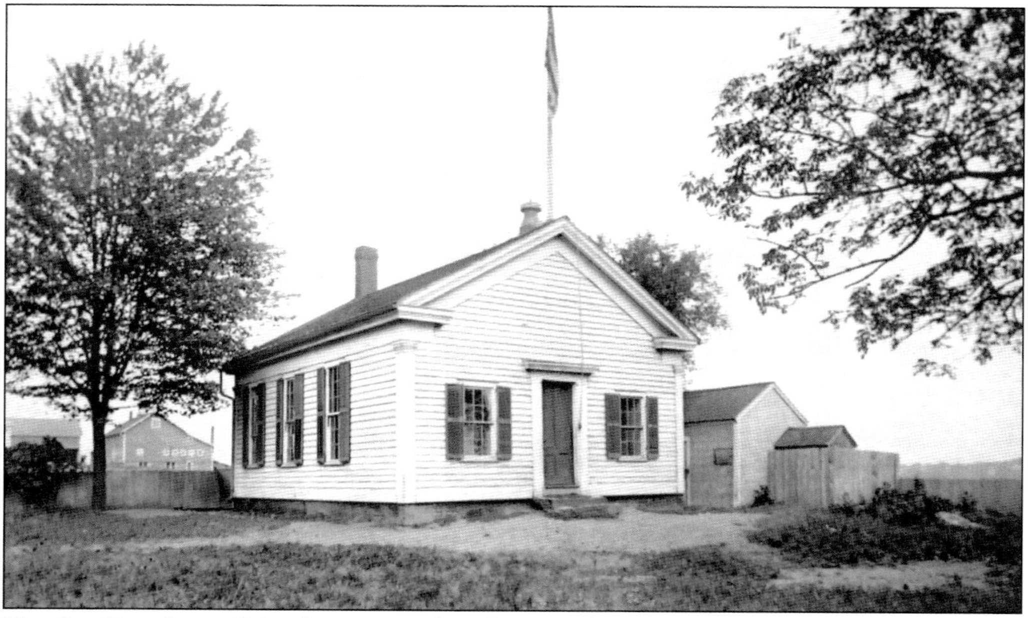

The first East Street School was one of 11 district schoolhouses in Suffield and stood at the corner of East Street and Guardlock Lane (later renamed Canal Road), near the present-day Enfield-Suffield Bridge. In 1914, student Walter Czyz had to leave school to help support his family. He recalled that his teacher made it possible to stay in school longer by paying him to start the fire each morning. (Courtesy KML.)

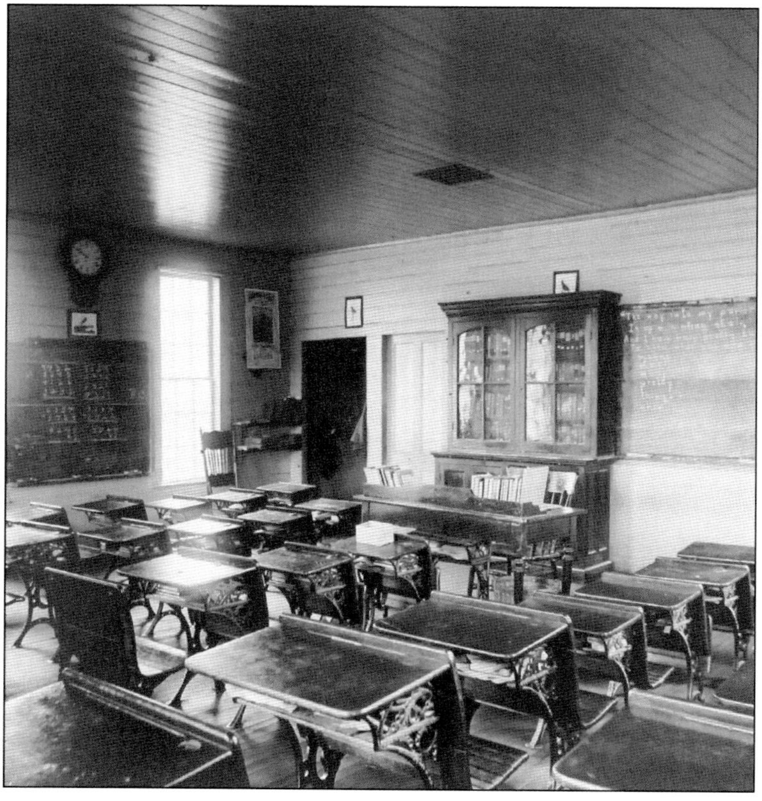

Close inspection of this photograph of the first East Street School classroom reveals a quaint poem written on the chalkboard. It reads "The way into my parlor / is up a winding stair / and I have many pretty things / to show when you are there." (Courtesy KML.)

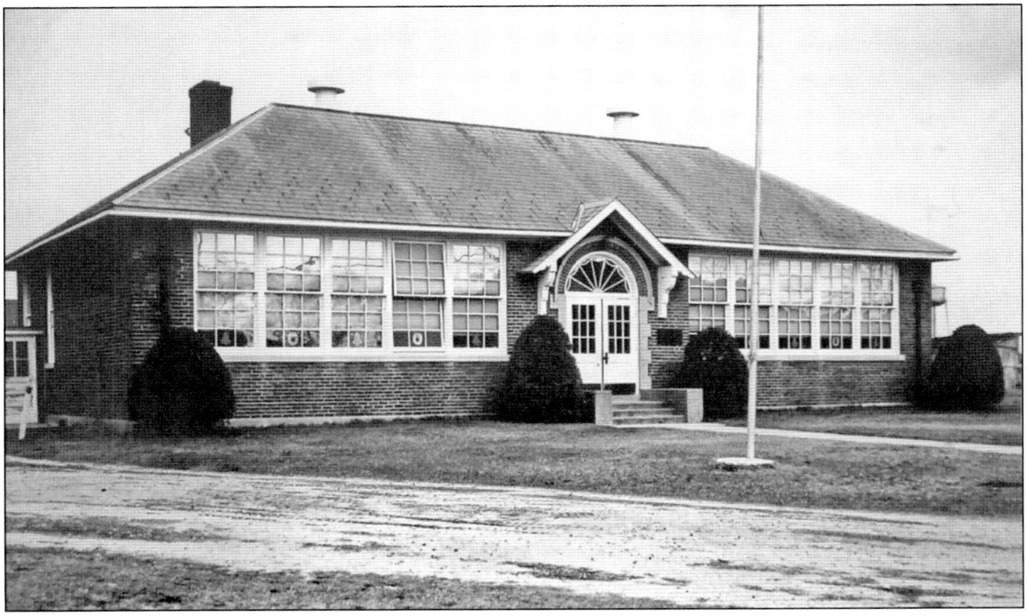

The town of Suffield purchased Thompsonville Road property from Michael Fleming for the second East Street School. It was a two-room brick building that opened around 1930 and closed in 1962. Sullivan's water tower is visible at the far right. The East Street Fire Station now occupies this location. (Courtesy KML.)

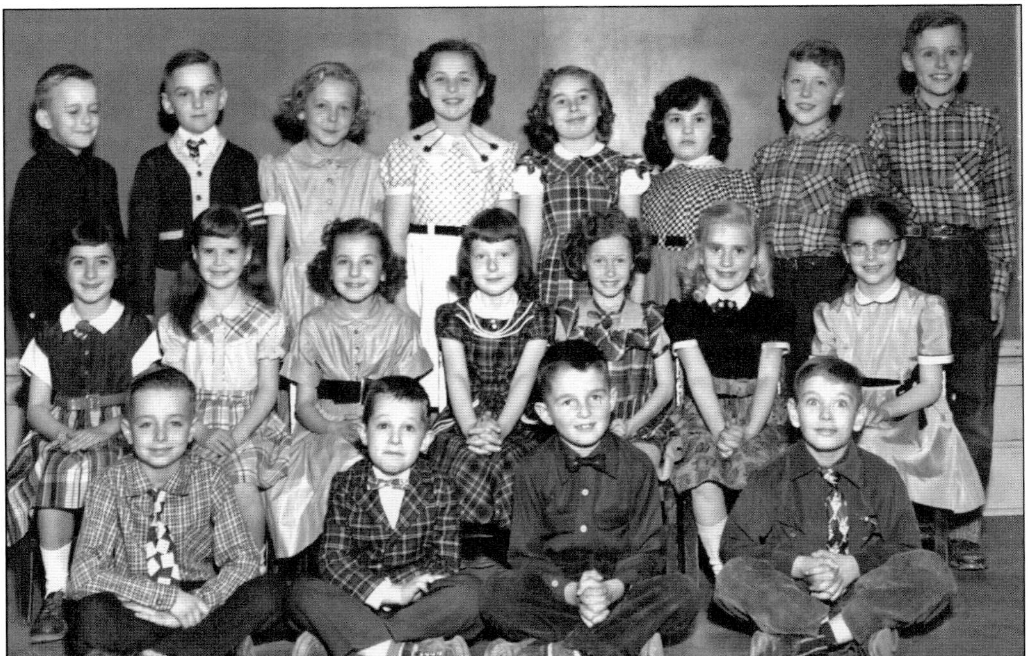

Students at the second East Street School pose in 1952. Seen here are, from left to right, (first row) Howard Blaisdell, Stanley Grigitis, Arthur Merrill, and Roger Stiles; (second row) Bonnie Mays, Dorian Love, Dorothy Gonsior, Patricia Zmitruk, Ann Brown, Linda Realini, and Marcia Cannon; (third row) Bobby Steward, Michael Krupa, Shirley Gonsior, Carol Wezowicz, Andrea Furman, Margaret Cassotta, Russell Mills, and Marcus Dean. (Courtesy Dorian Love Taylor.)

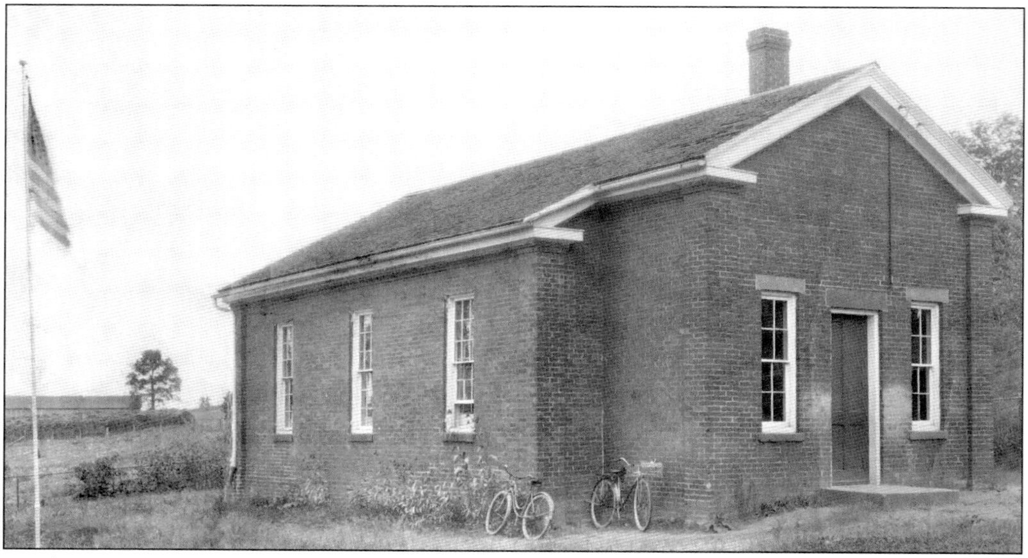

Mapleton School, serving the northeast district of Suffield, was situated on the sloping curve of Mapleton Avenue. It was a one-room, five-grade brick schoolhouse. The Hierls' strawberry fields at the far left and the Fullers' farm are visible in the background. The roster for the 1930s class picture below reads, from left to right, (first row) Jacquelyn Keeney, Marion Stebbins, Ruth Broughton, Claire Spaulding, Nancy Hinckley, Marilyn Orr, Shirley Gardner, Arlene Martin, Ellen Nichols, Doris Chapman, and Mona Smith; (second row) Hamilton Sikes, Lester Lloyd, Edward Karpinski, Carl Reed, Kenneth Dayton, Miss Eloise Covington, Ralph Dunn, Chester Gawel, Robert Snow, and Edward Gawel. The school opened in the mid-1800s and closed after the school year of 1944–1945. It is currently a private residence. (Courtesy George Fields.)

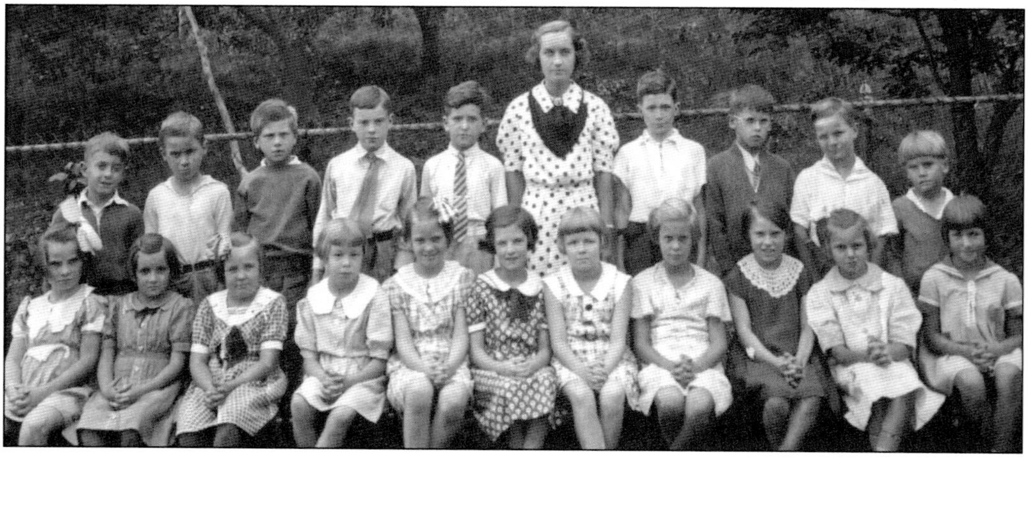

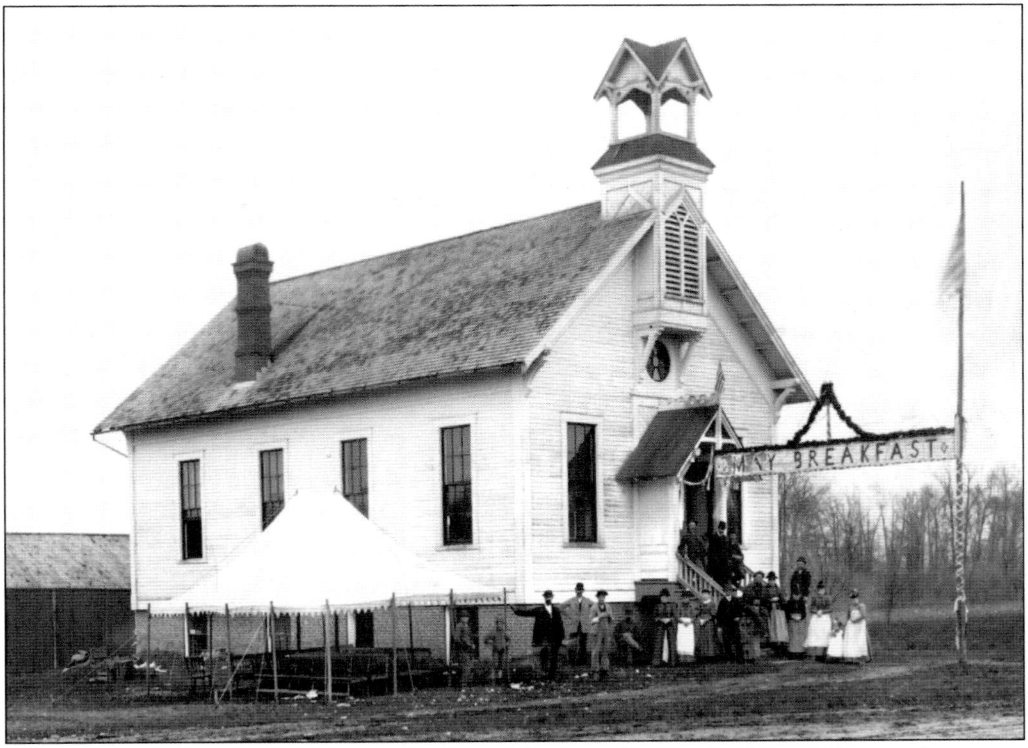

The history of this meetinghouse contains notable name changes. Built in 1883, it was known as Central Hall on Crooked Lane. By 1885, the Suffield Grange was organized, the street name of Mapleton Avenue was adopted, and the title Mapleton Hall followed suit. Annual May breakfasts drew crowds from as far away as Springfield and Hartford, arriving by trolley. The building is currently home to a popular theater group, the Suffield Players. (Courtesy Art Sikes.)

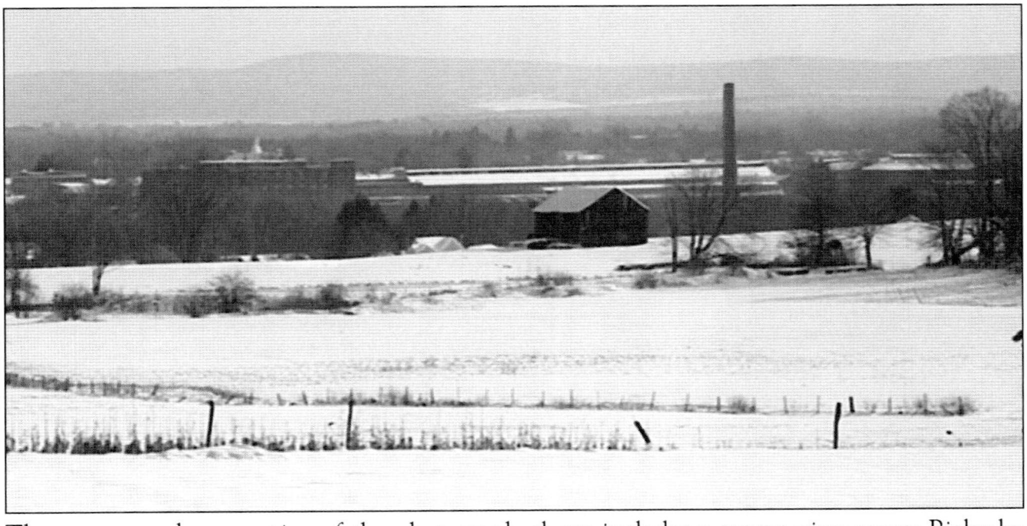

The compressed perspective of the photograph above includes a serene view across Bielonko Farm, East Suffield, followed by the Thompsonville carpet mill before the smokestack and long factory complex (center) were razed. Beyond that is the expanse of Enfield. The horizon is a silhouette of Soapstone Mountain in Somers on the northern part of the Shenipsit Trail. (Courtesy Laurie Tavino.)

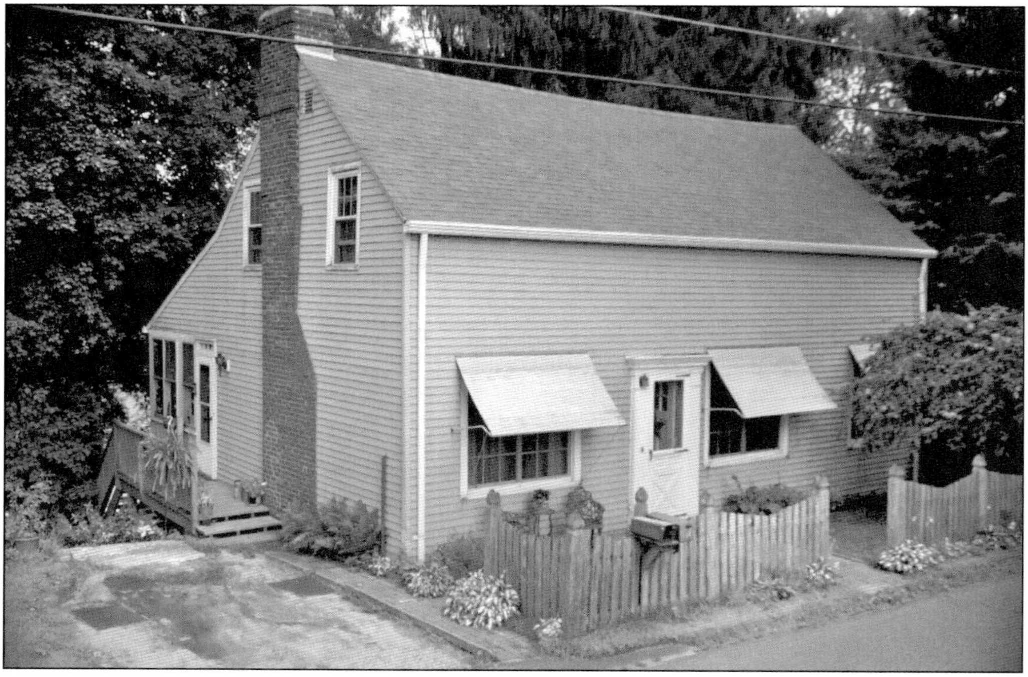

Wes and Charlotte Soloshun have called this building on River Boulevard home since 1986. It is little known that it was built in the 1930s as a clubhouse for the Sea Scouts. Founded in Massachusetts in 1912, this organization was sponsored by factories and industry. The Soloshuns' backyard is a steep slope down to the Connecticut River. Large basement doors opened to house the Sea Scout vessels. (Courtesy Lester Smith.)

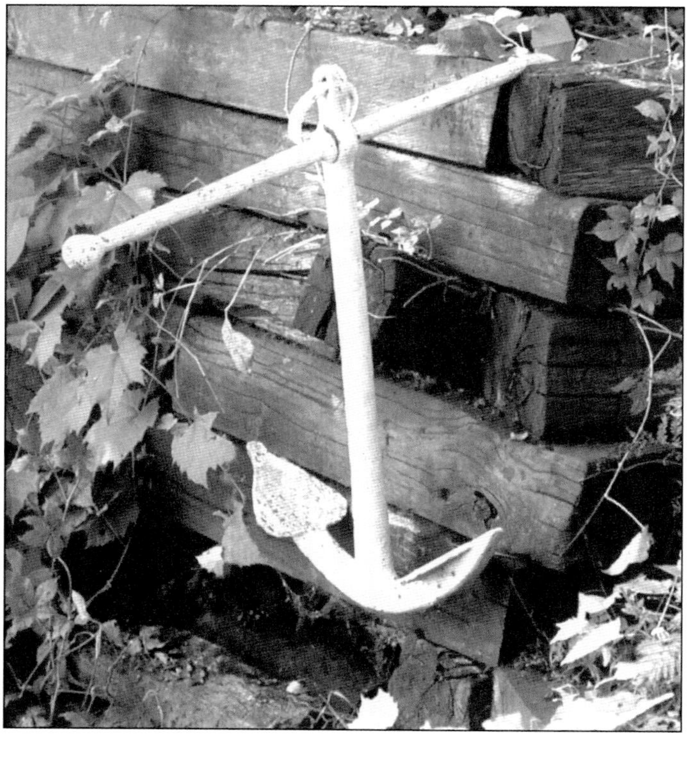

With strong support from 1929 to the early 1970s, the Sea Scouts decreased in number when industry started to leave Connecticut. A title search showed 1930s ownership of the property as the Sea-Gull Association in Enfield, Connecticut, probably the sponsor of the Sea Scout unit. While boating in the 1950s, Wes found this anchor and hoisted it up just offshore from where he would later live. He uses it to decorate his garden today. (Courtesy Ray Pioggia.)

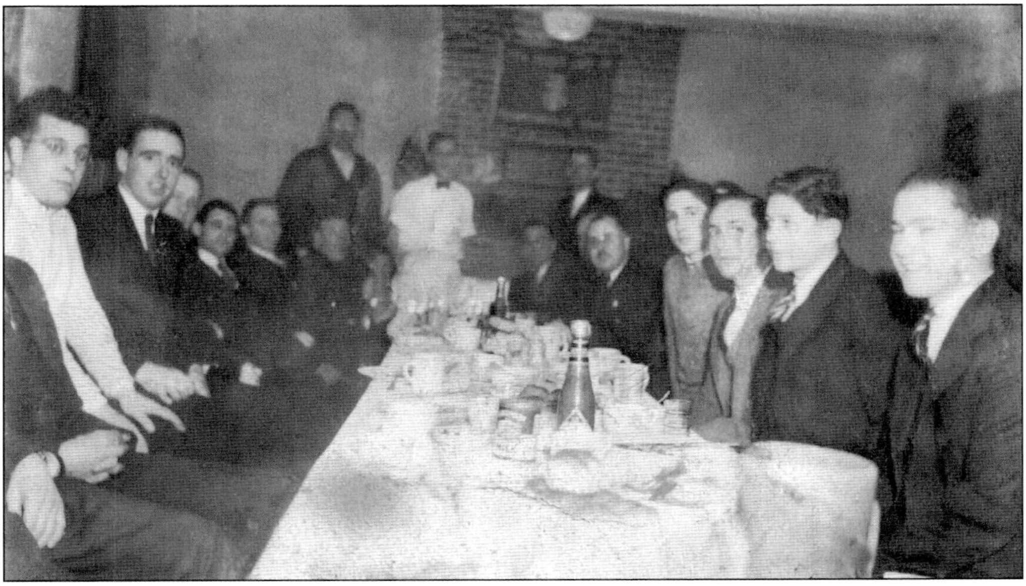

This rare photograph, recently discovered, is evidence of the River Boulevard clubhouse. Inscribed on the back is "Sea Scout Party 1936" with the names Ed Czyz, Kingy, H. Robinson, and F. Youngjohn. Sea Scouting promoted values and self-reliance, with the prospect of waterborne adventure as the lure. Paul Siple, a prominent Sea Scout from Ohio, accompanied Adm. Richard Byrd to Antarctica in 1928. (Courtesy Alice Dudek Czyz.)

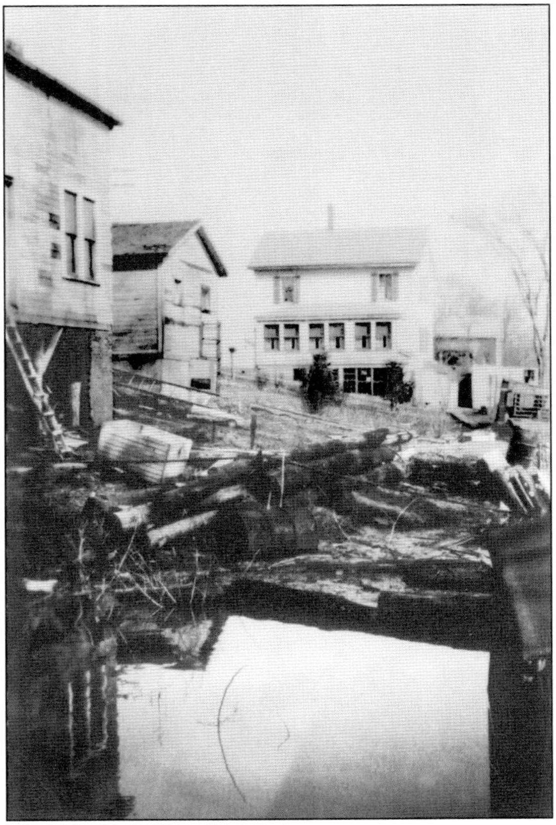

River floodwaters recede from the backyards of the Sea Scout clubhouse (far left) and neighboring houses on River Boulevard. During the great flood of 1936, Charlotte Soloshun's uncle Joe Albert, a Sea Scout who helped build the clubhouse, paddled a canoe right into its front room. Albert also took part in the Scouts' notable group trip down the Connecticut and up the Hudson River. (Courtesy Tavino family.)

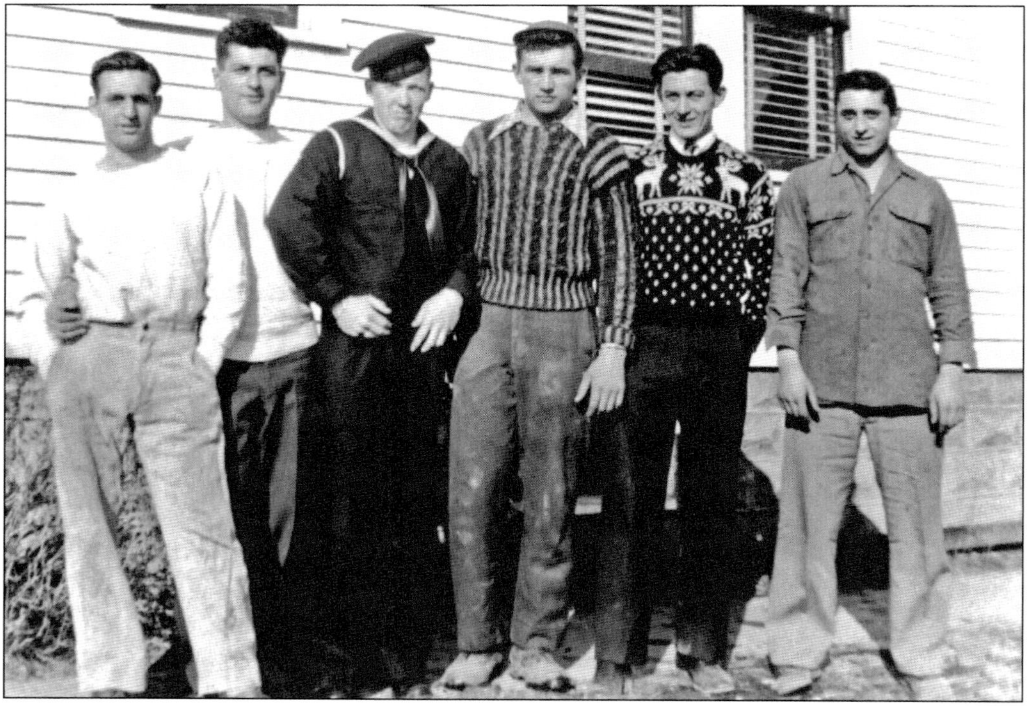

In the early 1940s, local teenagers formed a group called the East Suffield Boys Club. These lifelong friends exemplify the quintessential all-American youth descended from diverse ethnic backgrounds. In many families, the parents still spoke their native language at home but adapted to the American language through their children. In the photograph above are, from left to right, Duke Conte and Larry Tavino, who were first-generation Italian; John Conley, in uniform, who was third generation Irish; John Bielonko and Stas Zukowski's parents were Polish immigrants; and Christy Alexopoulos's parents were from Greece. Seen below are, from left to right, (first row) Chick Damon (of English and French descent), Duke Conte, and John Bielonko; (second row) John Conley, Larry Tavino, and Mike Alexopoulos. They all lean against the Bielonko farm truck for this photograph. (Courtesy Tavino family.)

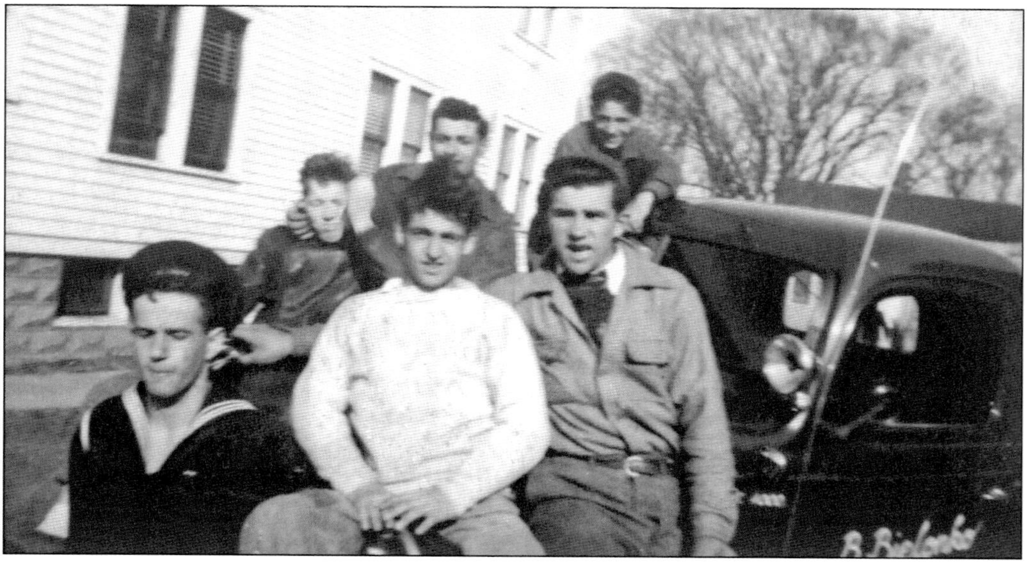

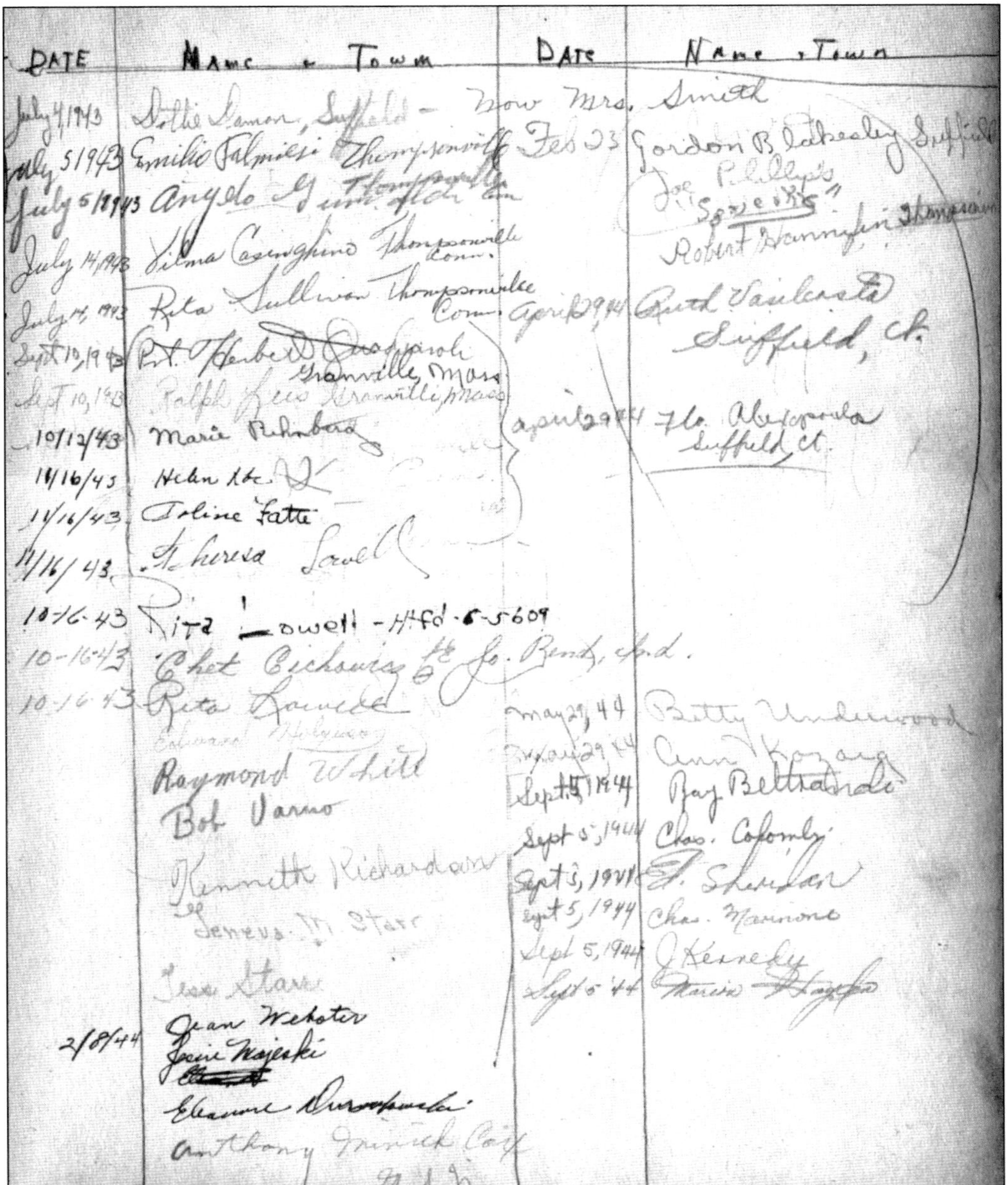

Pictured above is one of the guest sign-in pages from the World War II–era East Suffield Boys Club scrapbook. Among the pages of signatures was a list of members and photographs of neighbors and classmates. Mike Alexopoulos, the only surviving member, described the club meetings as where the group discussed sports, listened to the radio, played cards, and staged boxing matches. They also played on local baseball and boccie teams (boccie is a bowling game of Italian origin, played with wooden balls on flat, narrow outdoor courts.) The official clubhouse was an upper room of Lorenzo Tavino's barn on River Boulevard. One night someone had an idea and suggested putting a red light in the barn window, visible all around the neighborhood to alert members of a meeting. Aghast at this, Larry Tavino's three older sisters quickly put an end to the red light signal. (Courtesy Ida Lamagna.)

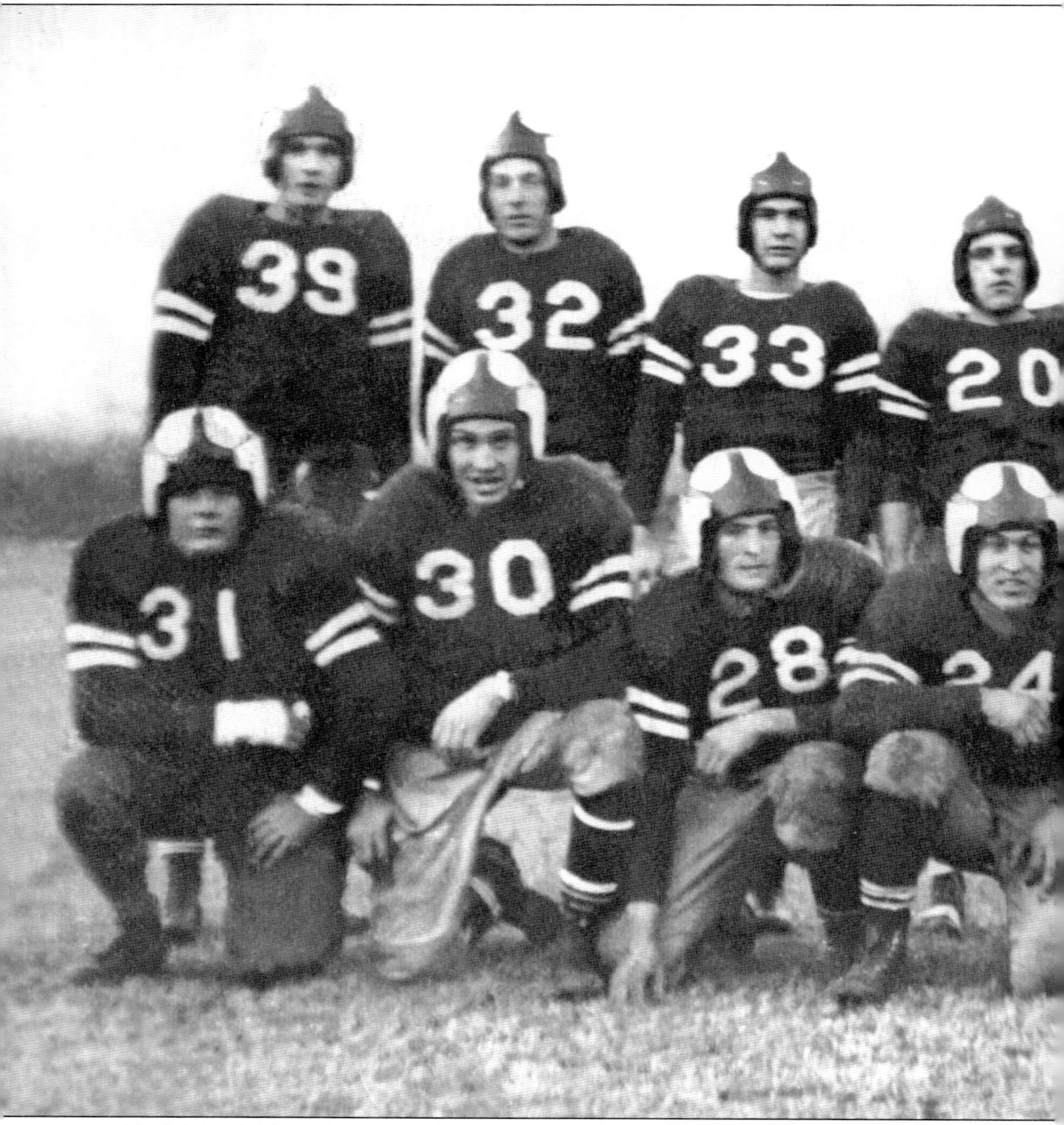

Suffield AA (Athletic Association) was a semiprofessional football team consisting of players from Suffield and surrounding towns. It was formed during World War II and lasted only a few years. These teams kept the sport of football going while so many men were serving overseas. This picture shows the Suffield AA on the morning of the Springfield Intercity League and Greater Springfield Senior Championship game in 1945. They overtook the champions of the City League: the Worthy AA from Springfield, Massachusetts. Seen here are, from left to right, (first row) No. 31, Prent Jenks (Agawam); No. 30, Bill Spear (Agawam); No. 28, Everett Brown (Agawam); No. 24, Bill Drewnowski (Feeding Hills); No. 35, Larry Tavino (Suffield); No. 21,

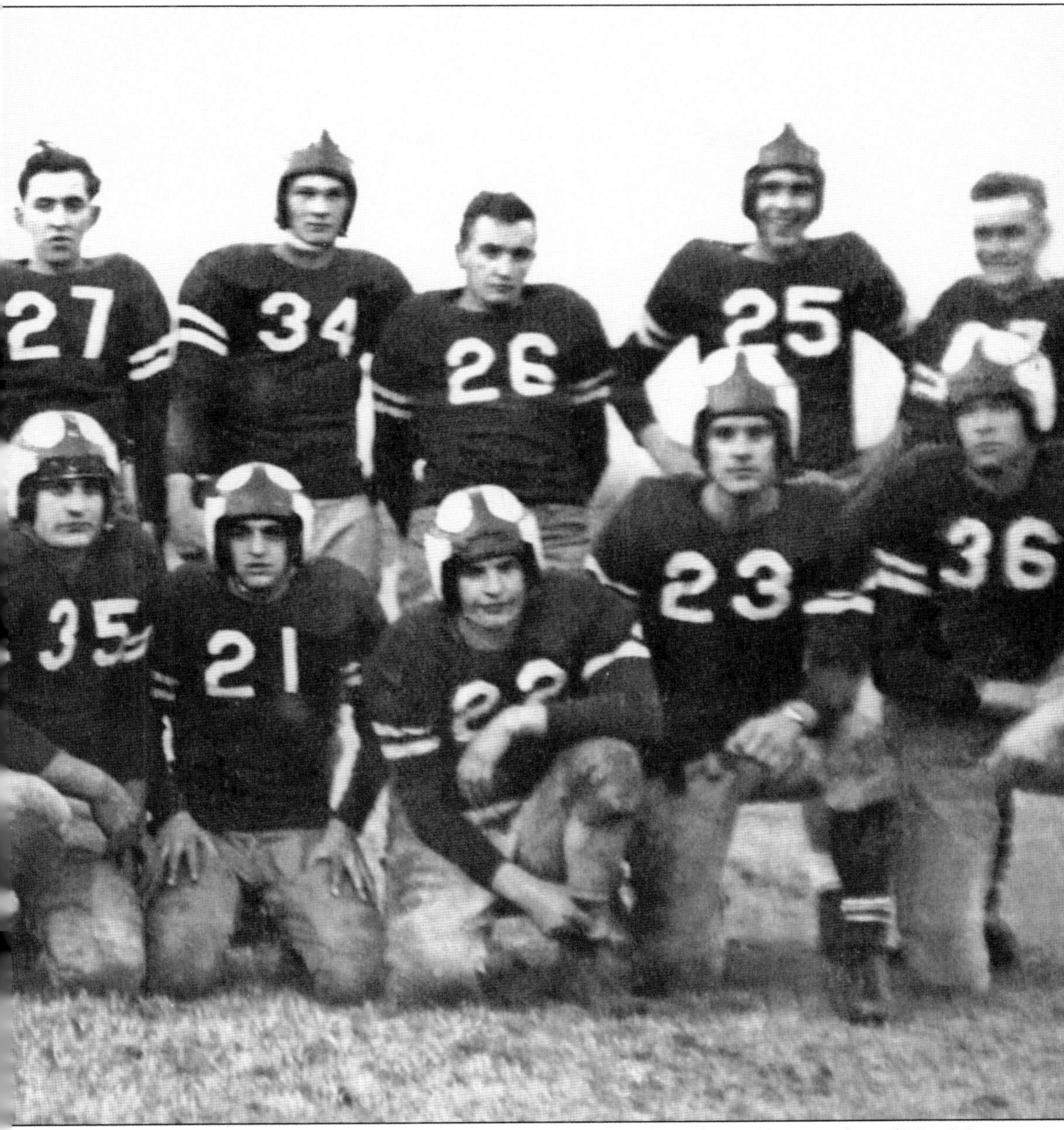

Duke Conte (Suffield); No. 22, Joe Danise (Suffield); No. 23, Jake Pohner (Agawam); and No. 36, Howard Krogh (East Granby); (second row) No. 39, Noel Brown (Feeding Hills); No. 32, Doug Cass (Feeding Hills); No. 33, ? Arsenault; No. 20, Joey Napolitan (Feeding Hills); No. 27, Henry Waniewski (Feeding Hills); No. 34, "Hammering Hank" Drewnowski (Feeding Hills); No. 26, Harm "Pat" Smith (Agawam); No. 25, Lenny Krogh (East Granby); and No. ?, Chan Duni (Suffield). Not pictured are manager Vick Jenson (East Granby) and team member John Conley (Suffield). (Courtesy Lenny Krogh.)

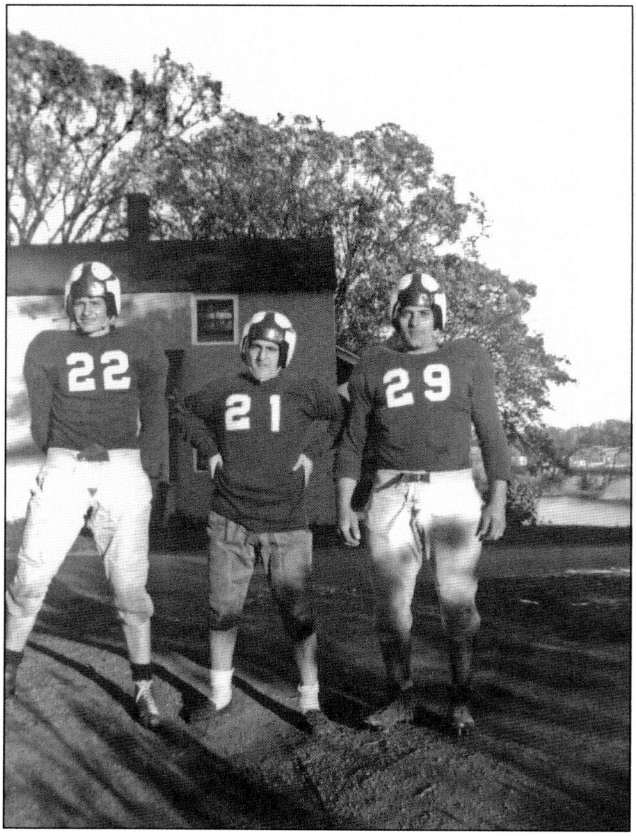

Geared up for a game are, from left to right, East Suffield's Joe Danise, Duke Conte, and Larry Tavino. The "Tobacco-Town Eleven" became the champions of their league. Just days before their big game two feet of snow fell. They cleared the field and went on to win the Intercity Crown. That was their last game. To quote Lenny Krogh, "We were tough! The beginning of the first game Duke Conte broke his nose, but he played the whole game." (Courtesy Romie Tavino.)

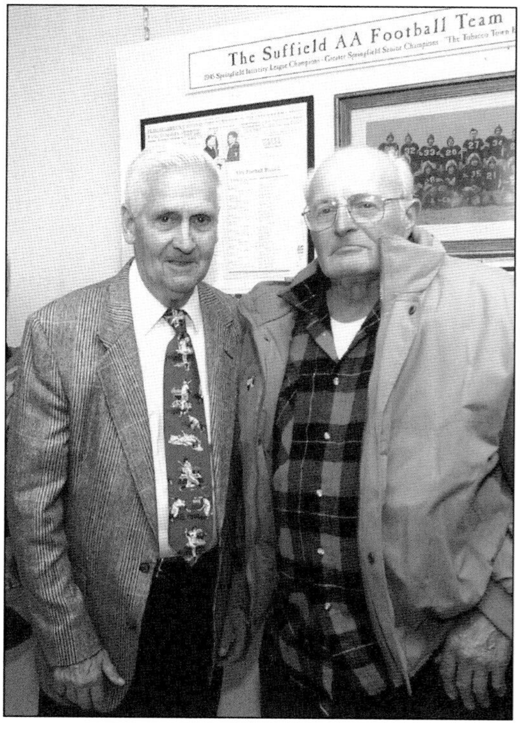

The *Suffield Southwick News* wrote: "Today surviving team members Noel Brown of Feeding Hills and Everett Brown of Agawam are still farming; Lenny Krogh in East Granby and William Drewnowski in Agawam are retired; and Henry Waniewski owns Waniewski Farms in Feeding Hills." Pictured here over 60 years after the team's glory days are teammates Lenny Krogh (left), quarterback, and Everett Brown, backfield positions and end. (Courtesy Heather Lockwood.)

Four

FAMILIES, FARMS, AND BUSINESSES

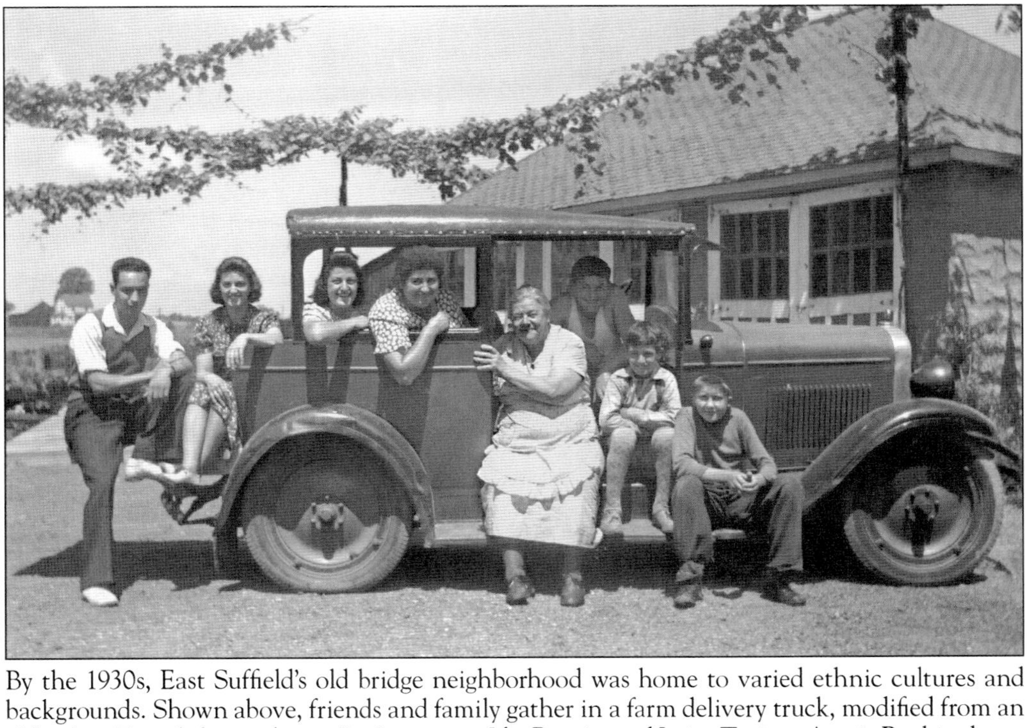

By the 1930s, East Suffield's old bridge neighborhood was home to varied ethnic cultures and backgrounds. Shown above, friends and family gather in a farm delivery truck, modified from an old sedan. From left to right are Pat Lamagna, Ida, Romie, and Luisa Tavino, Annie Buckingham, Larry Tavino, Duke Conte, and Johnny Czyz. This is a picture of contentment despite the hard times of Great Depression–era America. (Courtesy Tavino family.)

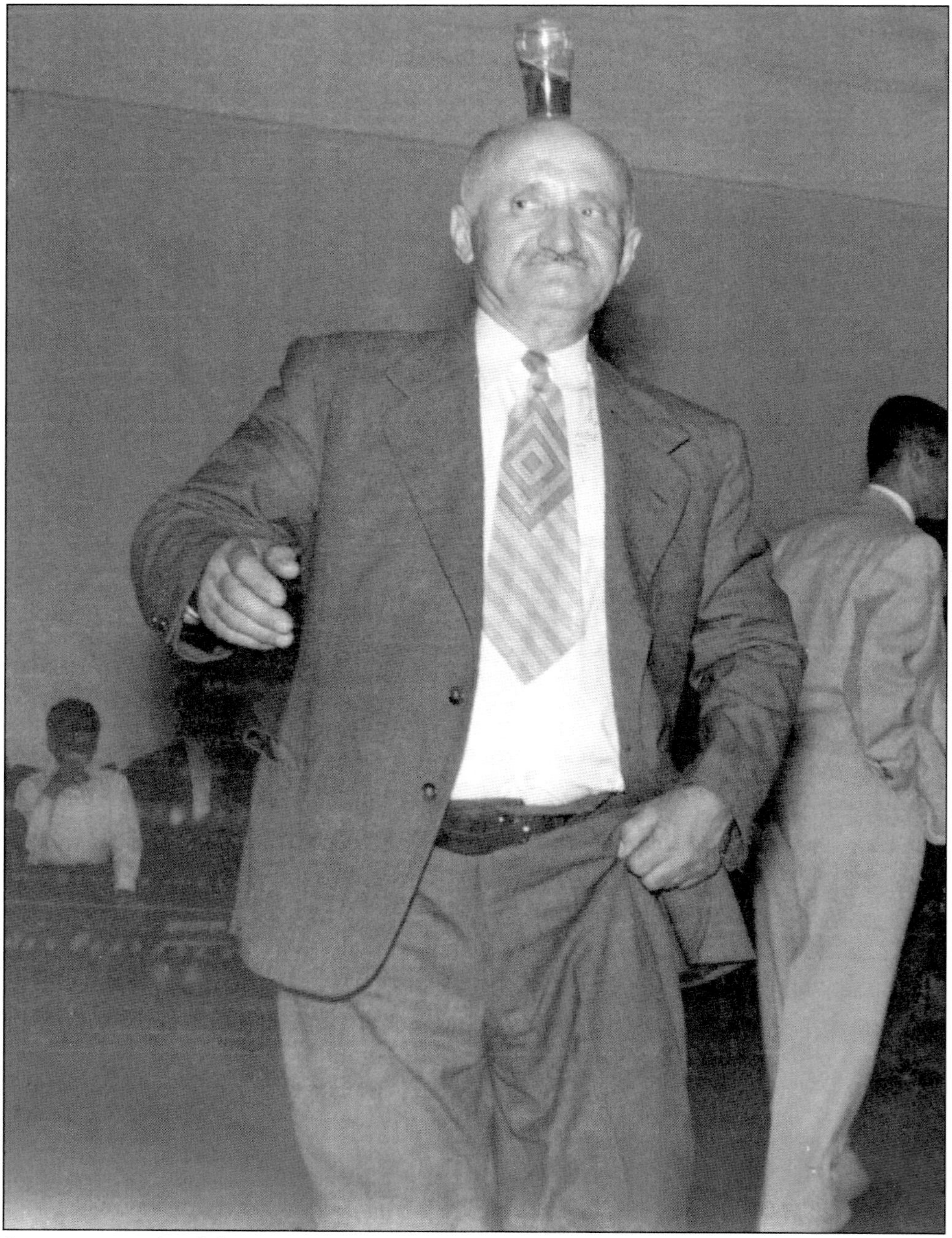

Almost one-tenth of the population in Greece came to the United States searching for work between the 1820s and 1930s. Gus Alexopoulos was one of them. Born in Koniska, Greece, in 1887, Gus married Irene Danos, who was from the Aegean island of Samos. Employed as a weaver at the carpet mill while living in Thompsonville, Gus saved his money. A lot was accomplished with those savings. It paid the fares for his in-laws to come from Greece and stay with them. After working for a few years at $7 a week, Gus was able to buy a house across the river in Suffield. He started his own business, Suffield Evergreen Company. As seen in this 1954 photograph, Gus enjoyed Greek dancing, often performing at weddings to the many traditional songs while balancing a filled glass on his head. (Courtesy Tavino family.)

By 1900, a considerable Greek population had established local businesses or worked in the nearby carpet industry. In 1916, Thompsonville's Greek community organized St. Nicholas Greek Orthodox Church. Gus Alexopoulos helped his father-in-law, Rev. Christoforos Danos, immigrate to Thompsonville and serve as one of St. Nicholas's first resident priests. Father Danos was also founder of the church's Greek Language School. He is pictured with his wife Calliopy. (Courtesy Mike Alexopoulos.)

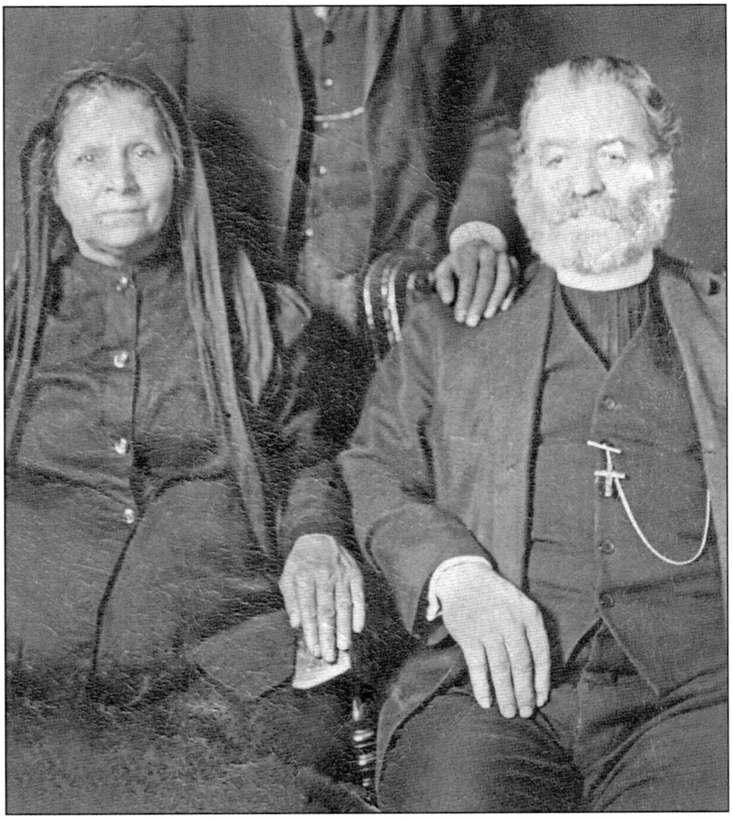

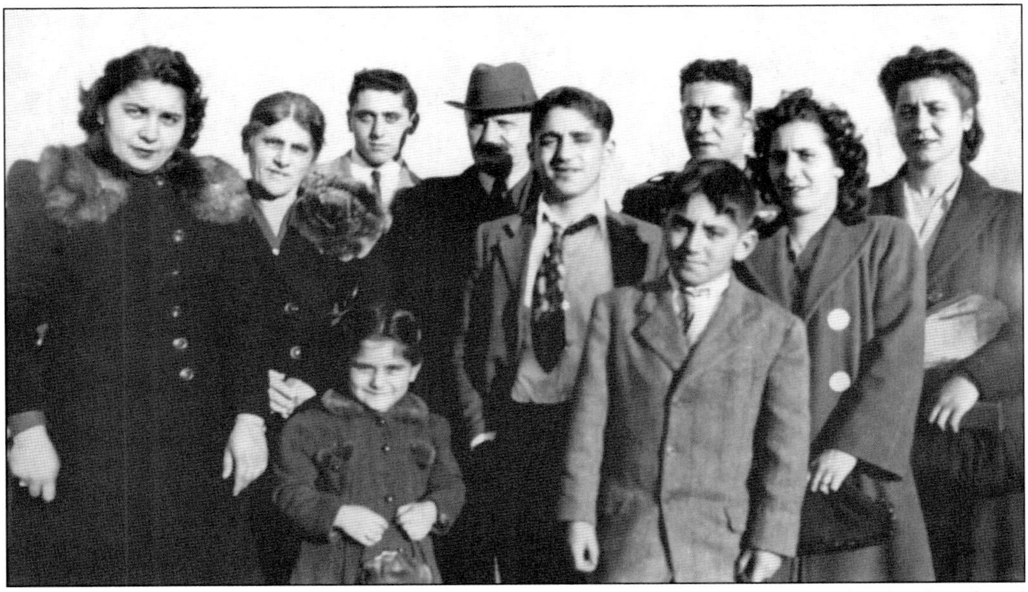

Irene Alexopoulos unexpectedly became ill and passed away at age 44, leaving her husband and eldest daughters to raise the large family. Pictured is the father Gus (with hat), eight of his nine children, and their aunt Zografo Caranassios (second from left). Son Lincoln (in back, third from right) brought great pride to the Alexopoulos family, having earned a Purple Heart in the Battle of Normandy. (Courtesy Elaine Alexopoulos Ford.)

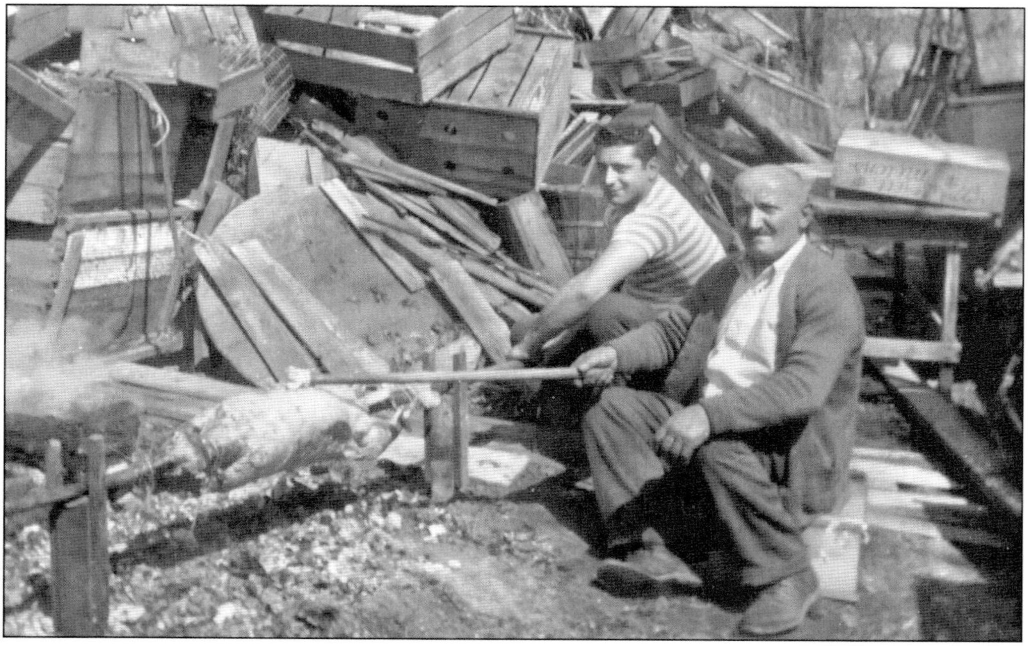

In 1954, utilizing kindling from evergreen crates, Gus Alexopoulos and his son Christy roast the traditional Easter lamb for dinner, which was an all-day affair. The family was largely self-reliant. They raised their own chickens and had a cow to provide fresh milk, from which they made yogurt and cottage and feta cheeses. Apple, pear, and cherry trees grew in the yard along with a substantial vegetable garden. (Courtesy Elaine Alexopoulos Ford.)

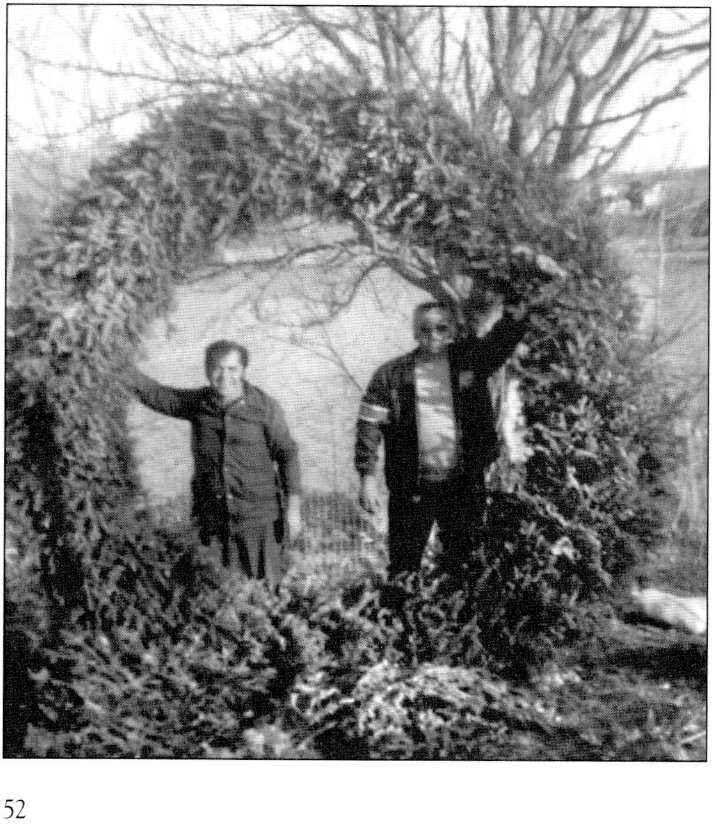

Brothers Mike (left) and Christy hold up a giant balsam wreath in 1978. The months of November and December kept the entire Alexopoulos family busy making wreaths and garland for the holidays. Balsam was piled high in their yard—the heavenly scent drifted through the neighborhood. Seven of the siblings worked in the evergreen business. Gus retired in 1972, and his son Mike continues to operate the Suffield Evergreen Company. (Courtesy Pat Alexopoulos.)

Benjamin J. Bielonko was only 16 years old when he embarked for America from Poland in the early 1900s. His goal to own his own farm and raise a family was achieved but sadly interrupted when his wife, Cora Sliwa (in this 1916 wedding picture), died of complications from childbirth. Friends helped raise the infant twins and three other children. Benjamin regrouped and married a second time to Anna Ruszala. They had two daughters of their own. (Courtesy Carol Wezowicz.)

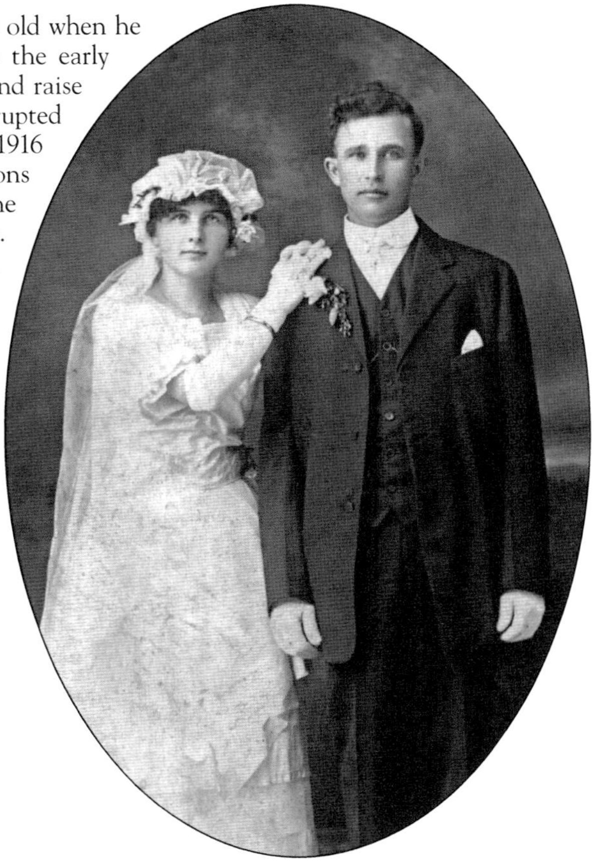

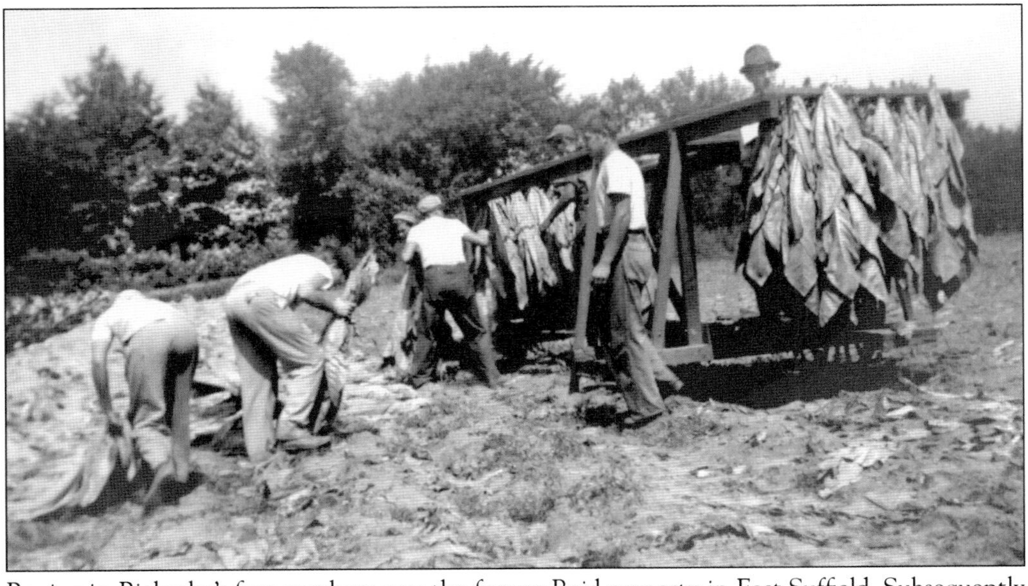

Benjamin Bielonko's first purchase was the former Reid property in East Suffield. Subsequently he acquired and combined additional nearby farms, forming a substantial dairy and tobacco enterprise. In this photograph, field-workers are gathering cut stalks of broadleaf tobacco and hooking them on laths for hanging in the sheds to dry. (Courtesy Marianne Petronella.)

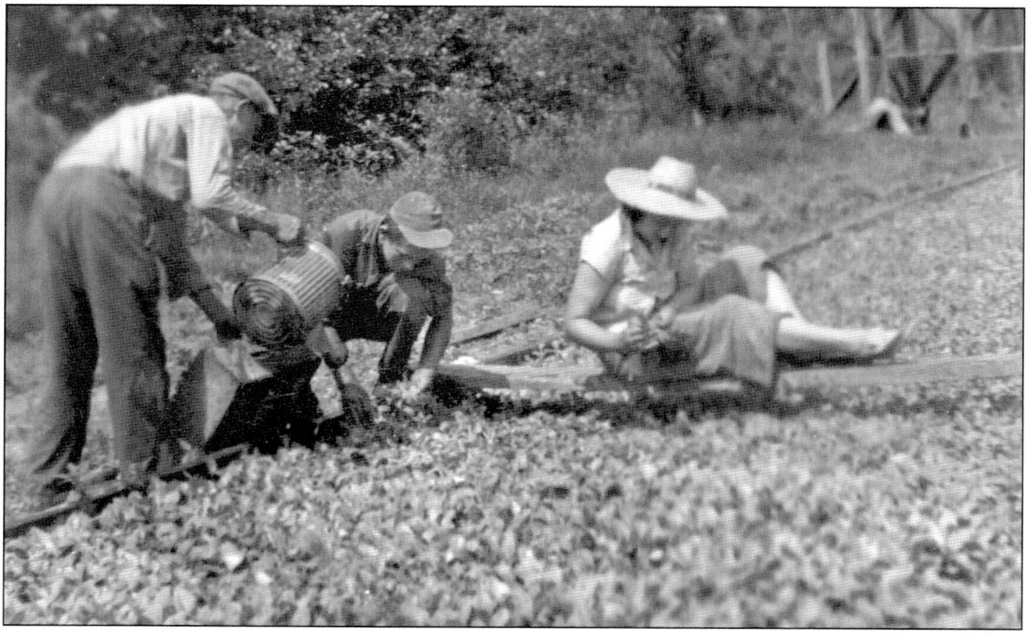

A 1930s photograph on Bielonko Farms depicts the delicate job of "pulling plants for reset." Small tobacco seedlings are gently uprooted and placed in boxes, then sprinkled with water to keep them fresh. The plants are then transplanted into the fields. The Bielonko farmstead still cultivates approximately 90 acres of tobacco in the same painstaking manner. (Courtesy Marianne Petronella.)

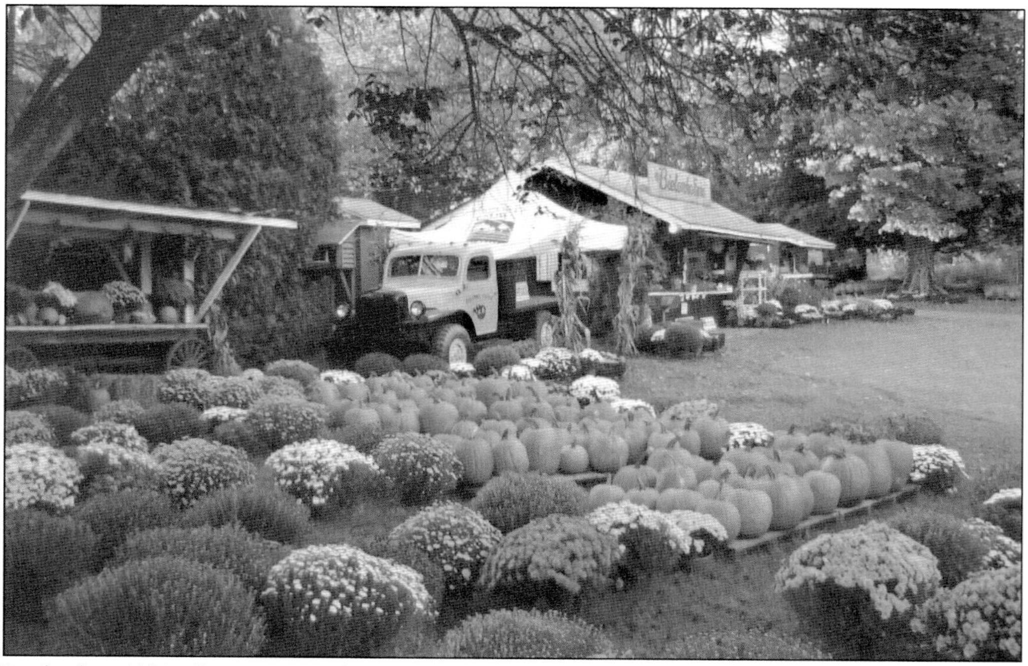

In the late 1950s, Benjamin Bielonko's son John and his wife, Irene Wlotkowski, introduced the vegetable aspect of the farm and became well known for their sweet corn. They initially sold their produce on a card table but soon switched to an antique horse-drawn wagon for their display. This led to the establishment of the Bielonko Farms roadside stand in 1970. (Courtesy Donna Bielonko.)

Now in its third generation, this century-old farm maintains a dairy with 150 cows, keeps close to 500 acres tilled every year, and has been noted in *Cigar Aficionado* magazine for its world-class broadleaf tobacco. Bielonko Farms has recycled and rebuilt tobacco sheds from all over East Suffield. The farm consistently wins awards for its produce and giant pumpkins, as seen in this photograph with sisters Klaire and Kelly Bielonko in 1997. (Courtesy Kathy Bielonko.)

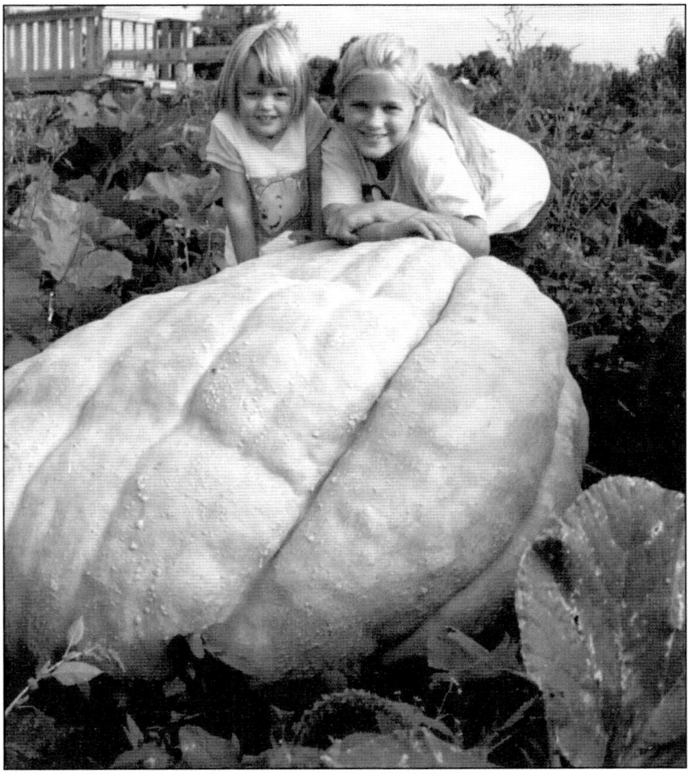

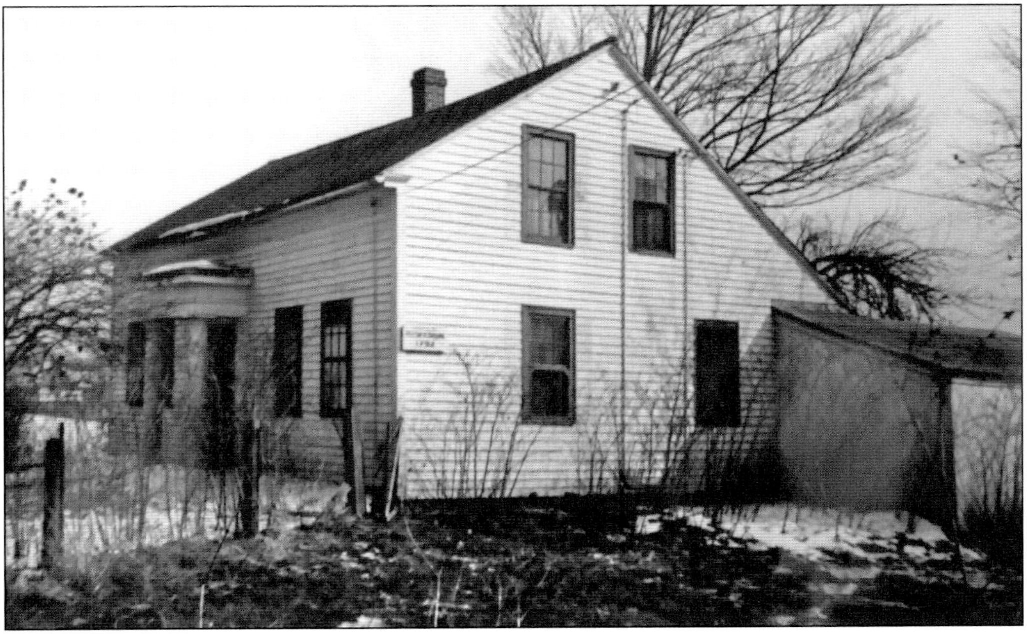

Little is known of Capt. Peletiah Allen Burbank, except that he built this saltbox-style house in 1792 on what is now known as Thompsonville Road. The house curiously faces north rather than aligning with the road. Notable are its 24-inch-wide pine floorboards, original raised panel wainscoting, and the fact that it has survived two fires. Painstakingly restored by the Rushlow family, it stands near their early American crafts studio. (Courtesy KML.)

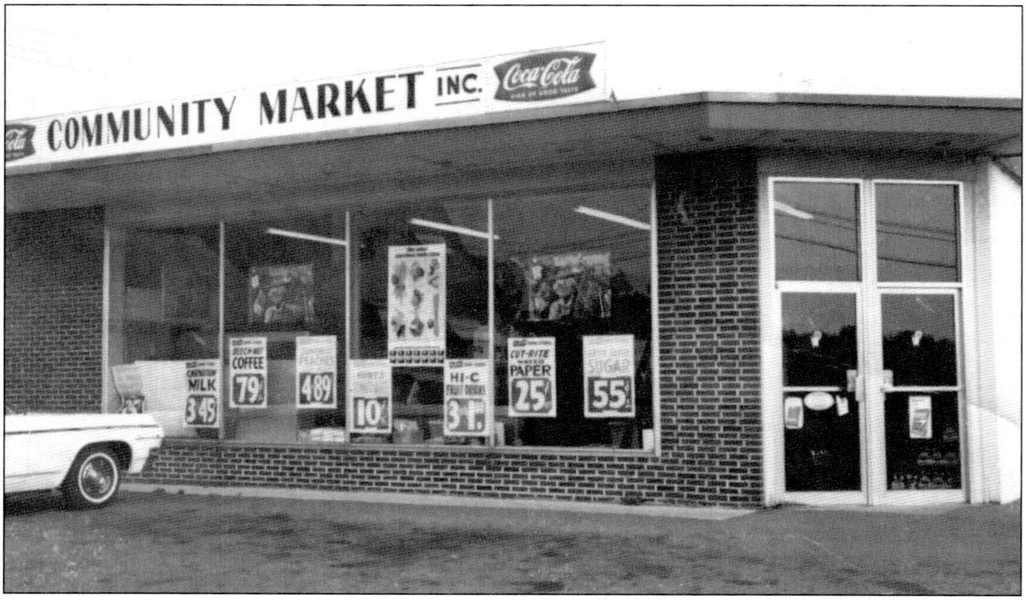

Brothers Saverio (Sub) and Vincent Gannuscio, with partner Chick Maniscalchi, purchased land on the corner of Thompsonville Road and Cowan Street. Here they built and opened Community Market in 1957. Maniscalchi moved on but the Gannuscios continued the business until the mid-1970s, closing soon after the old bridge came down. Ed Loiseau, a former tenant, purchased the space and consolidated it into his business, Bird Electron Beam. (Courtesy Rosalie Gannuscio Bakes.)

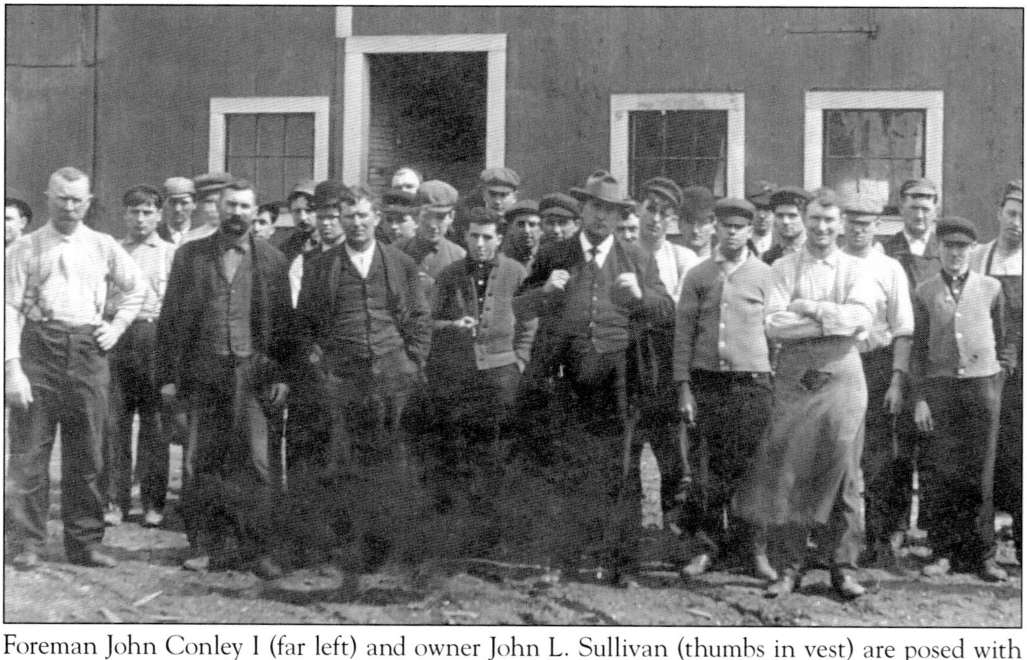
Foreman John Conley I (far left) and owner John L. Sullivan (thumbs in vest) are posed with employees in front of a tobacco warehouse. Conley's parents, Timothy and Margaret, reportedly were the first of this Conley lineage to come to America from Ireland. They settled first on Russell Avenue in Suffield, where Timothy was reportedly struck and killed by lightning. The family later relocated to East Street. (Courtesy Bob Sullivan.)

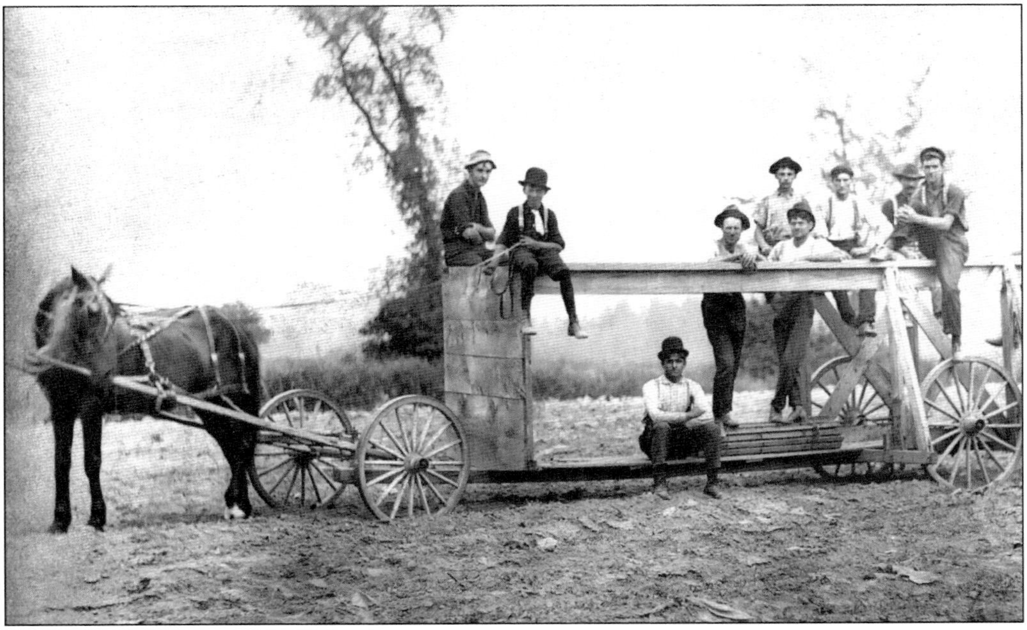

On Sullivan Farm, young John Conley II (second from left) is perched atop a harvesttime tobacco wagon. His father, John Conley I, had started a multigeneration working relationship with the Sullivan family. After serving in World War I, John II returned home, and his love of horses meant continued association and employment with the Sullivans. (Courtesy Sullivan family.)

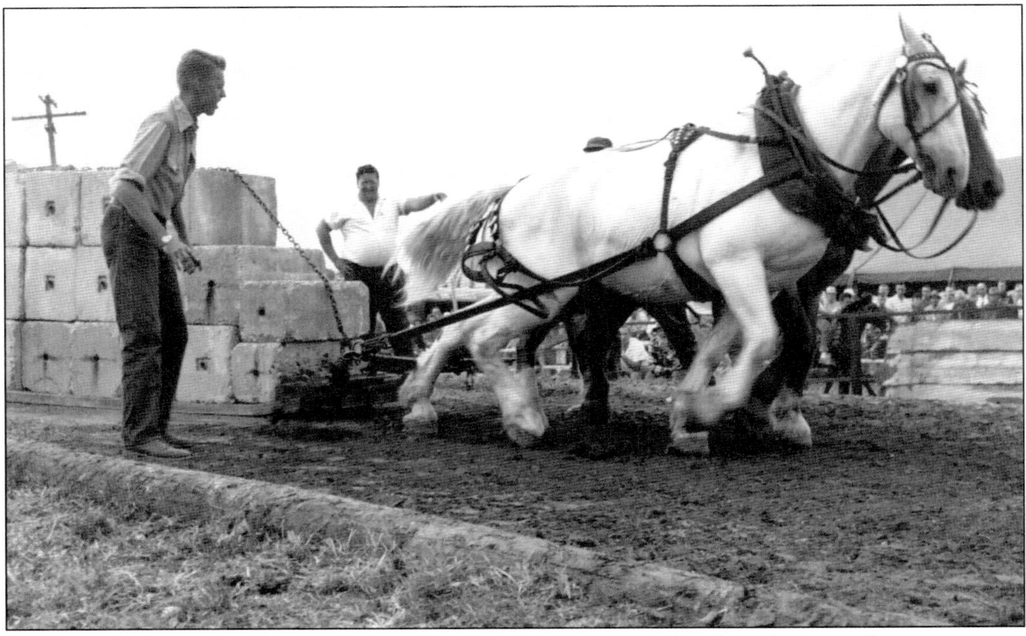

In 1953, John Conley III (center), works on the pit crew for the draft horse pull competitions at the Eastern States Exposition in West Springfield, Massachusetts. Like his father before him, John III served his country in a world war and was a skilled teamster. Today still residing in Suffield are the fourth, fifth, and sixth generations descended from Timothy and Margaret of Ireland. (Courtesy John Conley IV.)

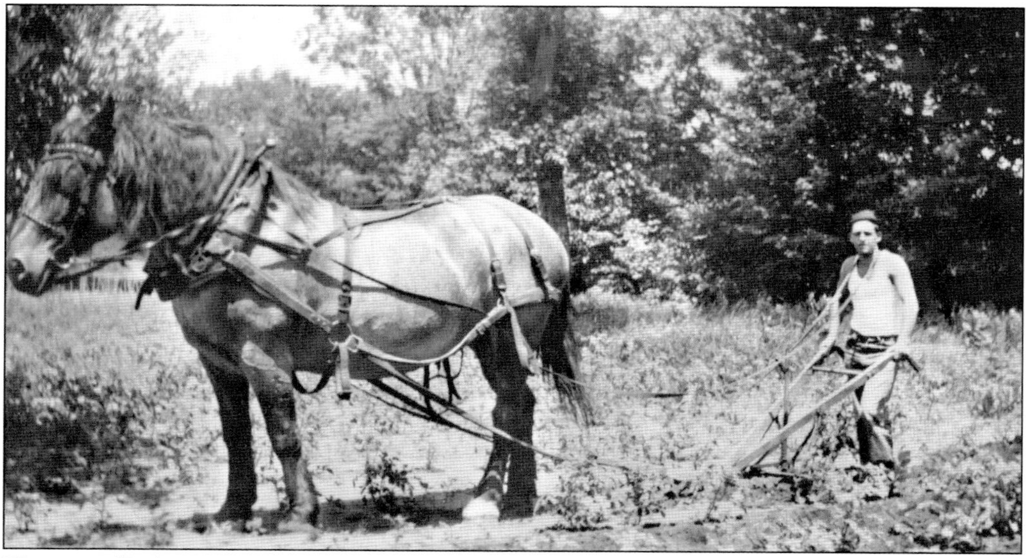

The son of Italian immigrants, Duke Conte was an outgoing figure from the old neighborhood. He was one of those all-American, first-generation characters who made the transition from old world styles through the Great Depression and upward to modern, postwar success. After serving in occupied Germany, he became an accountant for the state of Connecticut and held top posts in civic groups but unfortunately passed away at age 35. (Courtesy Ida Lamagna.)

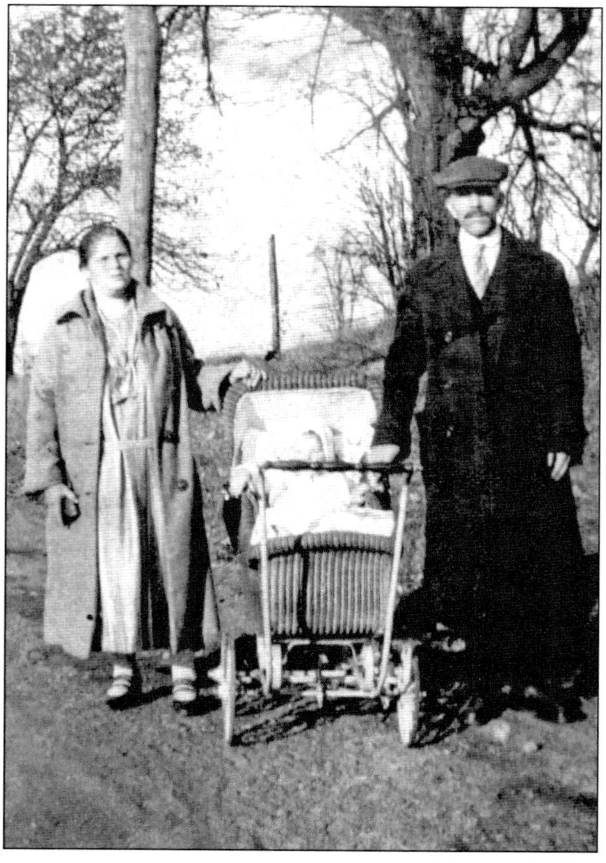

With every intention of returning to their homeland, Henry and Mary Pustelniak Czyz came to the United States from Poland around 1905. They settled close to Thompsonville in a small home on River Boulevard in East Suffield. The Czyzes had six children. Here they stand alongside a baby carriage with their youngest son, Johnny, in September 1925. (Courtesy Alice Dudek Czyz.)

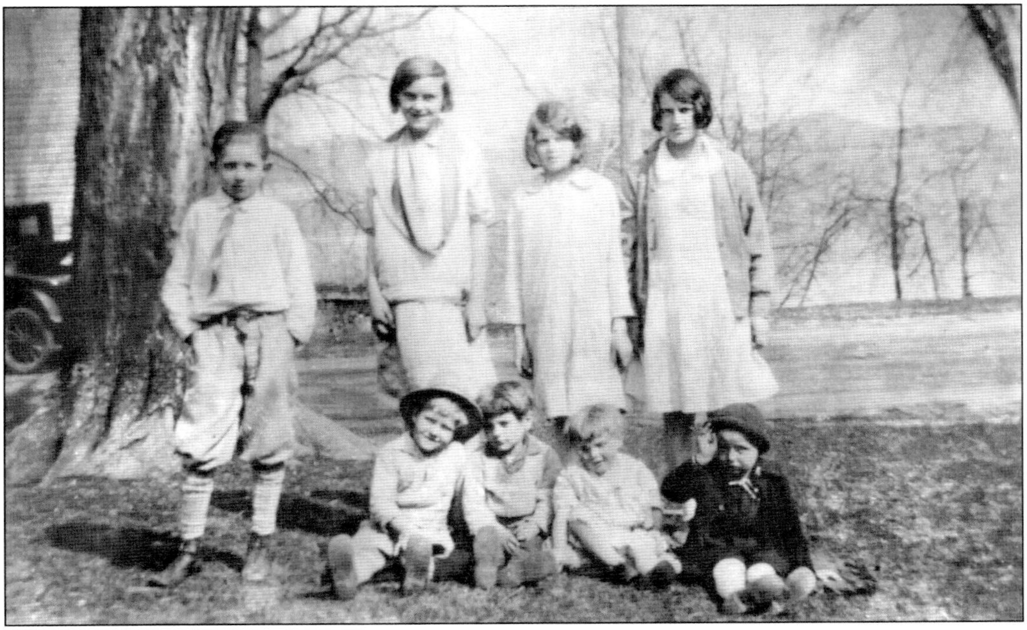

Henry Czyz, a gregarious and generous man, was particularly known for giving neighborhood children coins as he walked to and from work at the Bigelow-Sanford carpet mill. Around 1929, a group of local youngsters poses for a photograph with the river behind them. From left to right are (first row) Johnny Czyz, Larry Tavino, unidentified, and Sam Conte; (second row) Eddy Czyz, Arthur W. Bostick, Lucy Czyz, and Ida Tavino. (Courtesy Tavino family.)

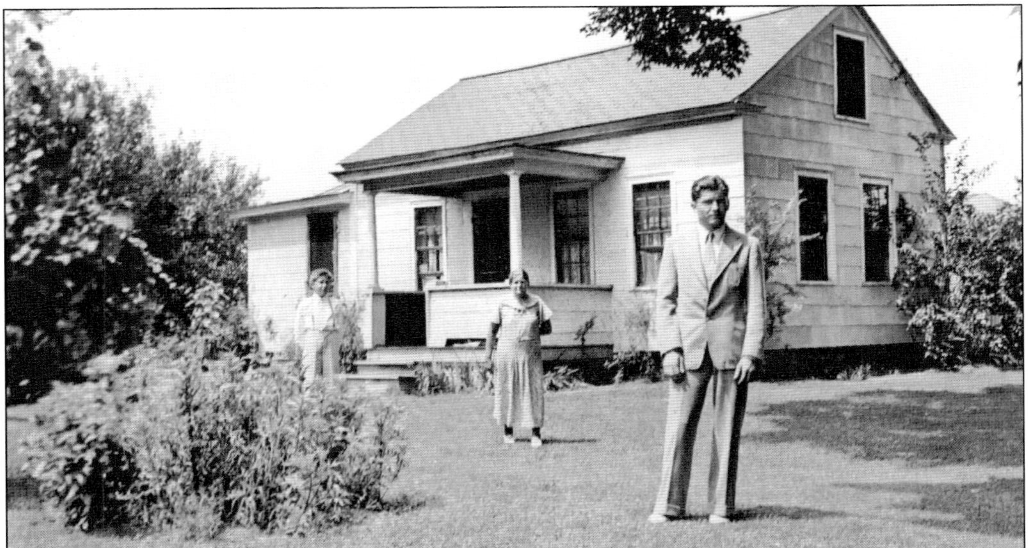

Little could have prepared the Cysz family for the loss of their two children, Tillie and Eddie, when they contracted tuberculosis and died. A few years later, father Henry and a third child unexpectedly died. Costly medical care depleted their savings. Until the late 1940s, attempts at finding cures for this disease were unsuccessful and many families were devastated. In this 1937 photograph, (from left to right) Johnny, Mary, and Joe Czyz stand before their home. (Courtesy Alice Dudek Czyz.)

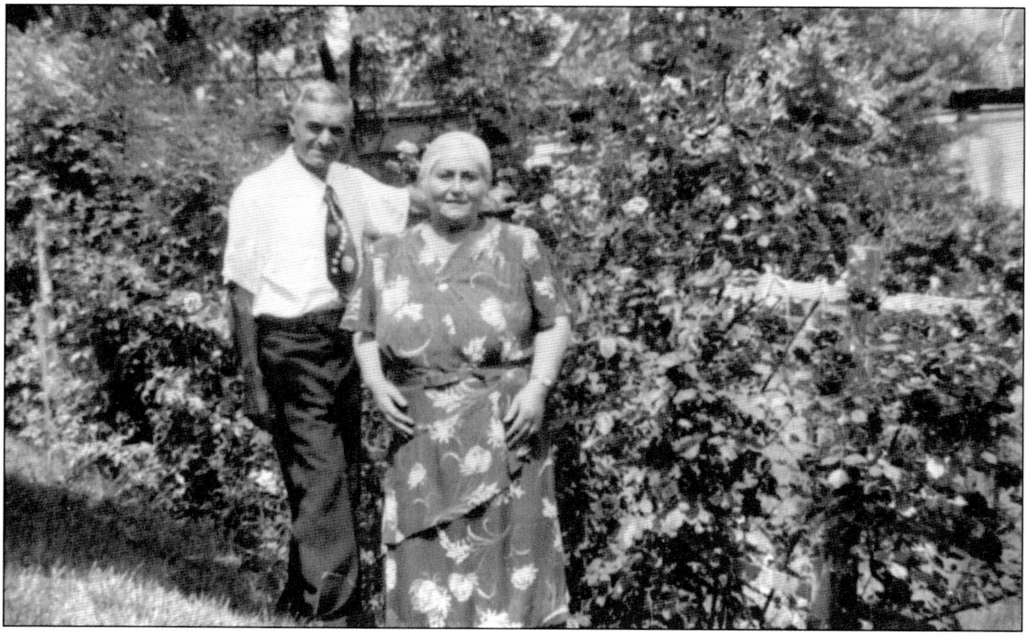

Ferdinando and Clementina D'Amato left Italy at the beginning of the 20th century for work in Thompsonville's carpet mill. Living on New Street in Thompsonville, the D'Amatos owned additional land in East Suffield's "Patch," where they raised vegetables and kept a goat. In 1942, they bought a large home overlooking the Connecticut River. This is where they raised eight children. (Courtesy Rose D'Amato Blickarz.)

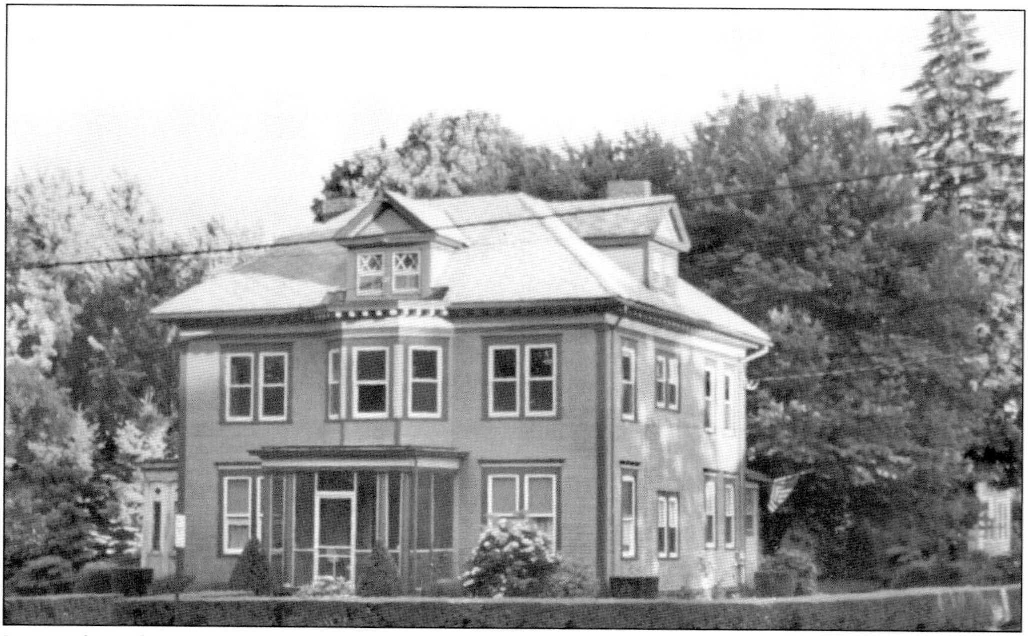

Located at the Thompsonville-Suffield Bridge, the D'Amatos' house rests on the site of the old Ferry Tavern built around 1775. Town records state that the tavern's "need was probably occasioned by the great passage of troops across the river during the Revolutionary War." This handsome home was constructed in 1907 by Ciely Viets after the tavern was taken down. It is presently owned by the Blickarz family. (Courtesy Rose D'Amato Blickarz.)

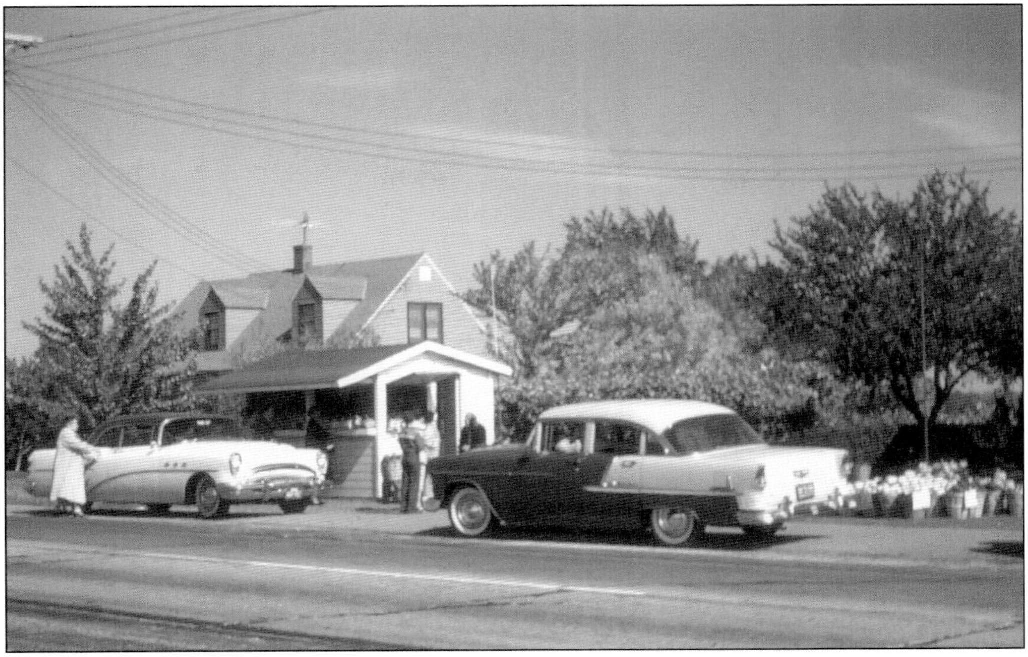

From the late 1800s up to World War I, droves of people from Bracigliano, Italy, left for North America. One of several principal destinations was Thompsonville. Vincenzo (Jim) Danise was one of these emigrants. He married Maria Romano and found employment with the New York, New Haven and Hartford Railroad. Shown above is a typical busy day at the Danise farm stand on East Street around 1956. (Courtesy Simonoko family.)

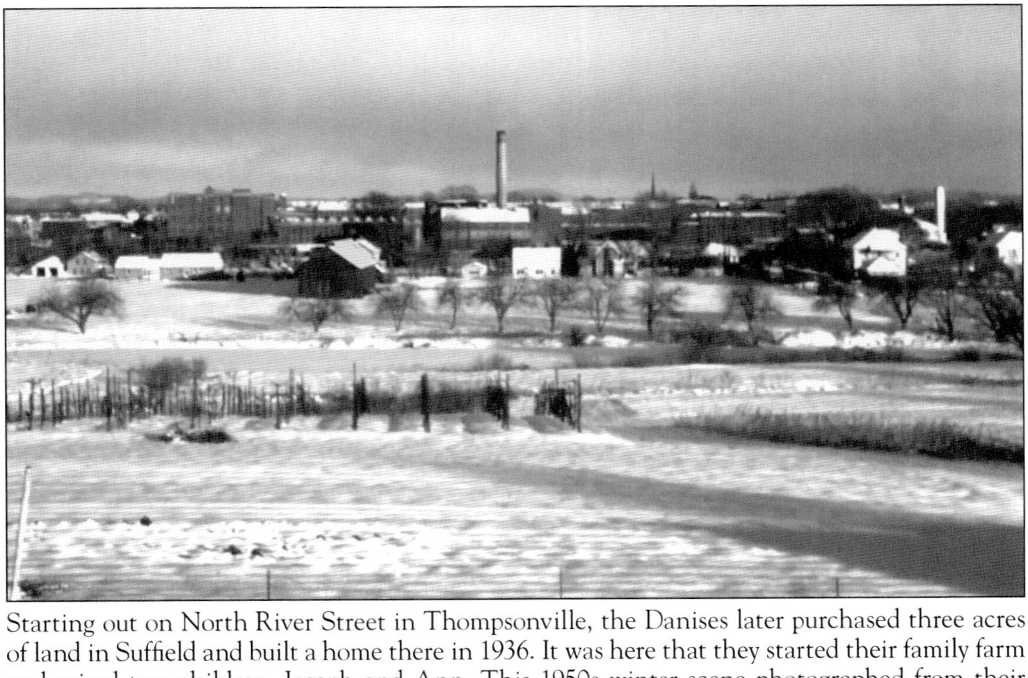

Starting out on North River Street in Thompsonville, the Danises later purchased three acres of land in Suffield and built a home there in 1936. It was here that they started their family farm and raised two children, Joseph and Ann. This 1950s winter scene photographed from their backyard shows East Suffield's snow-covered fields along River Boulevard with Thompsonville's carpet mill skyline in the background. (Courtesy Simonoko family.)

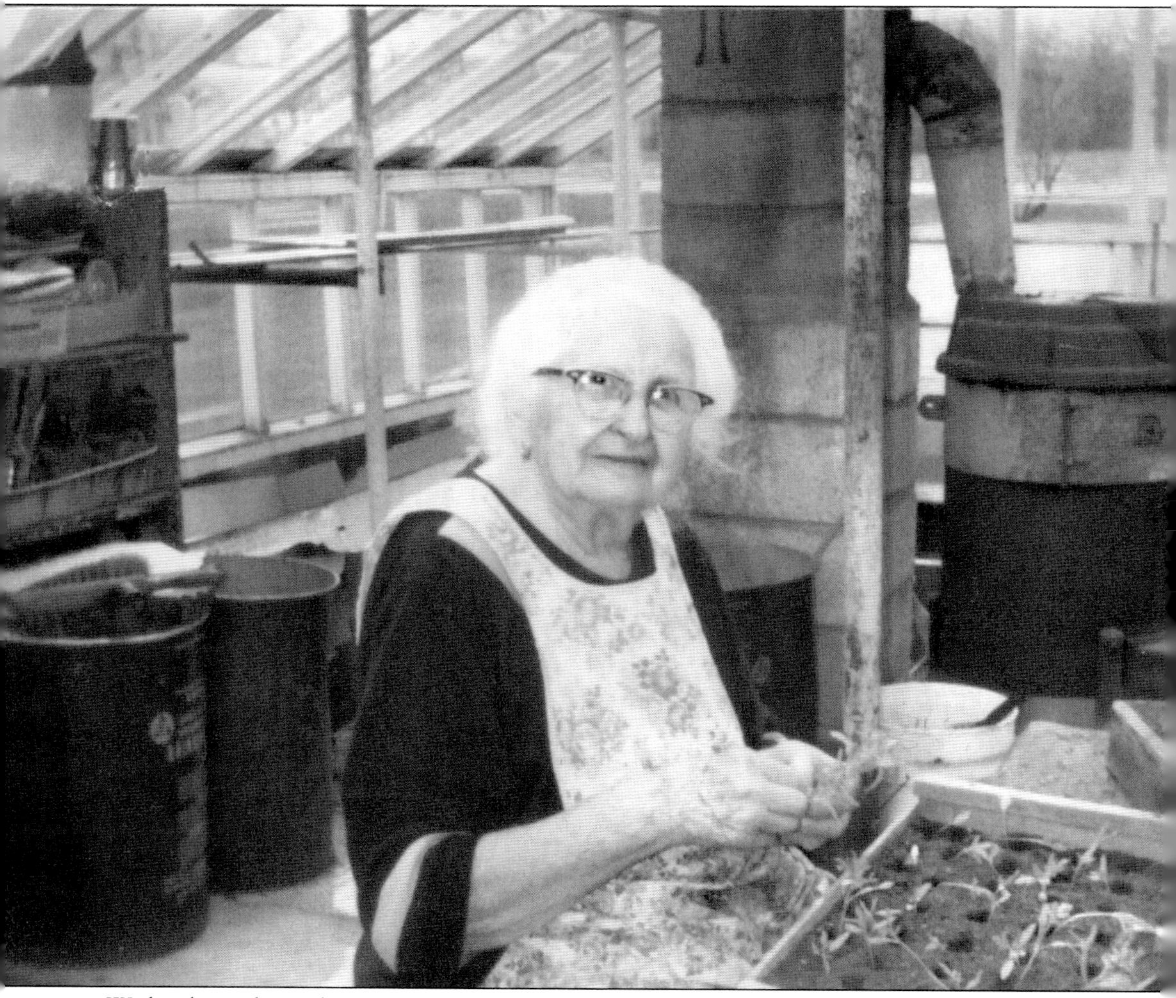

With a large, heated greenhouse and 15 hotbeds, the Danises raised tomatoes, peppers, squash, and assorted vegetables from seed. Maria, shown in this photograph, started the tomato seedlings in March, getting up in the early hours of the morning to feed the woodstove in the greenhouse. The Danises sold these starter plants in the spring and later in the summer marketed vegetables and flowers. Open from April to October, they offered fall products like butternut squash, pumpkins, and grapes. It was a self-sufficient enterprise. Every three months, the family purchased staple food items, such as pasta and cheeses, from the Italian Trade Company in Springfield. They bottled their own wine and for the most part lived off the land. Canning tomatoes was a family event that everyone, including children, took part in. (Courtesy Simonoko family.)

The Danises' small farm had a smokehouse where Jim Danise cured prosciutto and ham from the pigs that he raised. Here he tends a garlic patch with the landmark Sullivan water tower in the background. Devoted patrons kept their seasonal roadside stand busy until Jim passed away and Maria Danise retired. The business closed in the mid-1970s. The vegetable stand itself was moved further up the road and is used today by Bielonko Farms. (Courtesy Simonoko family.)

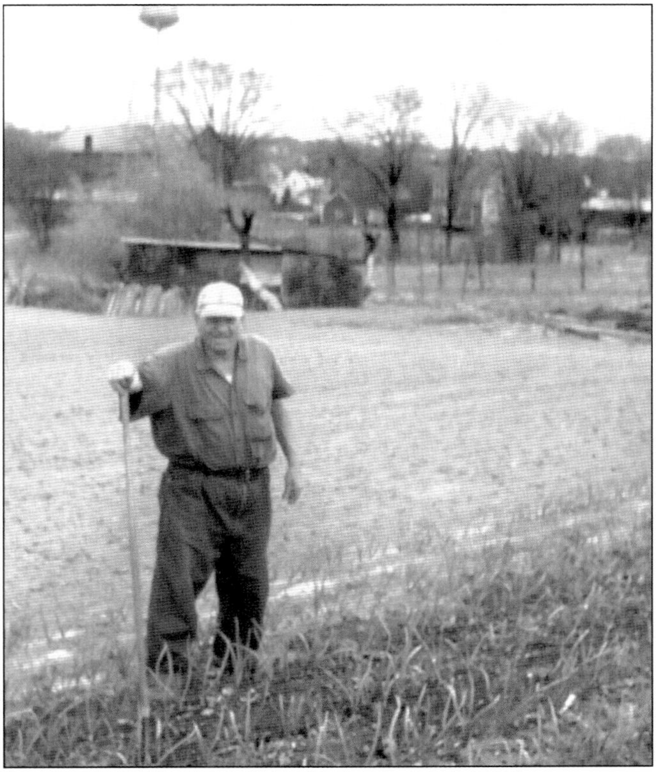

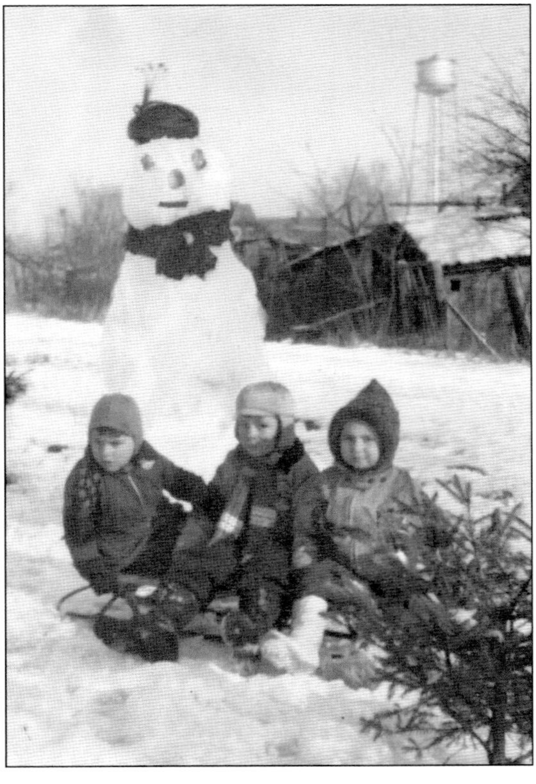

From left to right, cousins George Brassard, Salvatore Delore, and Florence Rinaldi go sliding at their grandparents' home on Douglas Street in 1952. The grandparents Salvatore and Nancy Delore emigrated from Sicily for employment opportunities in Thompsonville. In the 1940s, they achieved their dream of a home in East Suffield. As a youth, Florence walked over the bridge from Thompsonville to garden with her grandparents. She also made a home in Suffield and pursues a lifelong career as an educator there. (Courtesy Florence Rinaldi Falkowski.)

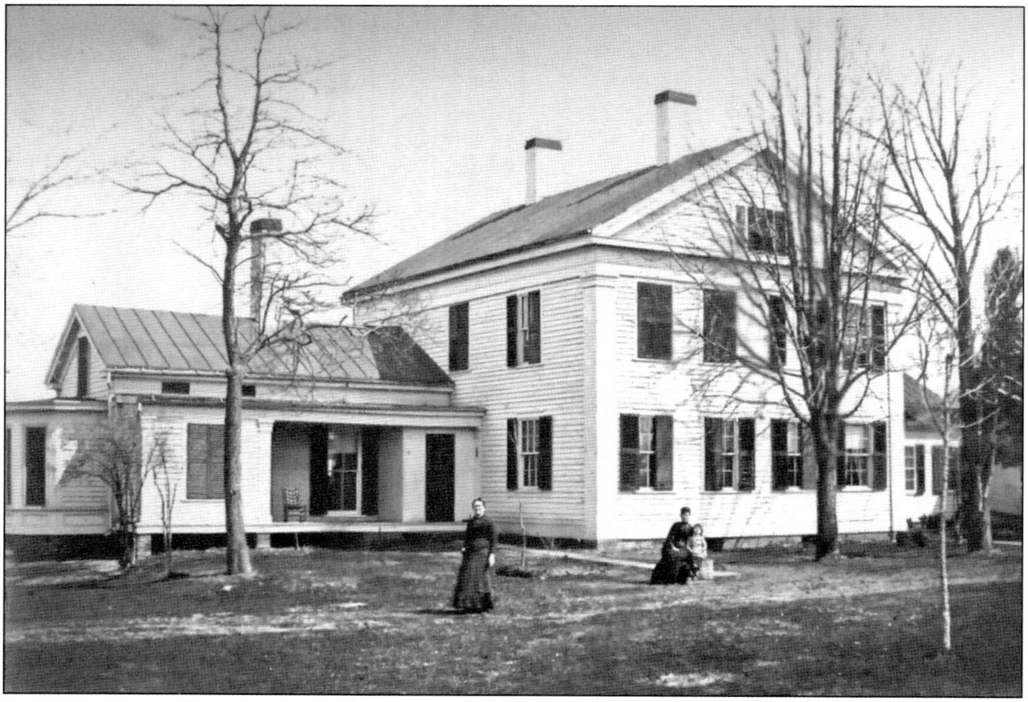

In 1830, Simon Douglas built this Greek Revival home on Thompsonville Road, nearest to the Ferry Tavern. The property was once a large tract of land running south along the river, including a sawmill on Rawlins Brook. A side street in this neighborhood bears the family name now. In many old postcards showing the view from Thompsonville, the distinctive chimneys and open-pillared back porch of this house are visible. (Courtesy KML.)

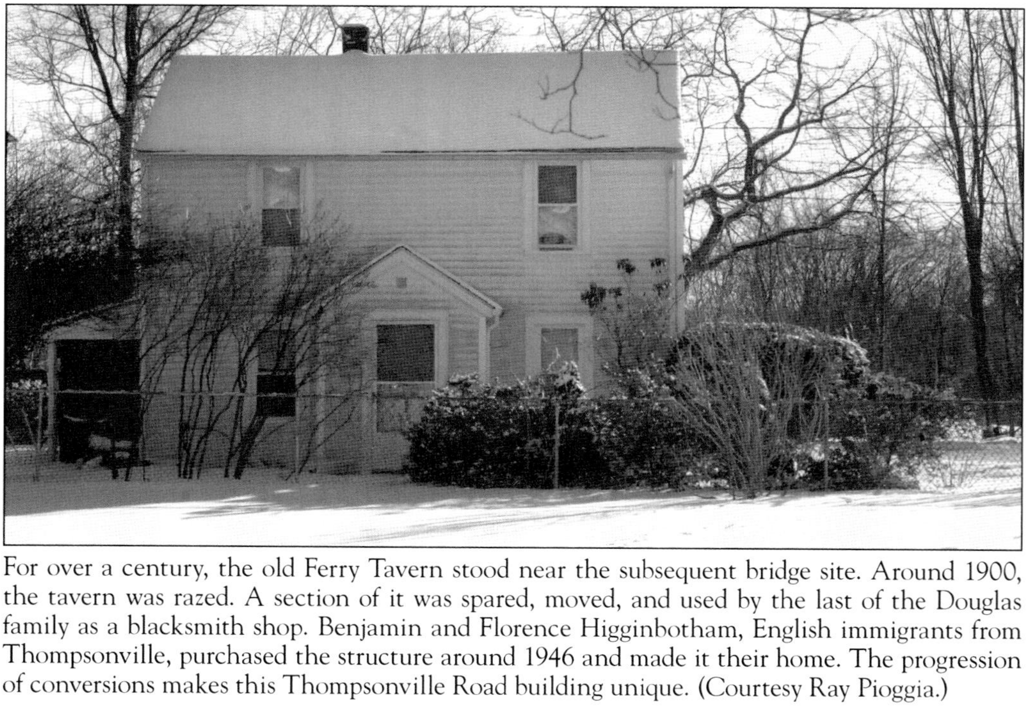

For over a century, the old Ferry Tavern stood near the subsequent bridge site. Around 1900, the tavern was razed. A section of it was spared, moved, and used by the last of the Douglas family as a blacksmith shop. Benjamin and Florence Higginbotham, English immigrants from Thompsonville, purchased the structure around 1946 and made it their home. The progression of conversions makes this Thompsonville Road building unique. (Courtesy Ray Pioggia.)

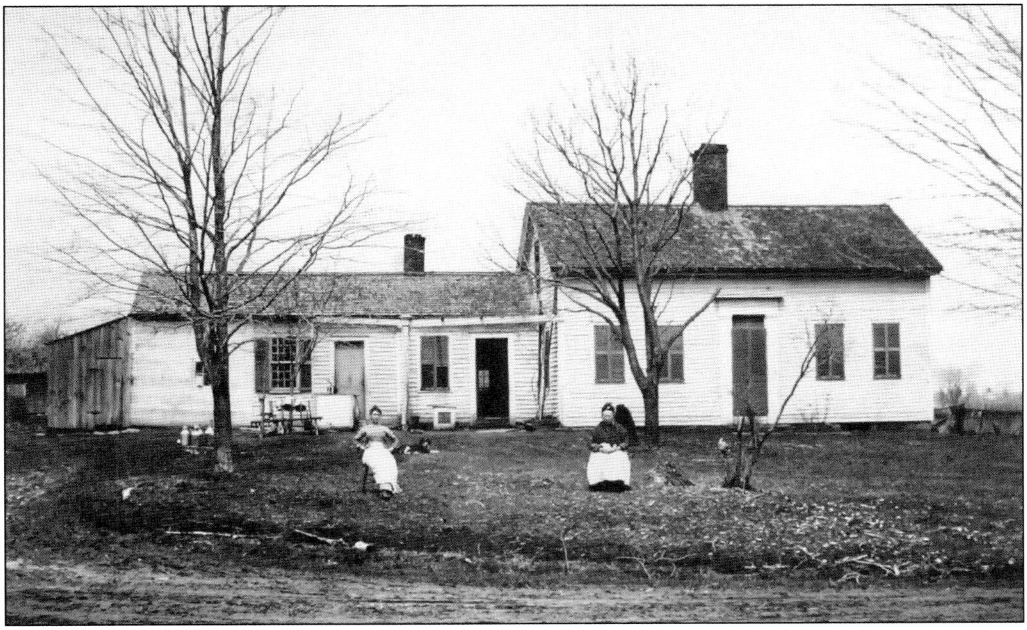

Born in Ireland about 1862, Michael Fleming came to America in 1874 with his parents, John and Catherine. Located on the northwest corner of Thompsonville Road and East Street, this house, destroyed by fire in 1913, marked the site of the present-day Fleming farm. Because of its location west of the river, the original property was known as the West Side Farm. (Courtesy KML.)

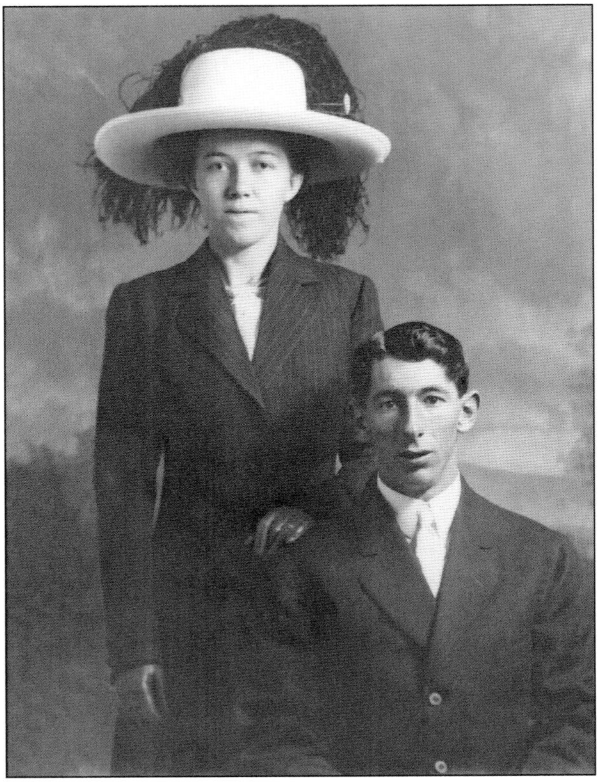

Michael Fleming and his wife, Bridget Galvin, had three children, John, James, and May. John opened a tailor shop in Thompsonville, and May got married and moved to southern Connecticut. James remained to run the farm, raising tobacco and operating the dairy. He married Catherine Burke, who had come to Connecticut from Pennsylvania to work in the Hartford Carpet Corporation in Thompsonville. This photograph shows James and Catherine on their wedding day in 1911. (Courtesy Pat McHugh Roehl.)

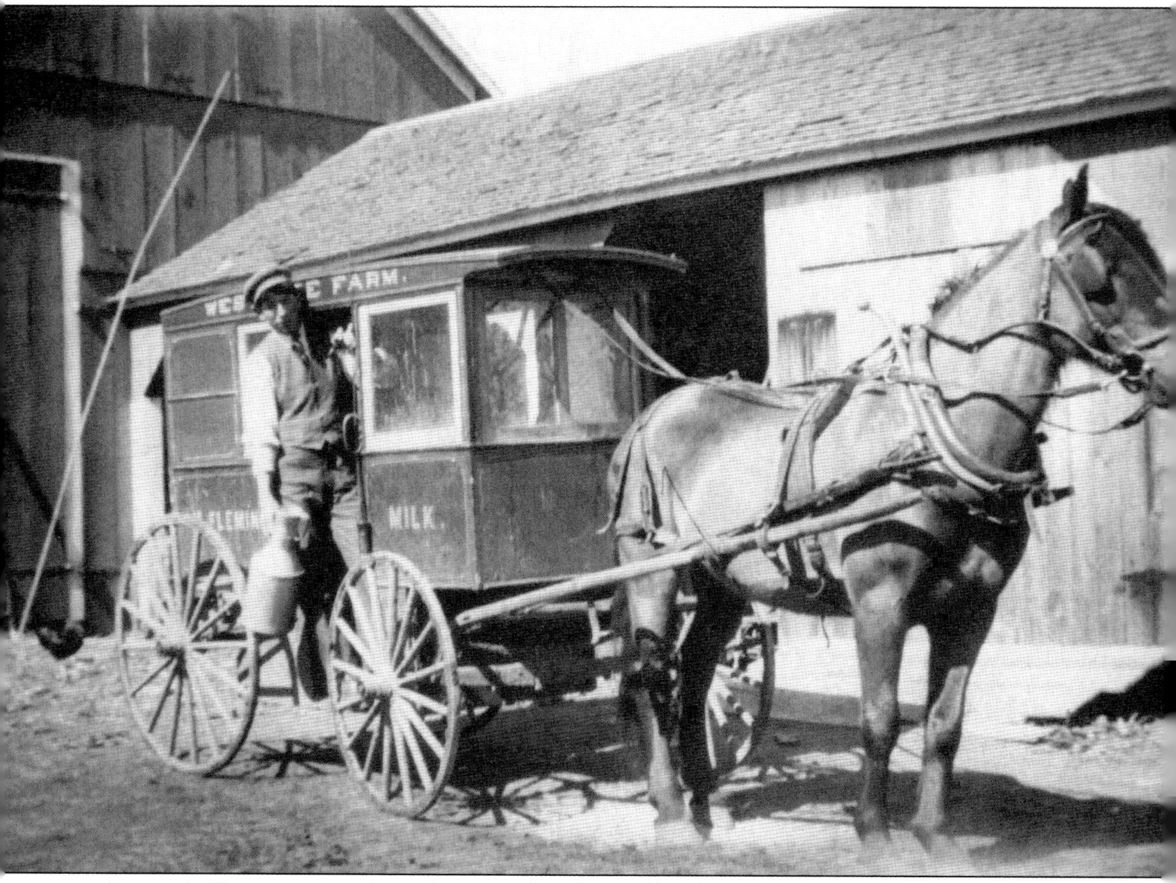

James A. Fleming poses for a photograph on his milk delivery wagon. He and Catherine had five children. Throughout their lives, they worked hard planting and harvesting tobacco and silage, as well as caring for and milking the cows. The Flemings delivered milk to customers in both Suffield and Enfield. In later years, daughter Mary made the early-morning deliveries by truck. In 1948, their son James E. (Jim) Fleming bought a flatbed truck and began delivering fertilizer and other farm products, as well as helping his father with the farm. He was reliable and hard working, and as time went on, he was able to increase his number of customers. Jim bought another truck and hired a driver, and by the early 1960s, the trucking business began to take up more of his time. The family then sold the cows and discontinued raising tobacco. According to Jim, the economy was such that "it started to cost more to raise the tobacco than you could get when you sold it." (Courtesy Pat McHugh Roehl.)

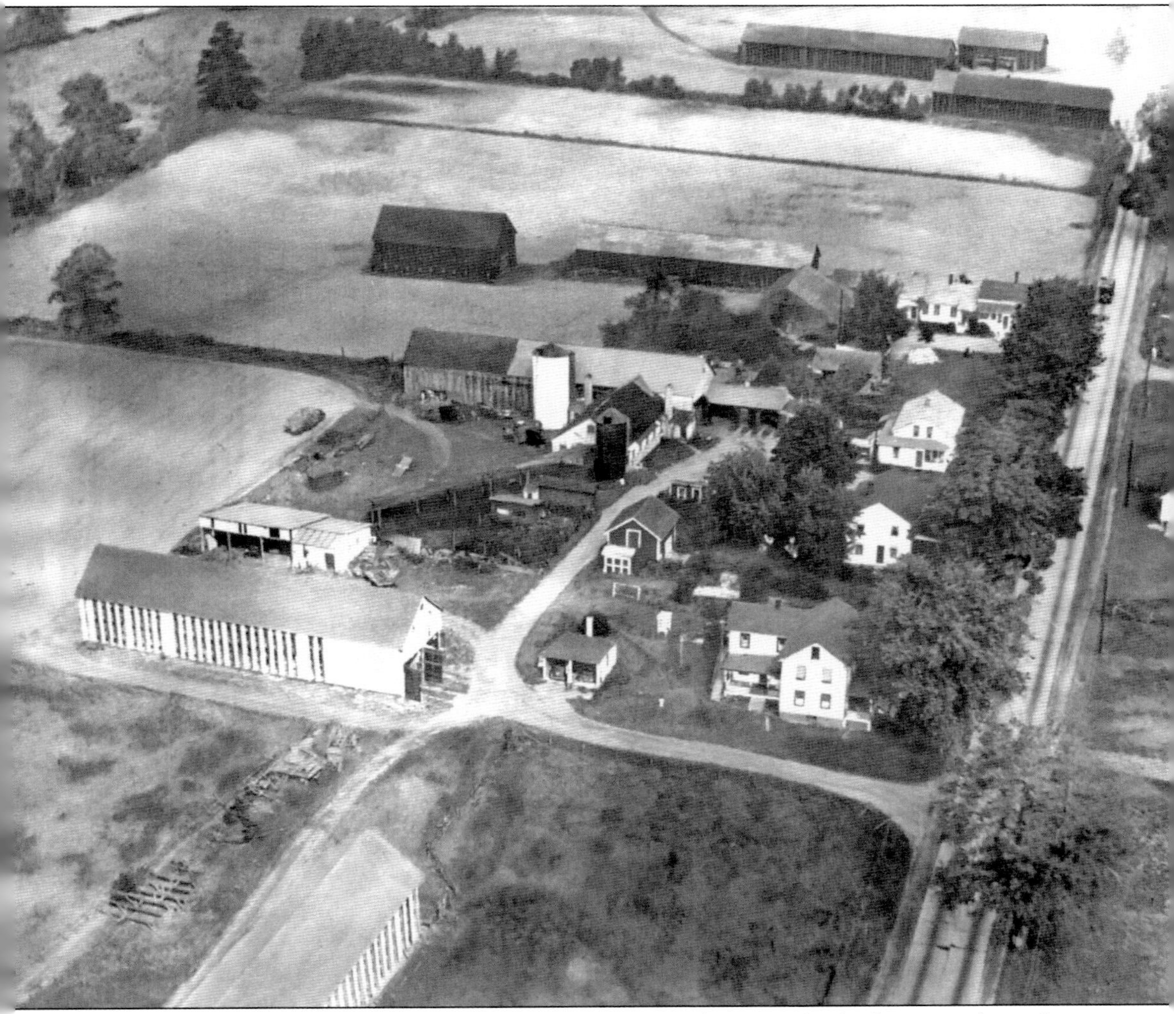

This aerial photograph shows the Fleming property around 1940. The highway at the right, running north and south, is East Street (Route 159). The three barns in the background belong to the Bielonko farm. Eventually James Fleming Trucking became one of the larger businesses in Suffield, and over time, Jim's entrepreneurial spirit enabled him to branch out into other businesses. These included a moving and storage business, snowmobile and motorcycle dealerships, and a service center. In the early 1980s, Jim returned to his farming roots when he established Fleming Farm and began breeding and raising Appaloosa horses. A large barn with over 25 stalls and an indoor riding arena was built where the tobacco once grew, and purebred show horses grazed where the cows were pastured. Today over 60 trucks and 200 trailers belonging to Fleming Transportation dominate the location. However, back in the barn and in the fields, Jim's mules and his family's horses still serve as a reminder that this was part of Suffield's farming history. (Courtesy Pat McHugh Roehl.)

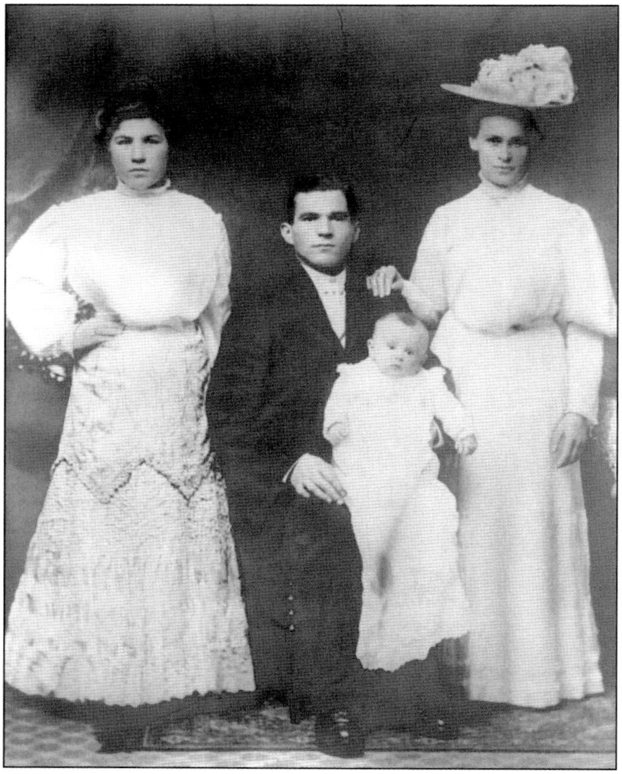

Mary Marszalek (with the hat) emigrated from Poland to Italy, where she and Vincenzo Galetta were married. They are pictured in this 1907 family portrait shortly after arriving in the United States. Vincenzo, known as "Jimmy the Ice Man," sold ice that he cut from the Connecticut River. A dugout near the old Thompsonville cemetery was used for storage. Delivered by horse and wagon, the blocks were placed into iceboxes, usually kept on back porches. (Courtesy Margie Osowiecki.)

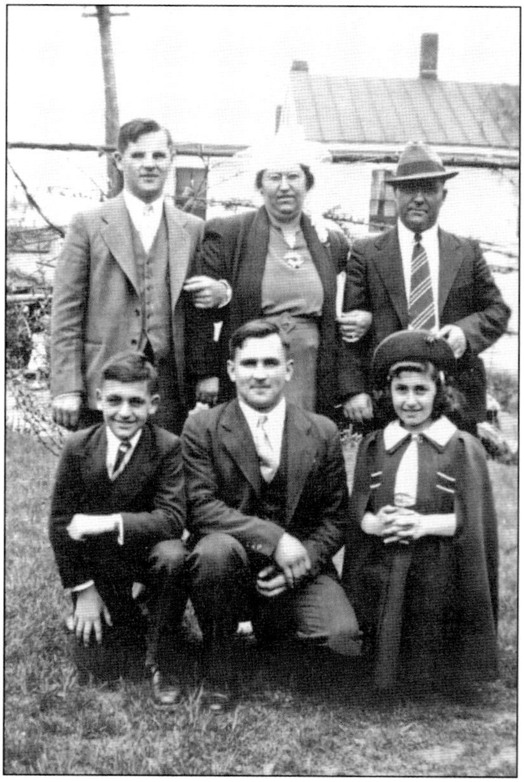

Pictured here are members of the Galetta family and their close neighbors, the Contes. Today much of the Connecticut River bank is thick with trees, but years ago, the Galettas kept every inch of their River Boulevard lot cultivated. A large terraced vegetable garden went part of the way down the steep riverbank. Jimmy sold this seasonal produce in Thompsonville. Planted on the lower section of the garden to the river's edge were grapevines and from its grapes, they made wine. (Courtesy Margie Osowiecki.)

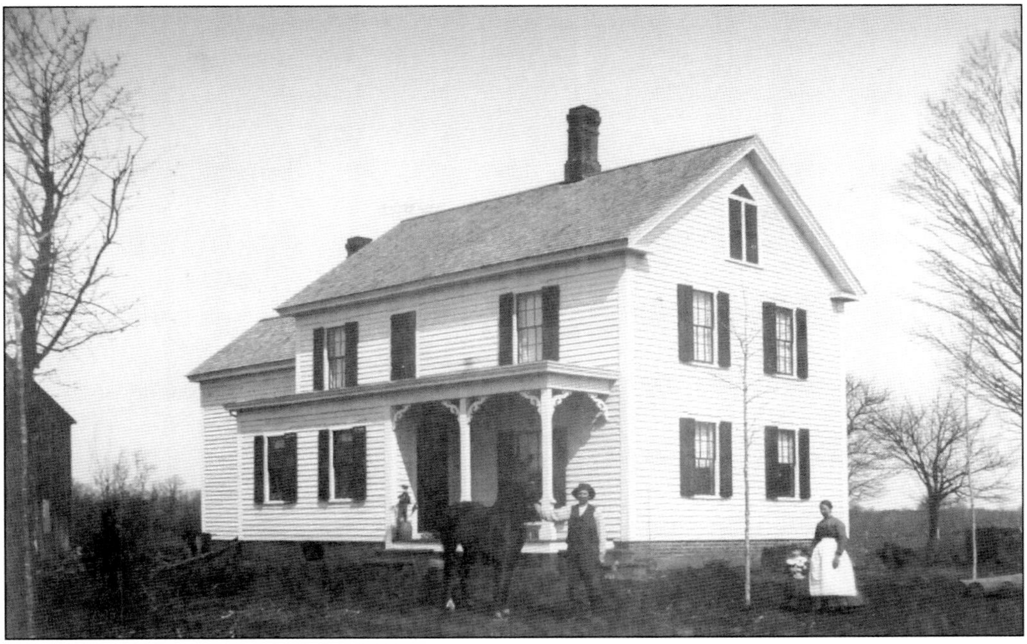

This early photograph is of the Tilden place, built on the site of the older Ebenezer King Sr. house on River Boulevard, which was destroyed by fire. Joseph and Mary Gonsior, immigrants from Poland, first found work in Thompsonville. In the 1930s, the Tilden farm went up for sale, and with three teenage sons, the Gonsiors seized the opportunity and started farming. (Courtesy KML.)

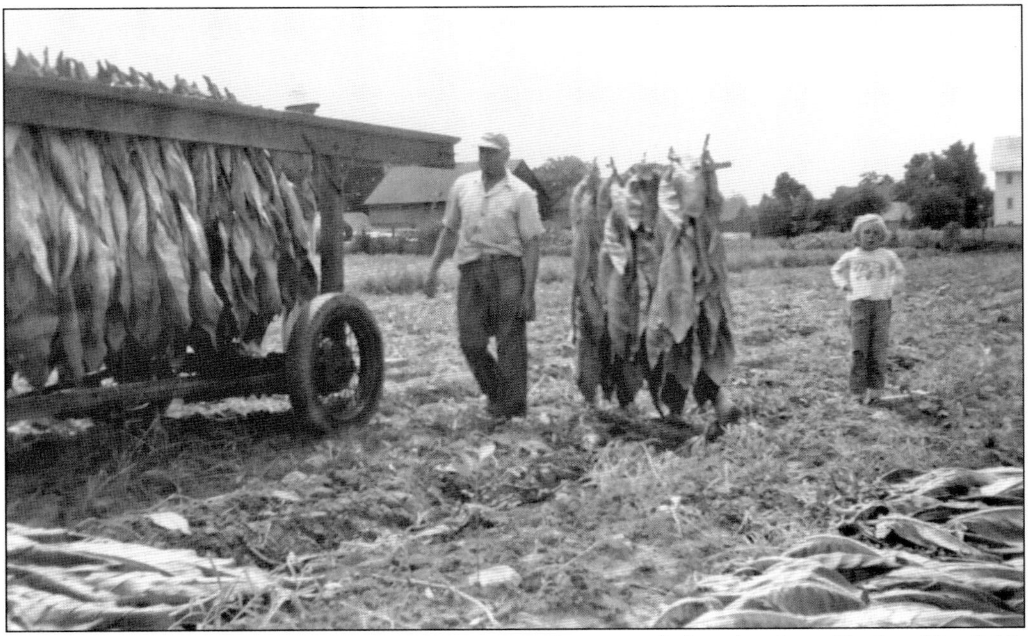

In this 1950s image, Stanley Gonsior harvests tobacco with his daughter Shirley. His fields reached from River Boulevard west to East Street. Initially the Gonsiors raised only tobacco, later adding crops of corn and strawberries that were sold at their East Street vegetable stand. The Sullivan warehouse is visible at the far right. (Courtesy Helen Rydzy Goncher.)

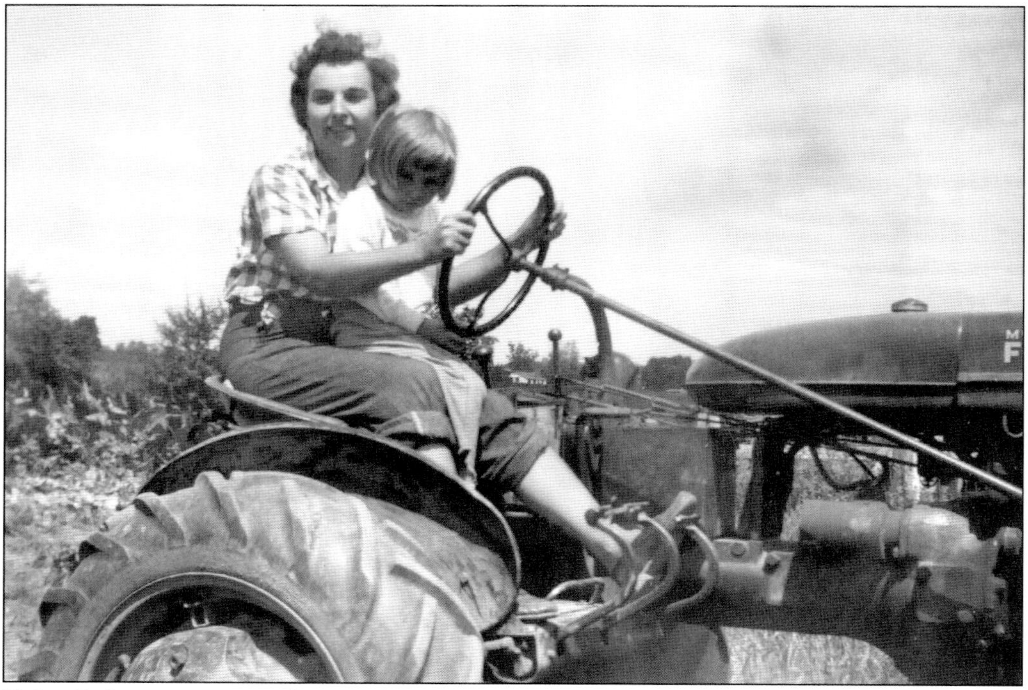

Helen Rydzy grew up on a dairy and tobacco farm in West Suffield and had plenty of experience driving a tractor. She married Edwin Goncher, Stanley Gonsior's brother, and helped out in the fields. Over time, the brothers' names had different spellings. Pictured here in the early 1950s is Helen with her niece Dotty Gonsior. (Courtesy Helen Rydzy Goncher.)

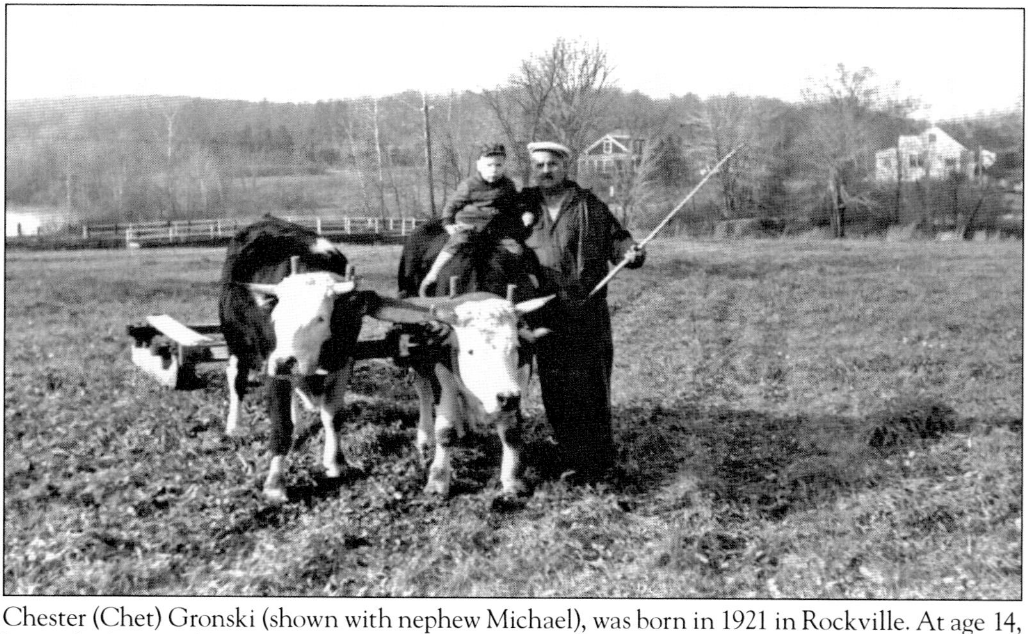

Chester (Chet) Gronski (shown with nephew Michael), was born in 1921 in Rockville. At age 14, he worked as a stable boy delivering ice by horse for Howard West of Tolland. Chet's calling was as a handler of large work animals, such as oxen, draft horses, and mules. He served in World War II and was awarded a Bronze Star. Chet and his wife, Hope West, made their home in East Suffield. (Courtesy Michael Gronski.)

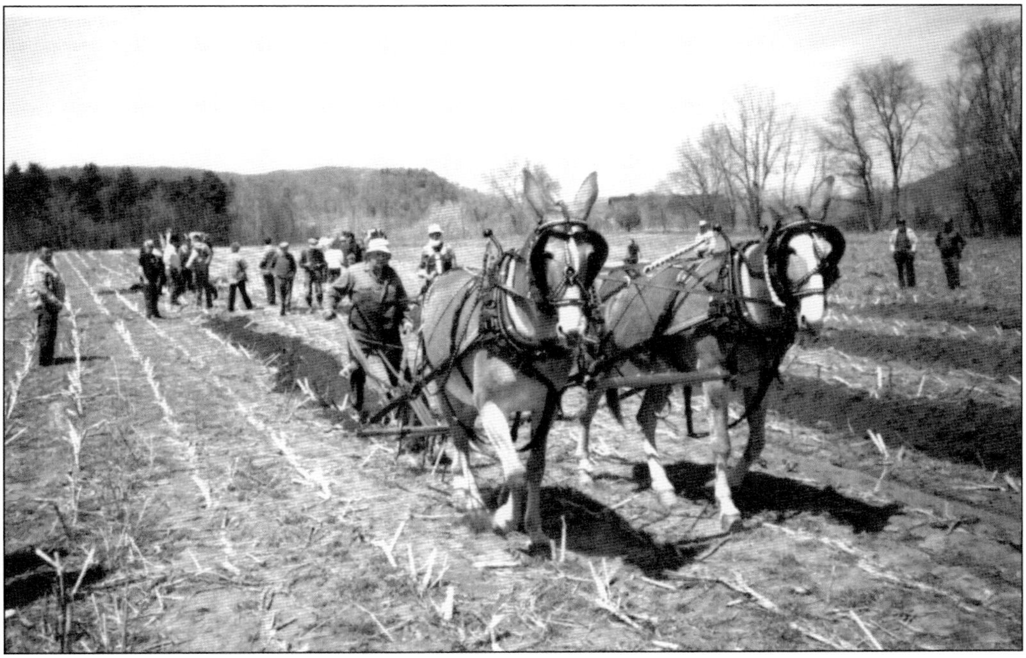

Employment as a steamfitter never interfered with Chet's career managing a horse farm and working as a draft horse teamster. On occasion he participated in an annual event in California called Mule Days. He enjoyed sharing old-time stories about his "mule man" reputation and is fondly remembered. This photograph shows Chet in his later years, still plowing with a team of mules. (Courtesy Michael Gronski.)

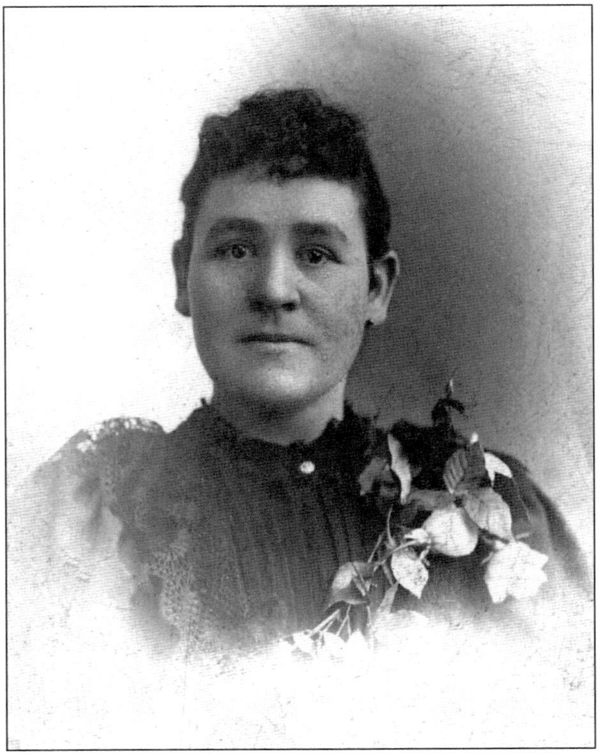

Between 1820 and 1920, over four million Irish came to the United States. They had an enormous impact on the workforce of America. Most found jobs as unskilled workers in mines and building the canal and rail systems. Some continued farming, as they had done in Ireland. Brigid Byrnes, pictured here, was born in 1872. She married Patrick Hogan from Birr, Ireland, and together they came to America in the 1890s. They settled in a small house near Rawlins Brook in East Suffield and raised five children. (Courtesy Alice Flasinski.)

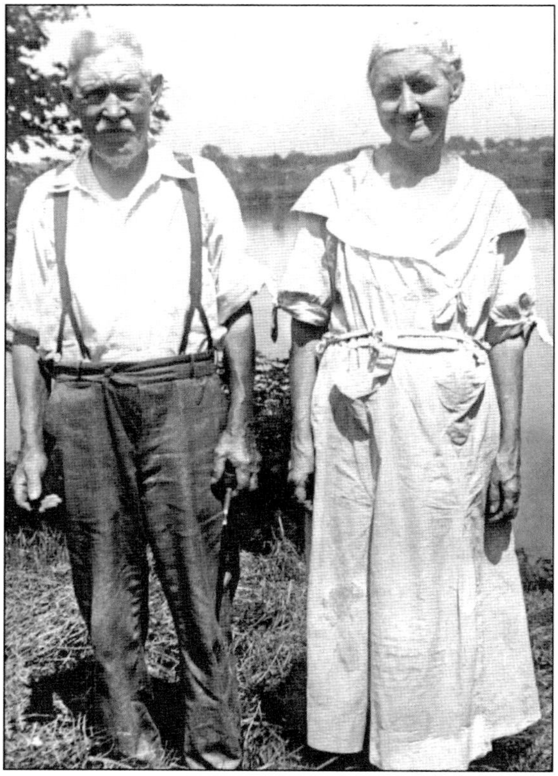

In 1902, the Hogans moved to River Boulevard. Pipe in hand, Patrick is seen here with Brigid in the early 1940s, the Connecticut River behind them. Patrick farmed for a living, occasionally working for the nearby Sikes family tobacco farm. He augmented his income fishing the river and selling his catch to neighbors. Like so many families, they raised and canned vegetables but also, in a remarkable way, blanketed their section of the riverbank with a multitude of flowers. (Courtesy Alice Flasinski.)

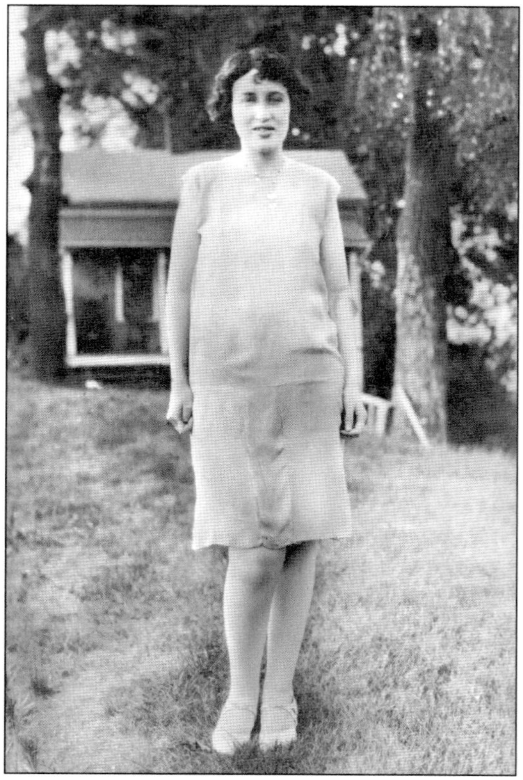

Brigid and Patrick's daughter Dora stands before their small family home atop the steep riverbank. Dora's daughter Alice now lives here with her husband, Stanley Flasinski. Up to five generations of the Hogan family have resided in this home. Stanley grew up in Thompsonville on a Kalish Avenue poultry farm. As a youngster, he and his mother, with horse and wagon, would head over the Thompsonville-Suffield Bridge to this same area to sell eggs. (Courtesy Alice Flasinski.)

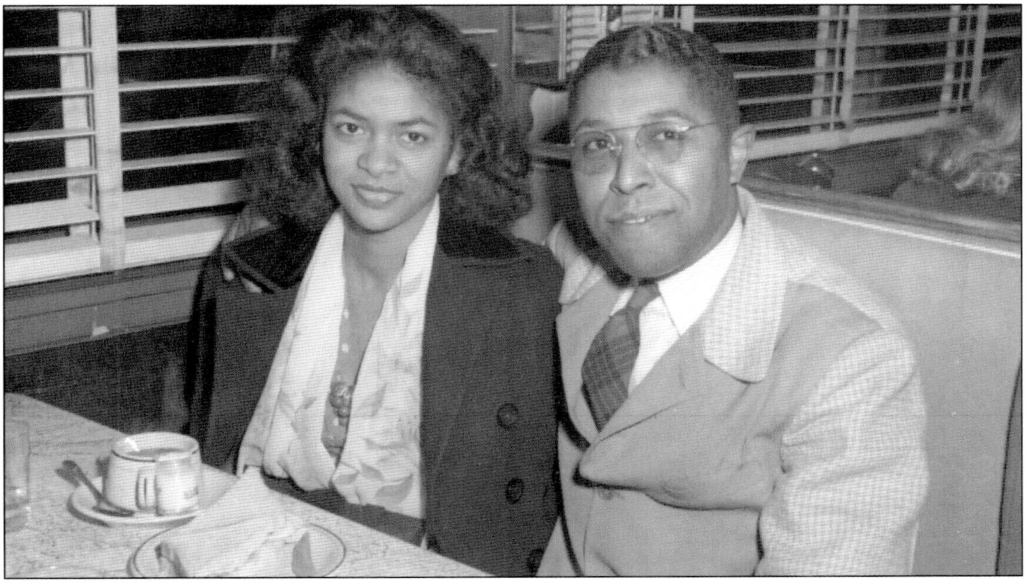

Charles Clyde Jones of West Suffield enjoys coffee with MaryEllen Vaughn around the time they were engaged in 1944. At the end of that year, Charles would be having Christmas dinner from his army boot camp mess kit. Being his first time away from home, his many letters tell of training and travel experiences, the conditions of the segregated South, and the perils during the liberation of the Philippines. (Courtesy Candy Jones.)

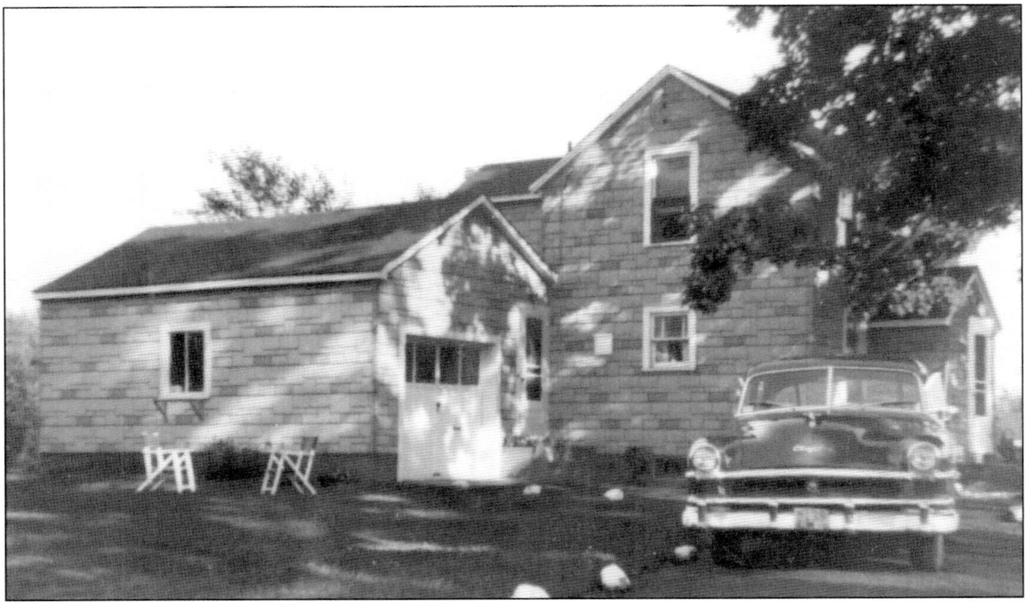

In 1948, Charles and MaryEllen Jones were married and later purchased this Thompsonville Road home. This structure was originally an ice-refrigerated milk house on an old dairy farm. The Joneses discovered farm artifacts in the walls and rafters during renovations. They raised two children here; James and Candy, who enjoyed living across the street from Papafil's General Store. Charles worked at Kaman Aerospace for 36 years before retiring. (Courtesy Candy Jones.)

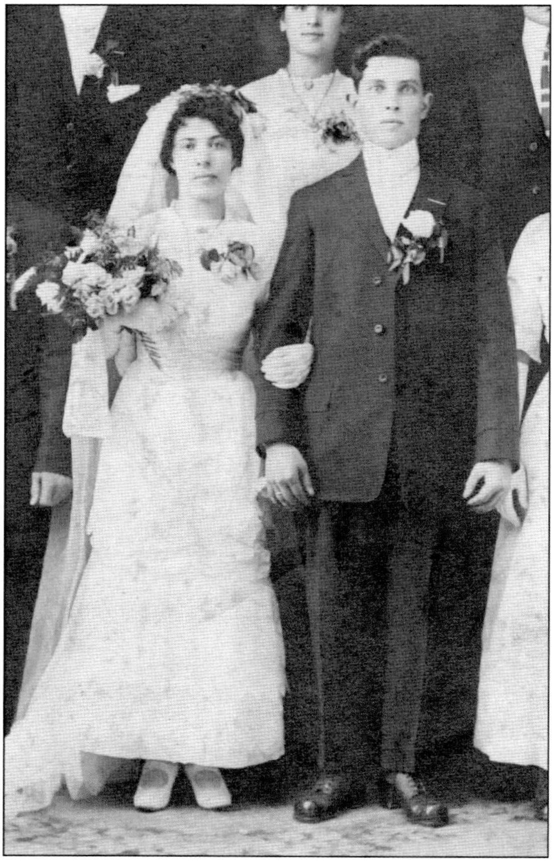

Caroline Sitarz, of Kamien, Austria-Poland, embarked for Ellis Island in 1907. Hers was not a voyage of necessity. She came to America simply because one of her girlfriends did. Proceeding directly to Thompsonville, Caroline started work at the carpet mill the day after her arrival. Eventually she met Jan Kida, from Lowisko, Poland, a coworker employed as a spinner. They married in 1913 at St. Patrick's Catholic Church. (Courtesy Grigitis family.)

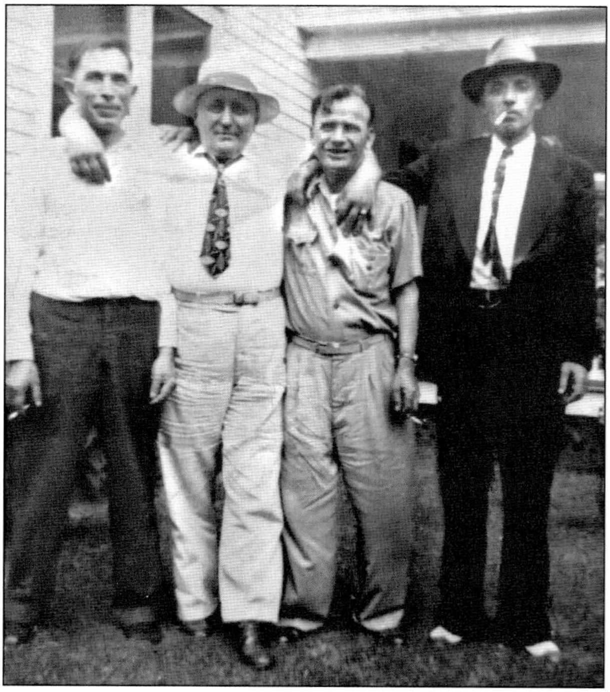

Jan Kida originally intended to return to Poland but never did. The Kidas bought a house and moved to East Suffield, where they raised five children. Friends and family from across the bridge visited often. In this photograph are, from left to right, Jan, Vincent Gongola, Matthew Golas, and Stanley Cholewa. Visiting was a chance to speak in their native language and catch up on news from the homeland. (Courtesy Grigitis family.)

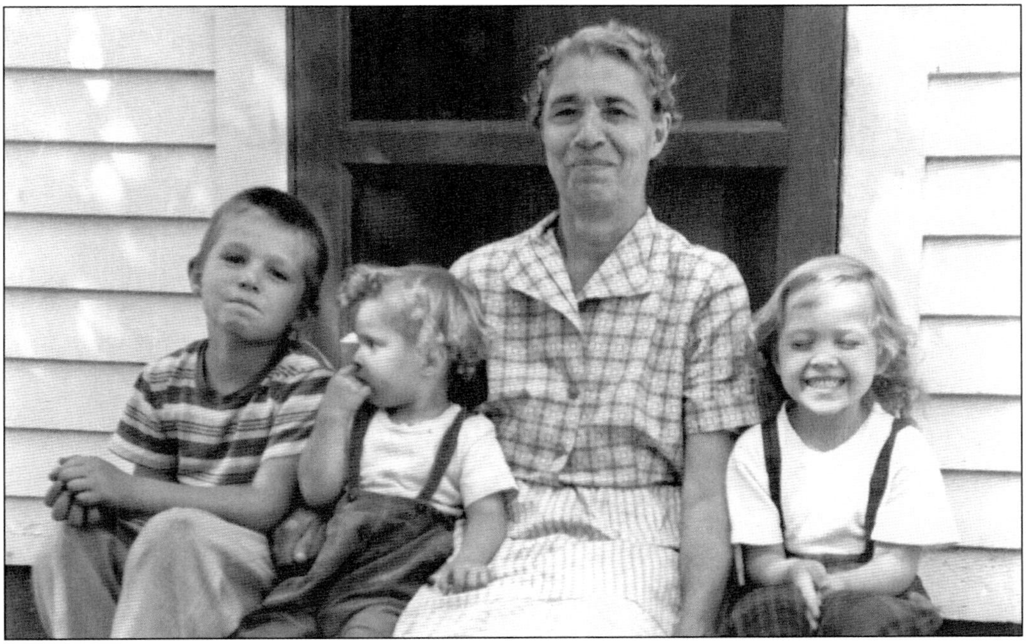

Later in life, Caroline Kida enjoys her grandchildren Stanley, Kathy, and Beverly Grigitis (right). Her life came a long way from the early days of sharing a tenement building apartment with other Polish immigrants, each carving their own mark on a loaf of rye bread and storing it in a common barrel. (Courtesy Grigitis family.)

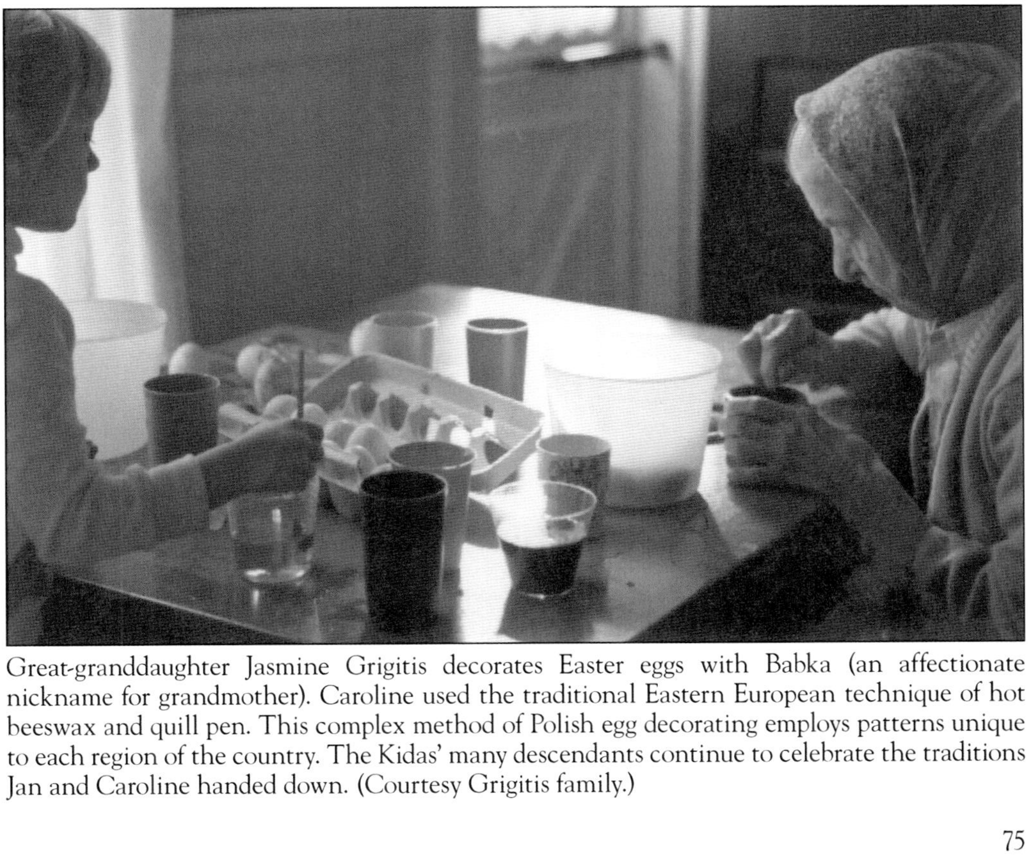

Great-granddaughter Jasmine Grigitis decorates Easter eggs with Babka (an affectionate nickname for grandmother). Caroline used the traditional Eastern European technique of hot beeswax and quill pen. This complex method of Polish egg decorating employs patterns unique to each region of the country. The Kidas' many descendants continue to celebrate the traditions Jan and Caroline handed down. (Courtesy Grigitis family.)

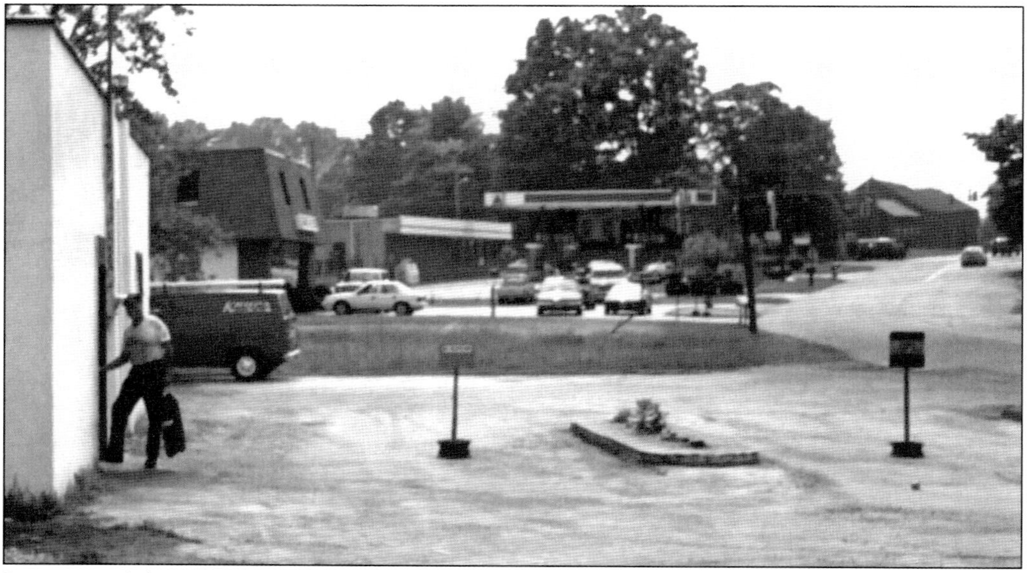

Born to Polish immigrants, the Krupa brothers, Chester and Albin, grew up on their family's farm on River Boulevard. Albin joined the U.S. Army during World War II. After the service, he attended trade school and at age 22 was the youngest man in the city of Hartford to receive his plumbing license. In 1948, he started Krupa's Plumbing, Heating and Water Conditioning. He installed the Thompsonville Road building in 1958 and later sold this property to his older brother Chester, who, along with his wife, Mabel, founded and operated Krupa Oil Company for over 50 years with their sons Thomas and Michael. Albin continued to operate his plumbing business out of his home until retirement and now maintains a 1,700-tree walnut grove. Pictured above at the left are the old Krupa Oil service station and Krupa Oil Company. (Courtesy Brian Scott.)

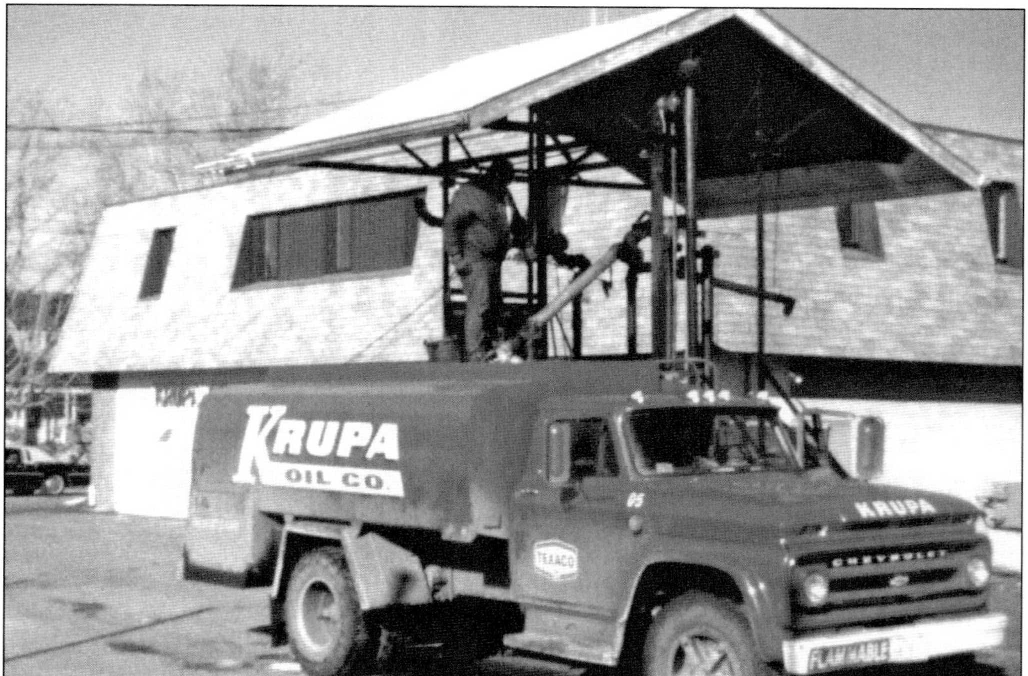

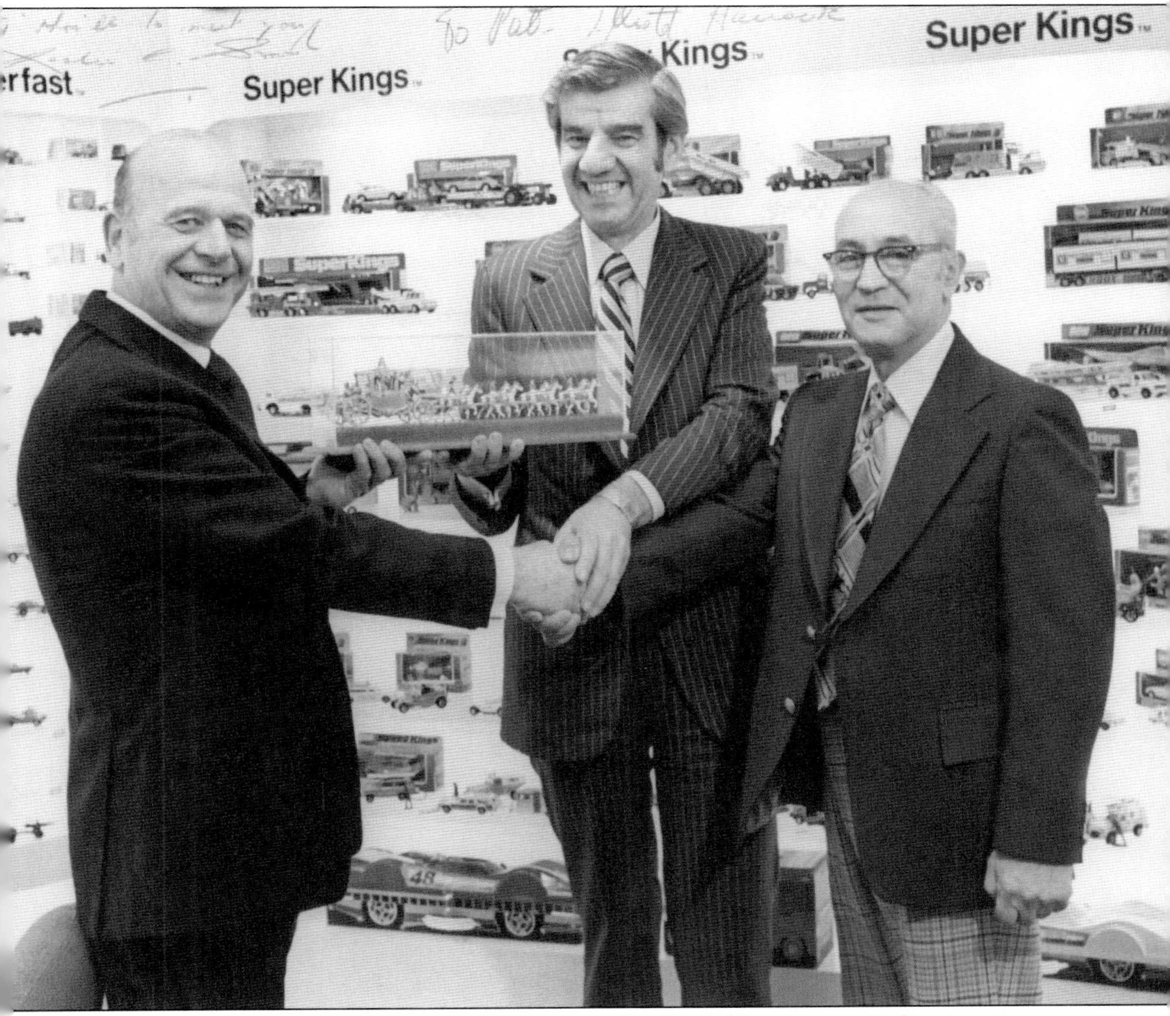

Pasquale (Pat) Lamagna (at the right above) was one of eight children born to Italian immigrants in Thompsonville. The family struggled financially, and although he was fortunate enough to have shoes, toys were scarce. As a young man, he met and married Ida Tavino from over the bridge in Suffield. After serving in the U.S. Navy during World War II they settled on her family's farm on River Boulevard. In 1968, recovering from a heart attack, Pat started collecting Matchbox cars. Some 25 years later, his hobby became one of the largest collections in the country. "He owns 3,500 cars and never drives one" wrote the *Daily Reveille*, the Louisiana State University newspaper in Baton Rouge, in 1983. His collection filled an entire room. The immaculate, illuminated cases covered the walls and windows from floor to ceiling. In the photograph, Leslie Smith (left), cofounder of Lesney Products, and Elliott Harrowe (center), president of Lesney Products, USA, return to Pat his King's Coronation model, refurbished and cased. The relaxing pastime eased Pat back to health; he knew that model cars were not just for children. (Courtesy Gary Lamagna.)

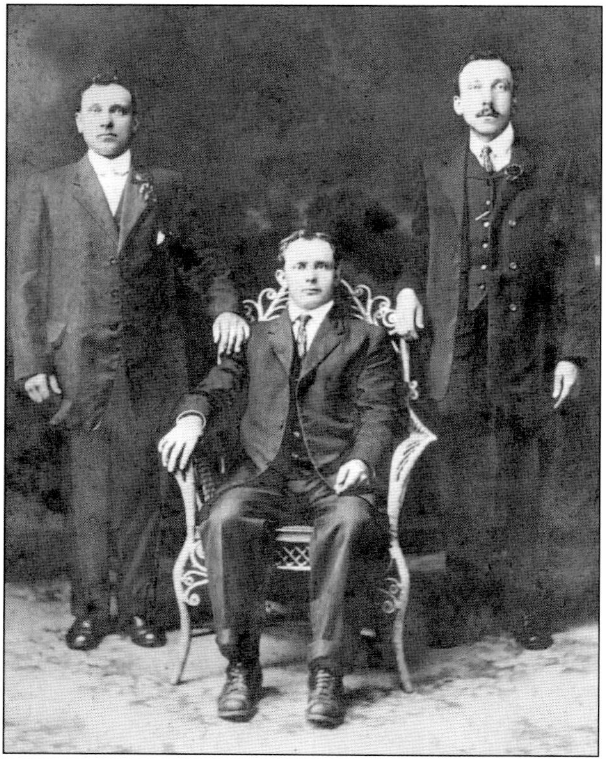

Three Matyskiela men, in succession, left the town of Suchowola, Poland, for Suffield. Pictured are, from left to right, Steve, John, and Frank. As they came over, each helped the next to follow. The first arrival was John in 1904. He sent money for passage to his half-brother Steve, who in turn, sponsored his cousin Frank. Via Ellis Island in 1921, Frank and his wife, Constance, came to settle on East Street, where they built their home. (Courtesy Rich Matyskiela.)

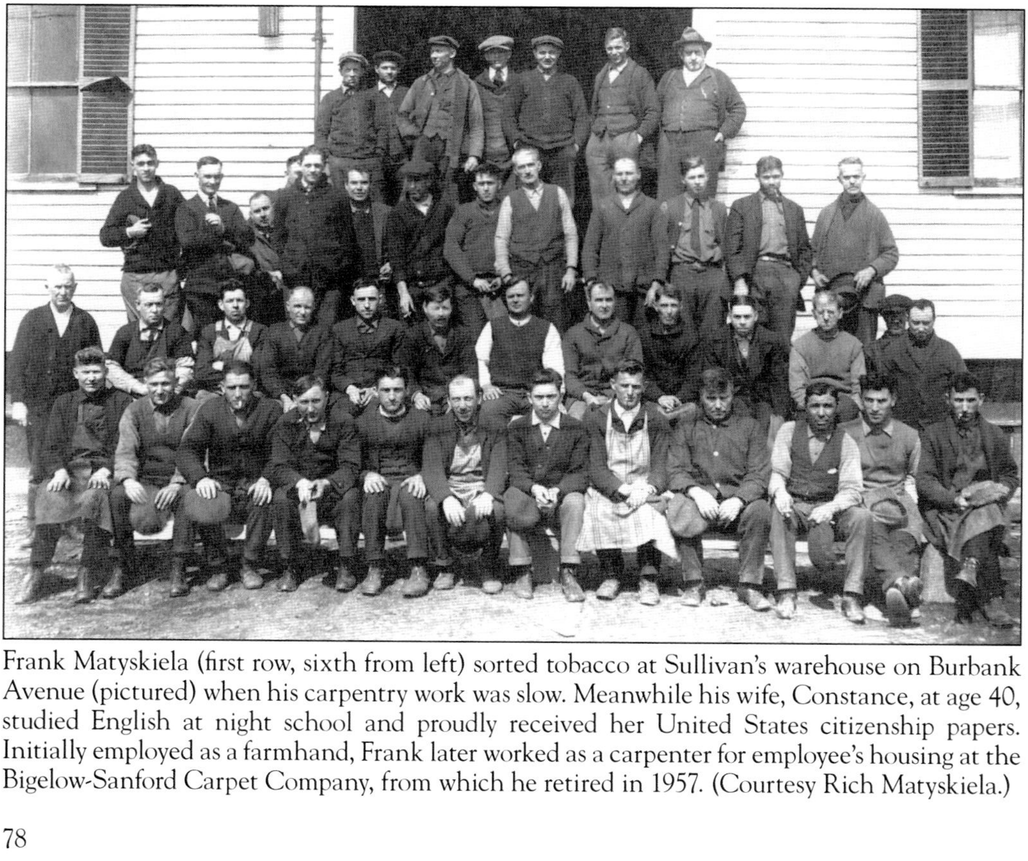

Frank Matyskiela (first row, sixth from left) sorted tobacco at Sullivan's warehouse on Burbank Avenue (pictured) when his carpentry work was slow. Meanwhile his wife, Constance, at age 40, studied English at night school and proudly received her United States citizenship papers. Initially employed as a farmhand, Frank later worked as a carpenter for employee's housing at the Bigelow-Sanford Carpet Company, from which he retired in 1957. (Courtesy Rich Matyskiela.)

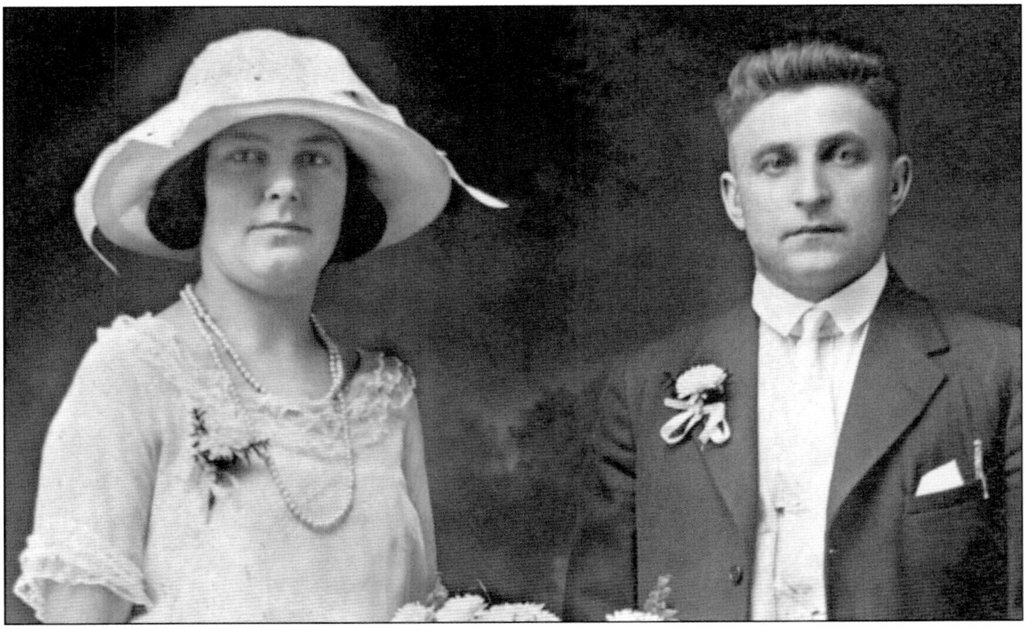

Helen Bucken and Terrance (Teddy) Matuck are pictured on their wedding day in 1920. Helen, of Polish ancestry, grew up on a 20-acre farm in Scitico, a section of Enfield. Teddy immigrated from Minsk, Russia, his voyage by ship taking 13 days. He did not talk much about his homeland, learned English right away, and decided not to teach his children Russian, because he was now an American. (Courtesy Margaret Matuck.)

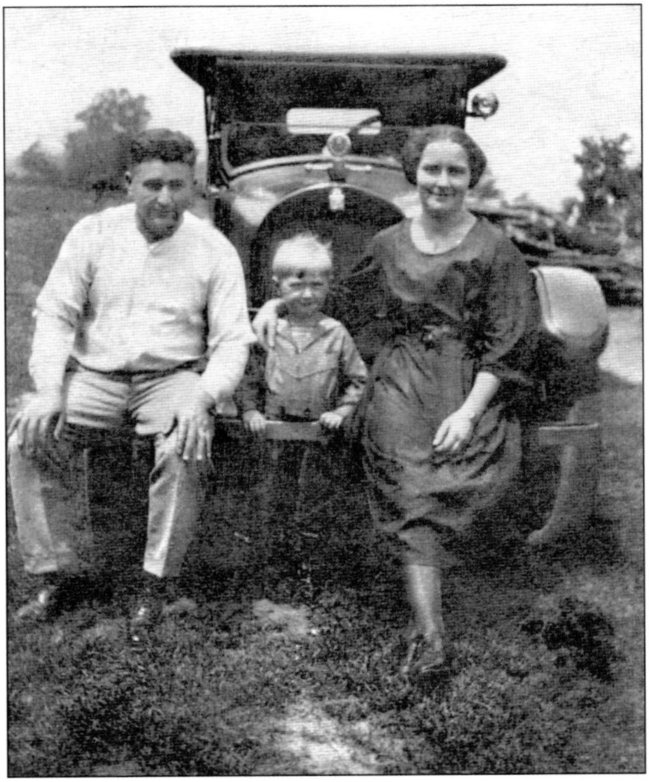

Teddy and Helen pose with their son Paul, seated on the bumper of their touring car in the 1920s. In 1947, the Matucks purchased a home on Woodworth Street, where they raised four children. At one time, the entire family was employed at the Bigelow-Sanford Carpet Company in Thompsonville. In 1996, their daughter Margaret was the last to move out of the family's East Suffield home, remarking later "this neighborhood was a great place to grow up." (Courtesy Margaret Matuck.)

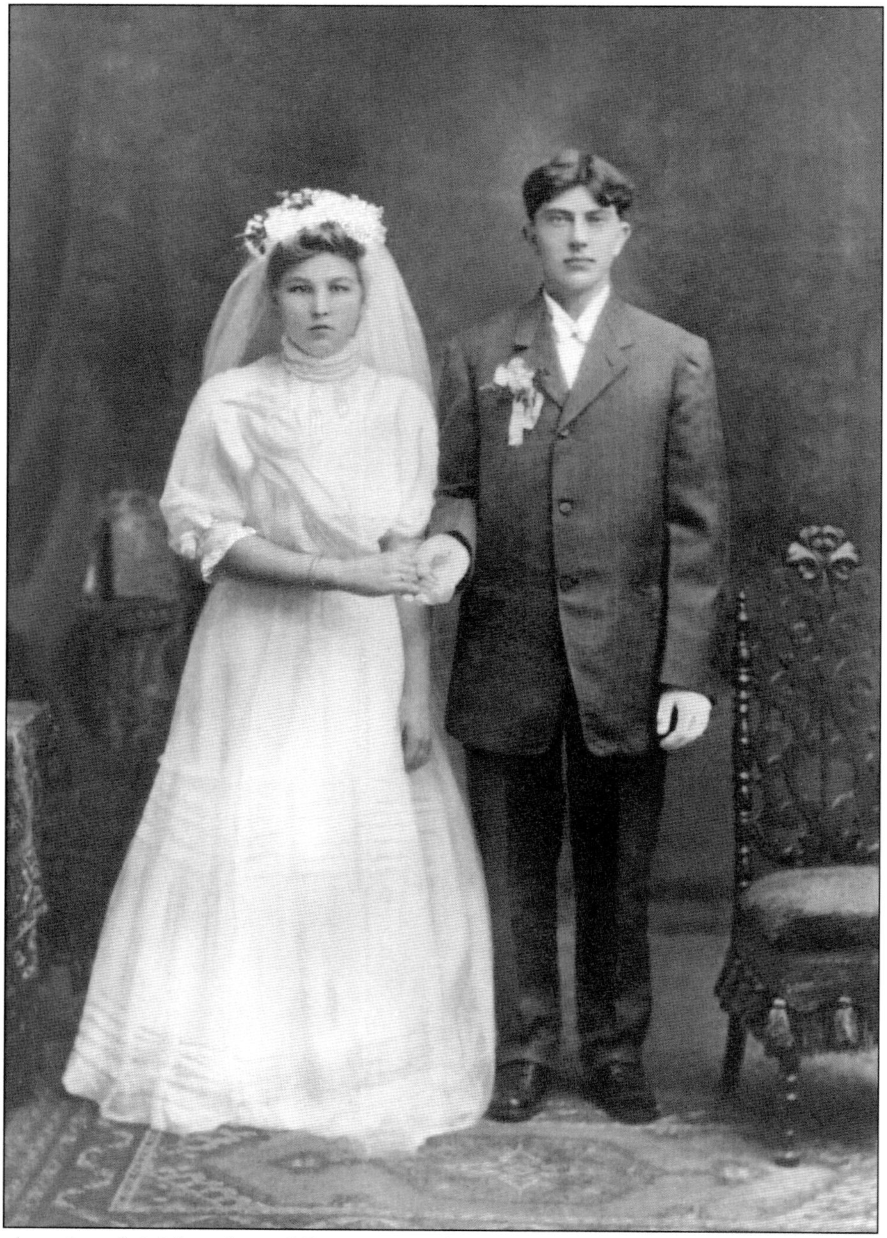

Pictured are Joseph Malinoski and Frances Ziemkiewicz on their wedding day, October 15, 1906. Frances was eight years old in 1897 when she emigrated from Poland to the United States. She stayed with family on Mapleton Avenue, across the road from what would become Hilltop Farm. The neighbors, finding the name Ziemkiewicz difficult to pronounce, simply called them "the Davises." Frances married Joseph W. Malinoski, who left Poland around 1903 and was living in Hatfield, Massachusetts. The couple liked Suffield, so Joseph sought employment at Spaulding Gardens. Although no jobs were available in the greenhouses, one of the Spaulding brothers hired him as a carpenter. Not caring for farming anyway, Joseph was well suited to his new trade and went on to become a successful finish carpenter. To his credit is the craftsmanship in the fine apartments along Fort Pleasant Street in Springfield. The Malinoskis bought a home on River Boulevard and raised a family of 10 children. (Courtesy Celia Malinoski.)

In this 1906 photograph, Frances Ziemkiewicz is 17 years old. As a youngster, she never attended school but taught herself to read and write English. She was employed for a time as a nanny for a professor at Smith College in Northampton, Massachusetts. In the evenings when her work was done, she went in the kitchen and studied how the cook prepared family meals. Never having learned how to prepare her homeland Polish recipes, she adopted the Yankee style of cooking. (Courtesy Celia Malinoski.)

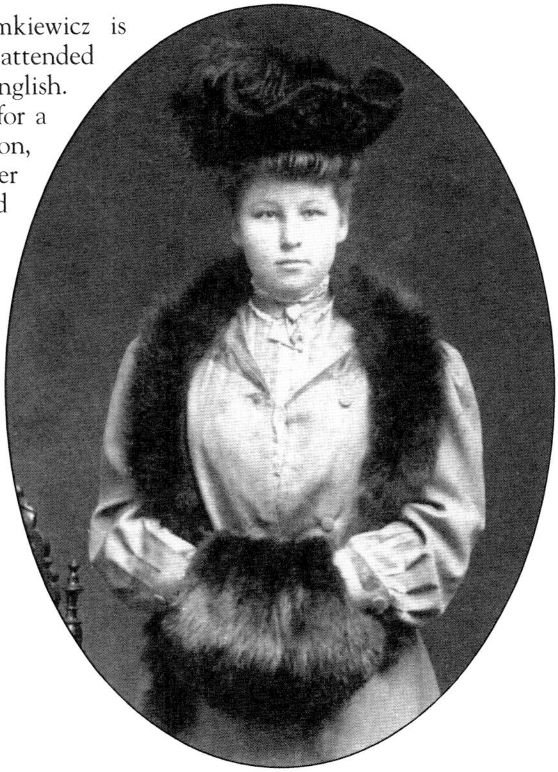

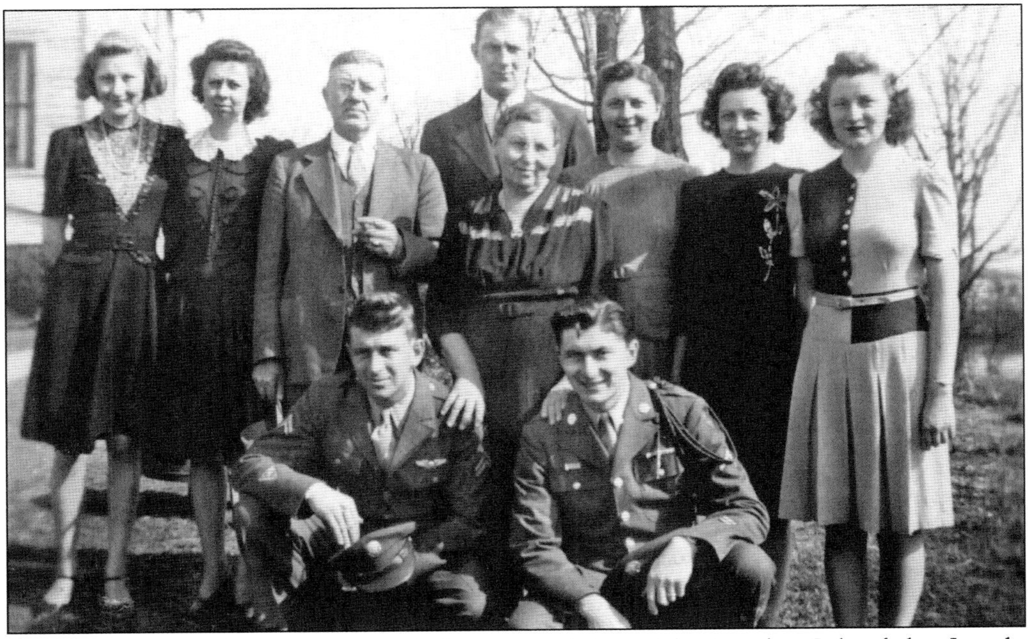

Members of the Malinoski family in 1943 are, from left to right, Martha, Celia, father Joseph, Andrew, mother Frances (center), Helen, Florence, and Leona. Al and Leo (in uniform) are in front. Joe Jr. is not pictured. Celia, born in 1916, was delivered by cesarean section. The procedure was rare in those days and three doctors were in attendance. Frances went on to have five more children. (Courtesy Celia Malinoski.)

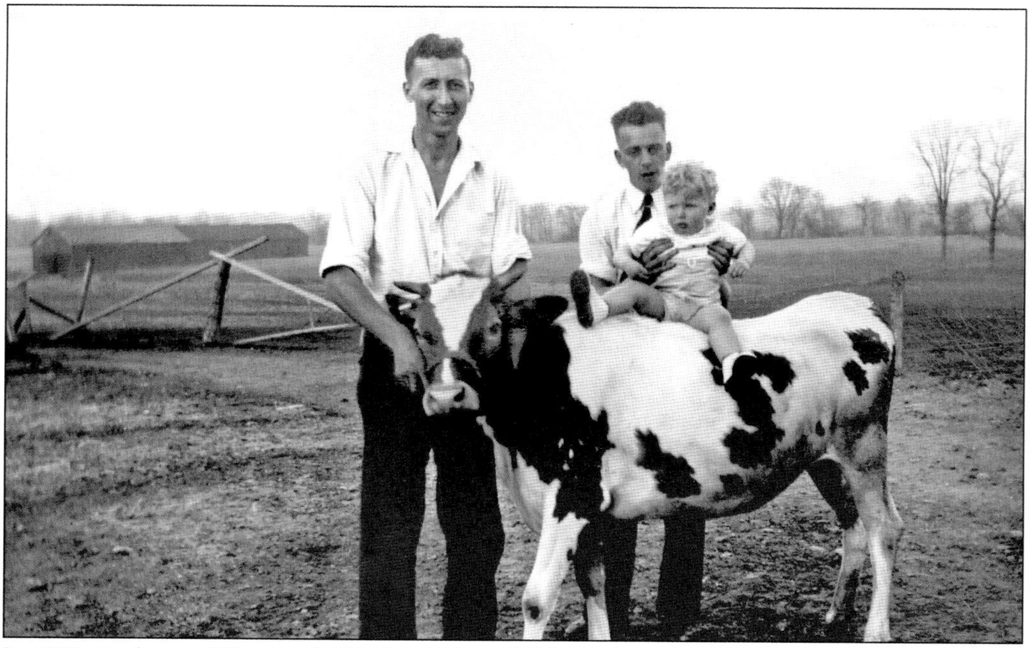

In 1938, Arthur and Bernice Mills, from Bloomfield, purchased a 60-acre dairy farm from Harry Reid at the north end of River Boulevard. Their son Russell describes the farm as stretching from East Street to the Connecticut River, where "there was good hunting and trapping." Along with the dairy, they raised tobacco and cultivated additional acreage on River Boulevard Extension. Pictured is Russell Mills (left), George Reid, and nephew Louis Clinton. (Courtesy Mills family.)

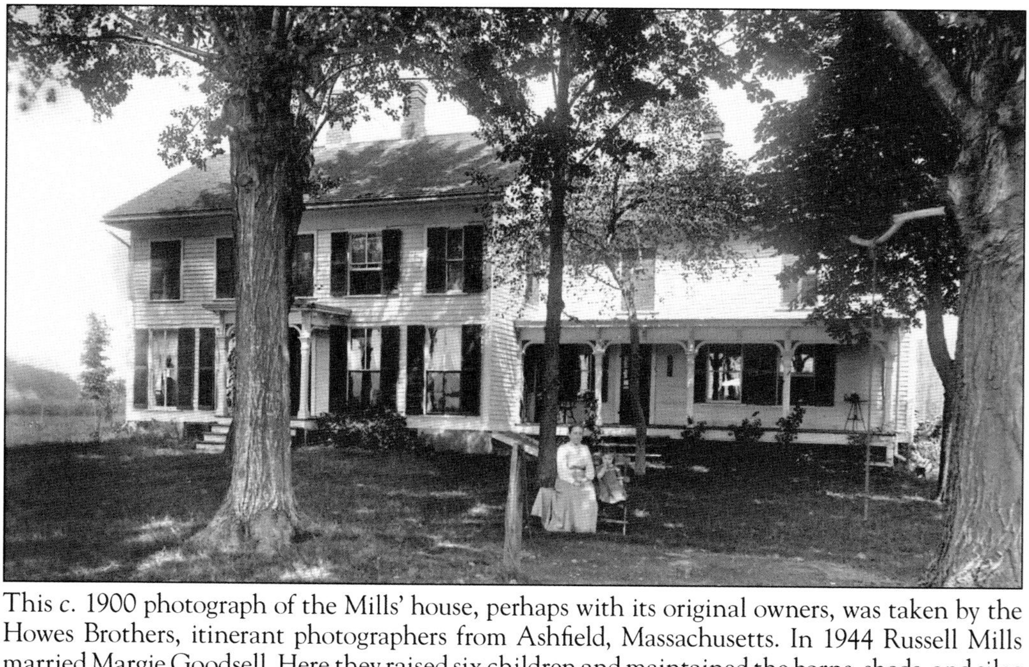

This *c.* 1900 photograph of the Mills' house, perhaps with its original owners, was taken by the Howes Brothers, itinerant photographers from Ashfield, Massachusetts. In 1944 Russell Mills married Margie Goodsell. Here they raised six children and maintained the barns, sheds, and silos of their farming enterprise. Their roadside market stand did very well on weekends with the flow of traffic to and from Riverside Park in nearby Agawam. (Courtesy Ashfield Historical Society.)

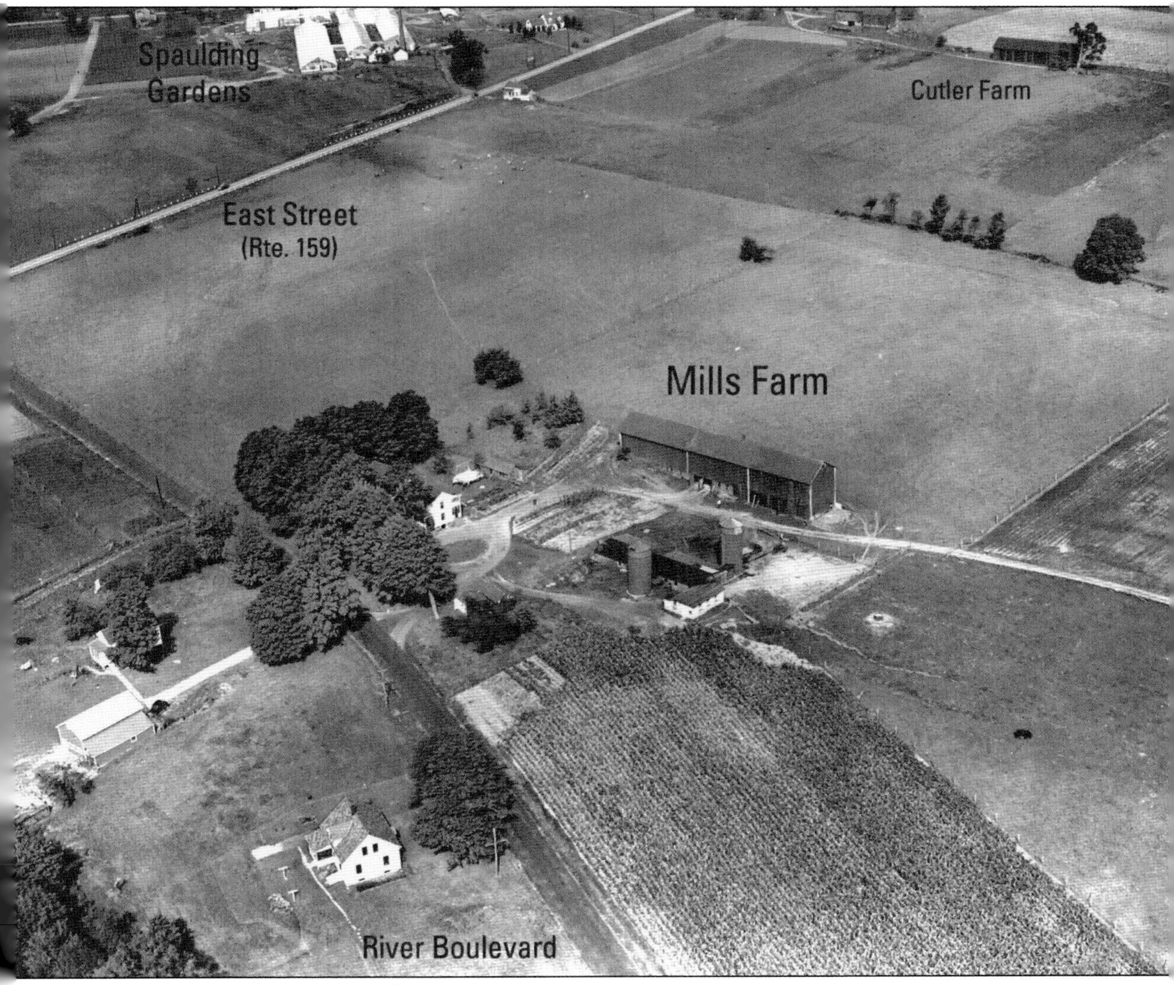

This aerial photograph is of Mills Farm on River Boulevard. In the early 1950s, the Mills family experienced an unusual event. Garments missing from the clothesline and their dog's barking alerted them to the presence of an intruder on the farm. They discovered the uninvited guest was a shell-shocked soldier, returned from World War II. He had wandered close to 30 miles south along the Connecticut River from Northampton and was taking shelter in their barn. He foraged for food from their fields, washed in the river, and helped himself to clean clothes when he needed them. The disoriented veteran was then reunited with his family. In 1960, the Millses sold their place to George and Pat Stewart, who formed Karandrew Turf Farm. Farming close to 600 acres of their own land, the Stewarts also leased additional acreage and sold turf wholesale to the cities of Boston and New York for athletic fields. Large sections of East Suffield resembled a golf course, with acres of thick, manicured turf. In 1999, George retired and the land was gradually sold and developed into residential neighborhoods. The Markowski family currently occupies the original farmhouse. (Courtesy Ginger Mills Seaburg.)

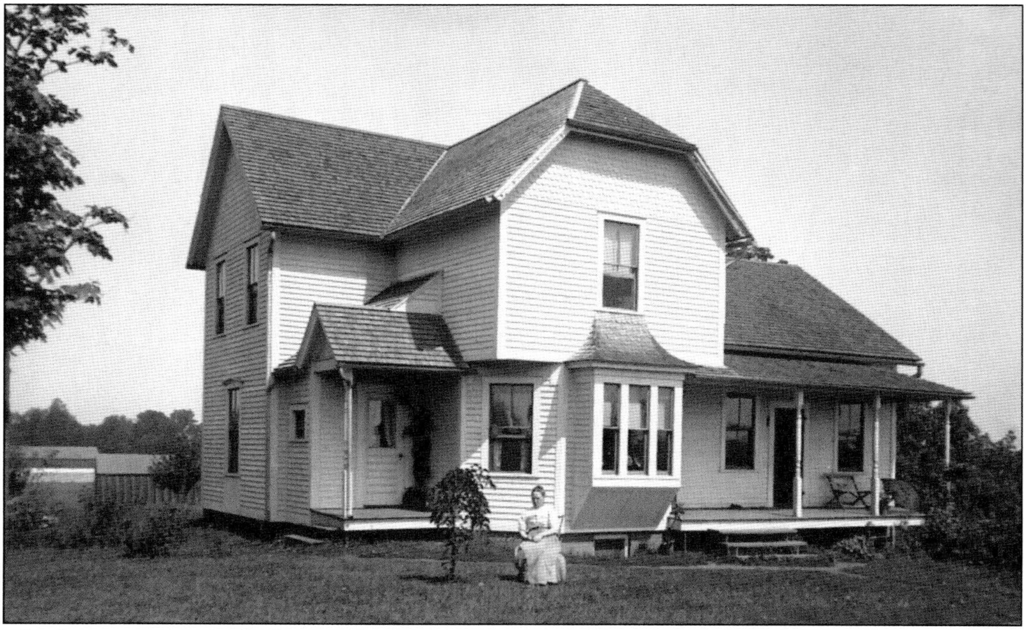

This house sits on the highest riverbank lot on River Boulevard, no doubt chosen for this reason when Willard C. Sikes built it in the late 1800s. Tony Moffett and his wife, Mary Romenius, were the children of early-20th-century Lebanese immigrants. They bought this property in 1957 and raised two sons: Toby, a former two-term U.S. congressman, and Bill, a professional musician and teacher of 35 years. (Courtesy Ashfield Historical Society.)

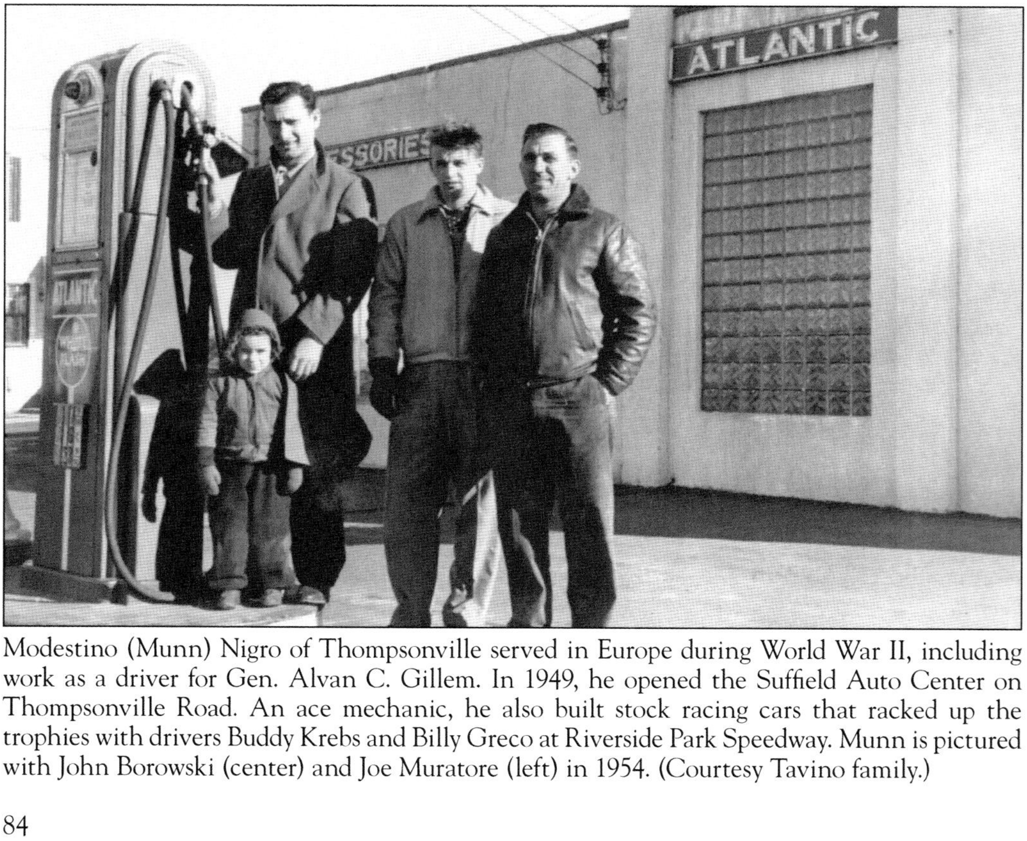

Modestino (Munn) Nigro of Thompsonville served in Europe during World War II, including work as a driver for Gen. Alvan C. Gillem. In 1949, he opened the Suffield Auto Center on Thompsonville Road. An ace mechanic, he also built stock racing cars that racked up the trophies with drivers Buddy Krebs and Billy Greco at Riverside Park Speedway. Munn is pictured with John Borowski (center) and Joe Muratore (left) in 1954. (Courtesy Tavino family.)

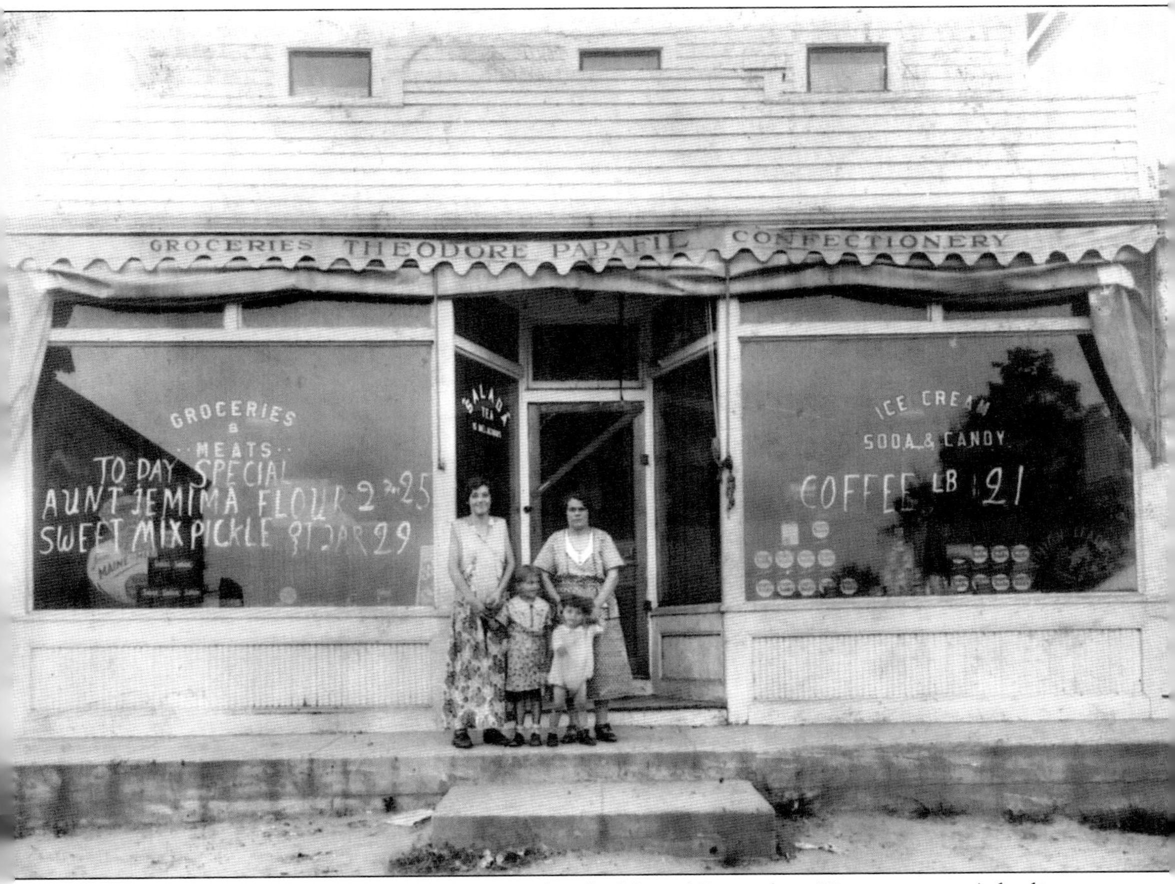

When 17-year-old Theodore Papafil immigrated to the United States from Kontovazena, Arkadias, Greece, he settled in Thompsonville and worked as a weaver at the carpet mill. Six months later, in 1914, he opened his own business across the river in East Suffield, called it Theodore's General Store and moved in above the shop. In 1921, after his tour of duty with the U.S. Army in Europe, he married Evangeline Poulopoulos, also from Greece. They raised three children, Alexander, Helen, and Nicholas, and made their livelihood operating the neighborhood store full time. In the 1930 photograph above, Peggy Fleming (left) and Evangeline Papafil, with her children Helen and Nicholas, pose in the doorway. Theodore's General Store was a local meeting place and the destination for every neighborhood kid seeking a cold soda and penny candy. (Courtesy Rookey family.)

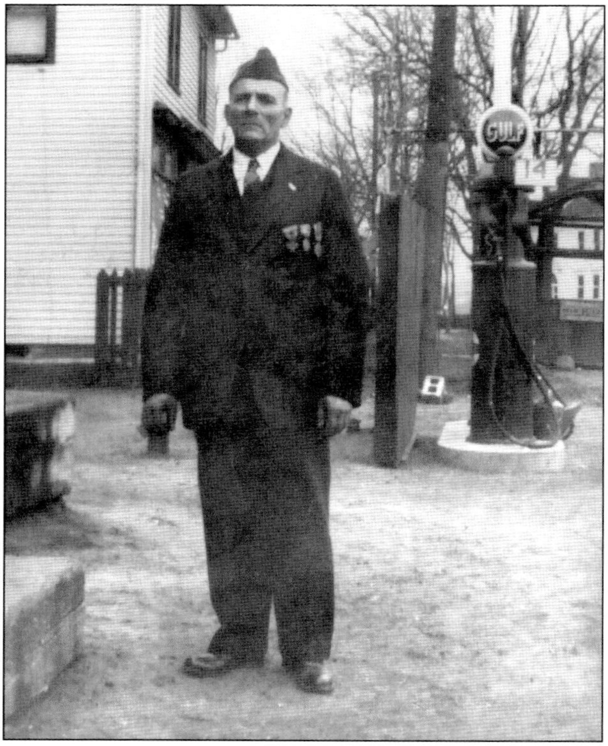

"Theodore Papafil, a U.S. Army veteran of World War I, was among the many people who were kind and helpful to the Polish immigrants," wrote Rich Matyskiela of Suffield's Polish Heritage Group. "He extended credit to those who lived in the area, worked in Thompsonville, and shopped at his store because most didn't own cars. They were 'on the books' and reimbursed him on payday. Some Polish farmers went several months on credit until their crops were sold. During the Depression, Theodore carried some people quite a while this way." (Courtesy Rookey family.)

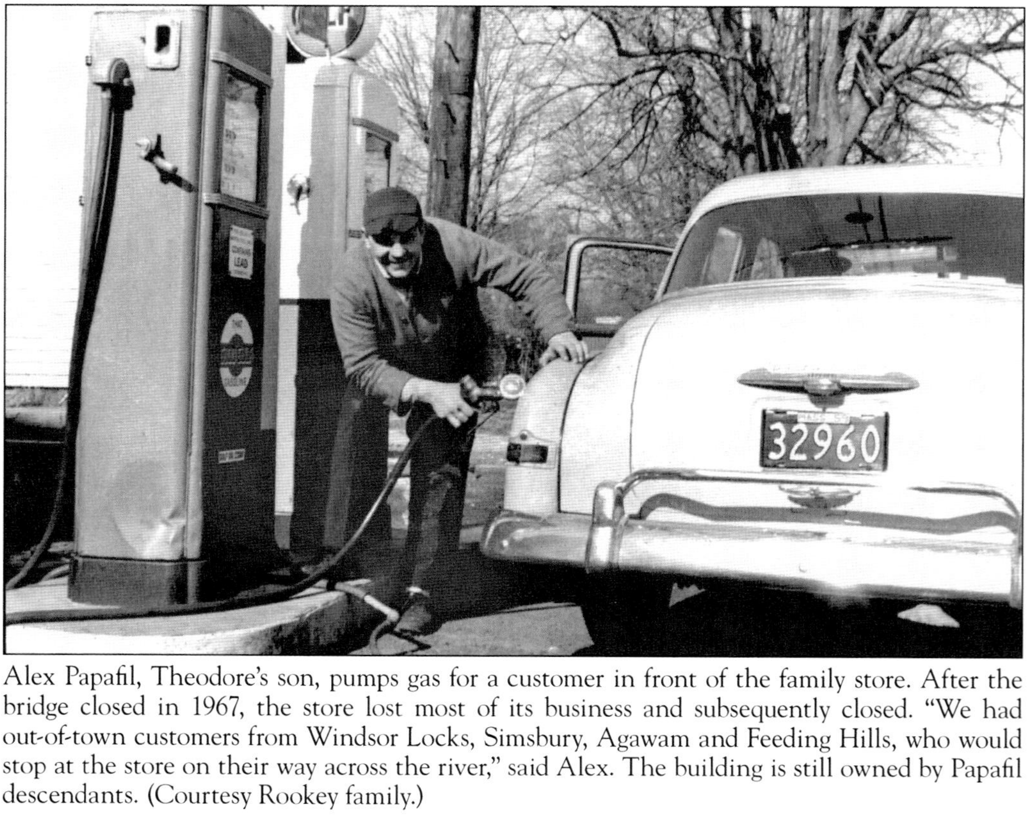

Alex Papafil, Theodore's son, pumps gas for a customer in front of the family store. After the bridge closed in 1967, the store lost most of its business and subsequently closed. "We had out-of-town customers from Windsor Locks, Simsbury, Agawam and Feeding Hills, who would stop at the store on their way across the river," said Alex. The building is still owned by Papafil descendants. (Courtesy Rookey family.)

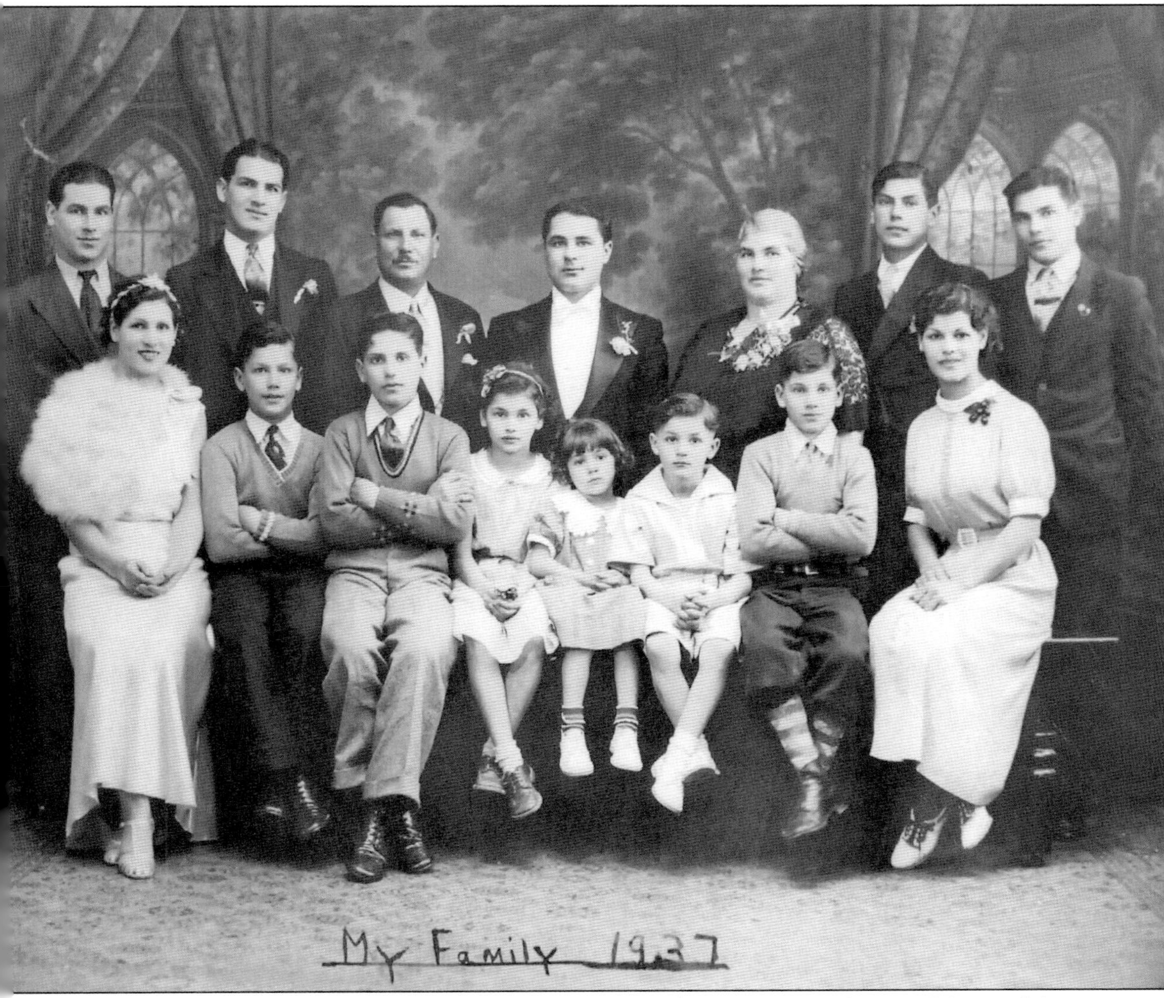

From their home in Naro, Sicily, in 1912, Luigi Reale sent his pregnant wife, Pace Maniscalchi, and two small sons to America, following them a year later. They settled in the Frenchtown section of Thompsonville, living first on Martin Street. From there, they moved to Douglas Street in East Suffield in 1925. In this photograph the couple is shown with their 13 children. Seen here are, from left to right, (first row) Lillian, Charles, James, Marie, Jean, Edward, Armand, and Rose; (second row) Rosario, Jerry, father Luigi, Joseph, mother Pace, Alphonse, and Thomas. Many of the sons served honorably in the military and survived World War II, five of them serving at the same time. Several sons were amateur boxers in the local area. Their father Luigi retired from the Bigelow-Sanford Carpet Company in 1951. Lillian, the eldest Reale daughter, spent much of her childhood acting as the family matriarch, kneading bread dough, washing, and cooking for 10 younger siblings while her mother tended the babies. (Courtesy Lillian Schreffler.)

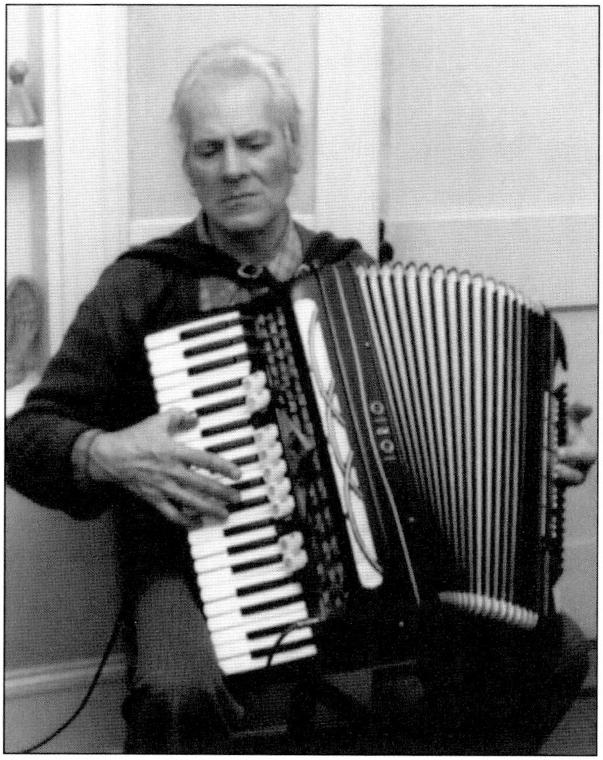

The Reale family was musically gifted. Luigi, the father, was a tenor and could be heard two streets away singing opera on Saturdays. Their Douglas Street home was filled with children and music. Almost all of the 13 children tried their hand at an instrument or two and continued playing throughout their lives. In this photograph Rosario is playing the accordion. (Courtesy Lillian Schreffler.)

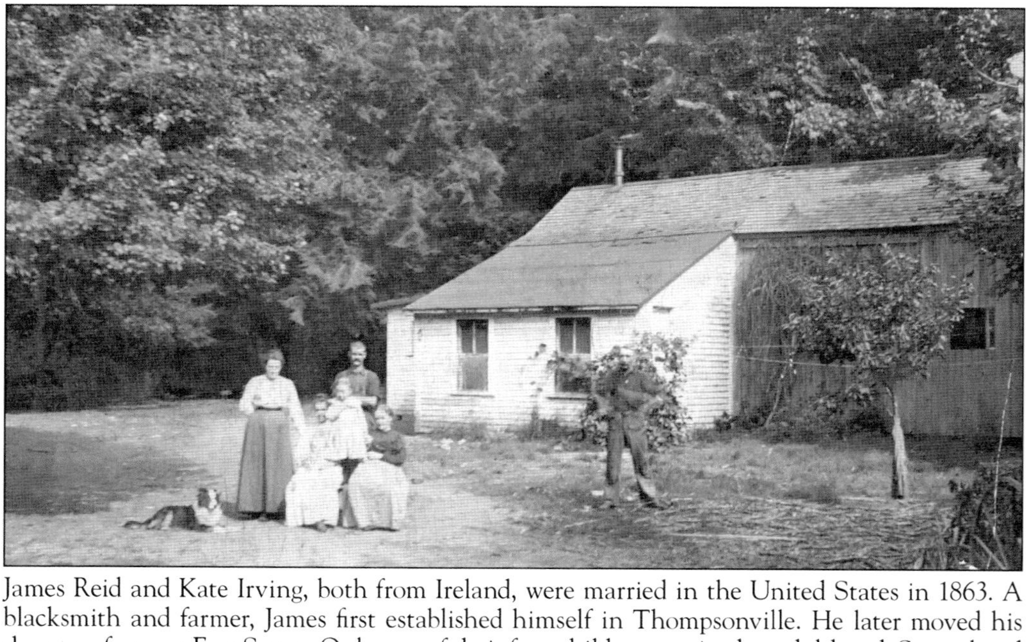

James Reid and Kate Irving, both from Ireland, were married in the United States in 1863. A blacksmith and farmer, James first established himself in Thompsonville. He later moved his shop to a farm on East Street. Only two of their four children survived to adulthood, Samuel and Kittie. This 1901 portrait is of the Reids and extended family in front of their home (currently Bielonko Farms). (Courtesy Dorian Love Taylor.)

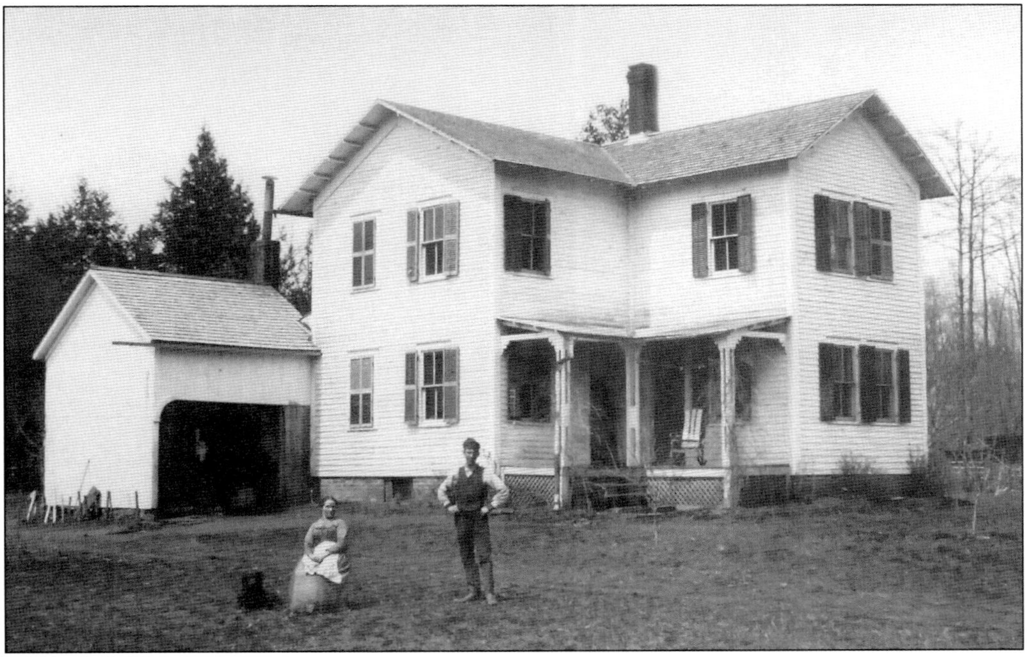

James and Kate built this "new" house on East Street in front of the original, smaller one. Their son Sam's wife, Sarah Adams, ran a tourist home here from 1930 to 1932. Travelers took overnight rooms and were served breakfast for $2. Reid descendants still possess the old guest register. Below, Sam and Sarah Reid stand flanked by their children Lillian and Harry. One rainy day Lillian was walking home from work across the bridge when Andrew Love kindly offered her a ride. The son of Scottish immigrants who worked as weavers in Thompsonville, Andrew was a butcher and made his deliveries by horse and wagon. Lillian and Andrew married soon after in the front yard garden of the family home on East Street in 1917. (Above, courtesy KML; below, courtesy Dorian Love Taylor.)

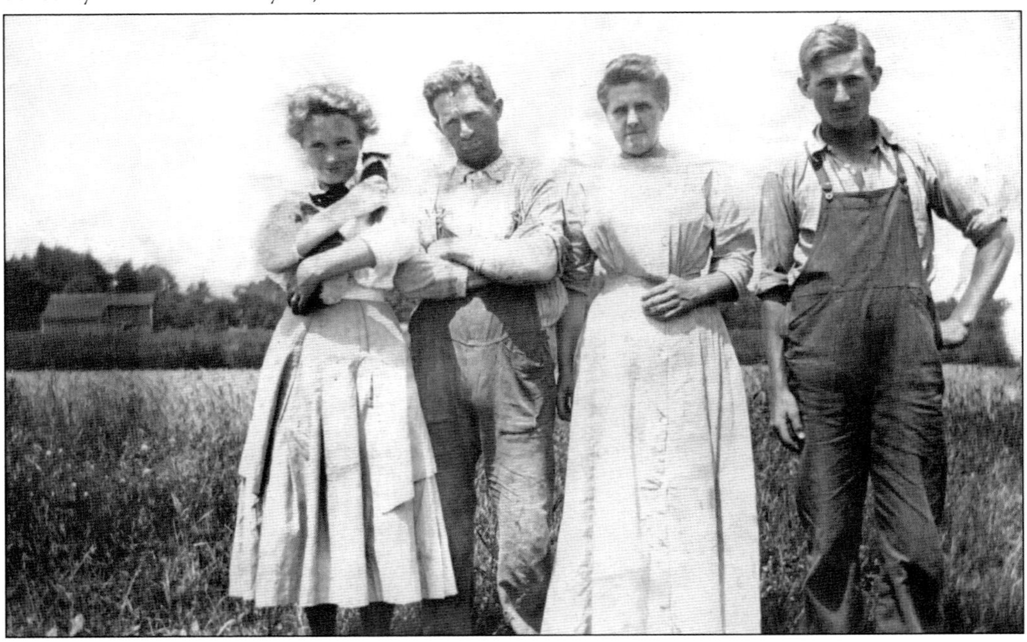

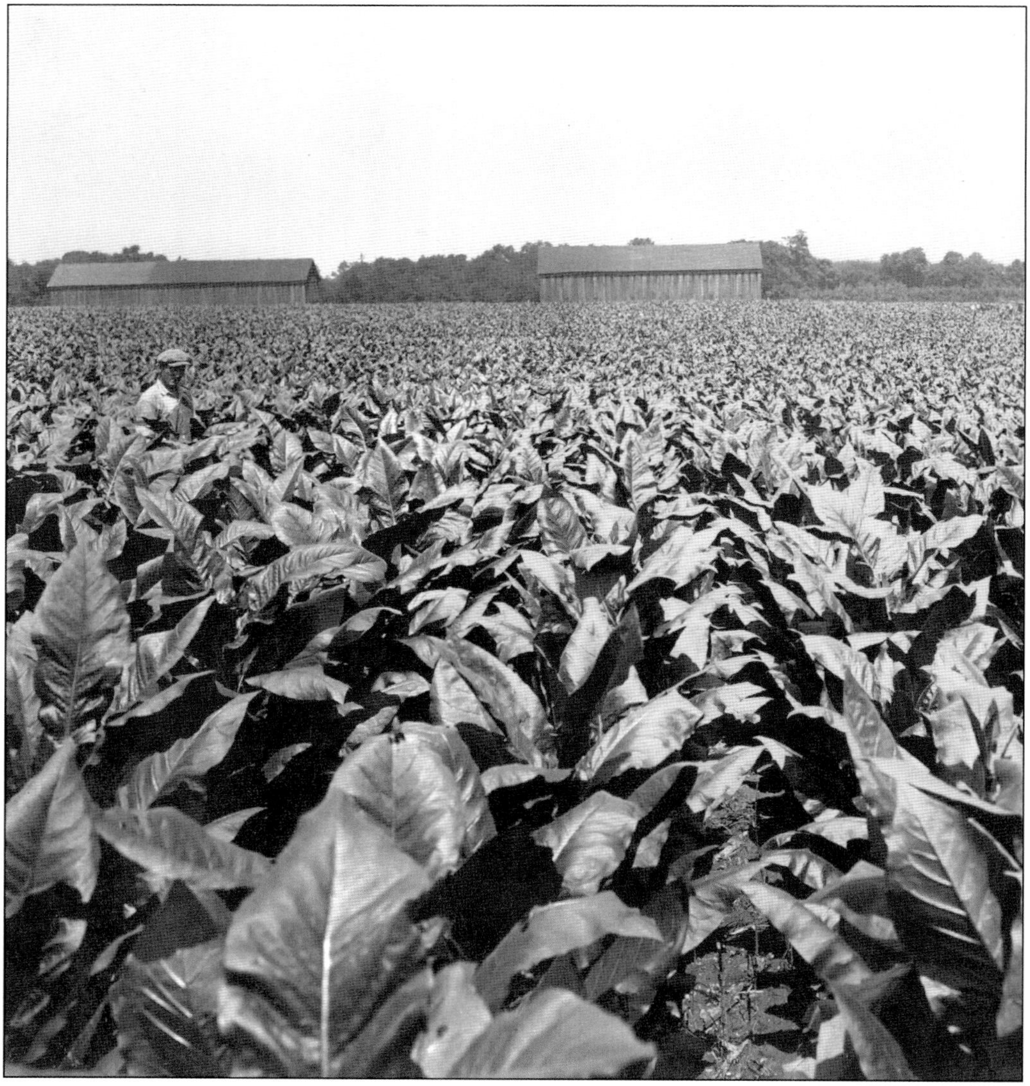

Inspecting plants, Sam Reid's son, Harry, stands in a sea of broadleaf tobacco on his family's East Street farm. The local section of the Connecticut River valley, also referred to as "Tobacco Valley," has the perfect combination of climate and soil factors for this product to flourish. The crops Harry's grandfather James originally cultivated were vegetables and fruit, especially strawberries, which were peddled with horse and wagon to Thompsonville and Springfield. The Reid family purchased food staples at Hilditch's Store in Thompsonville, on credit, as many farmers did. After the tobacco crop was harvested, cured, and sold, with a lump sum of cash on hand, accounts were settled. In the 1920s, Sam named the farm Edgehurst, meaning "edge of the woods." He expanded the enterprise by adding a herd of U.S. government–accredited Ayrshire cows in 1928. To celebrate the opening of the dairy, free glasses of milk were handed out. Harry continued with his own dairy farm on River Boulevard. In 1938, Benjamin J. Bielonko bought the entire Reid farm on East Street. (Courtesy Dorian Love Taylor.)

Born in 1877, George N. Remington Sr. inspects his broadleaf tobacco crop in this 1950s photograph. One of the original families to settle in Suffield, the Remingtons came to America from England in 1637. The family eventually moved to a farm in Suffield via Boston and Windsor, Connecticut. Suffield is now home to many Remington households, reaching into their 12th Suffield generation. (Courtesy Remington family.)

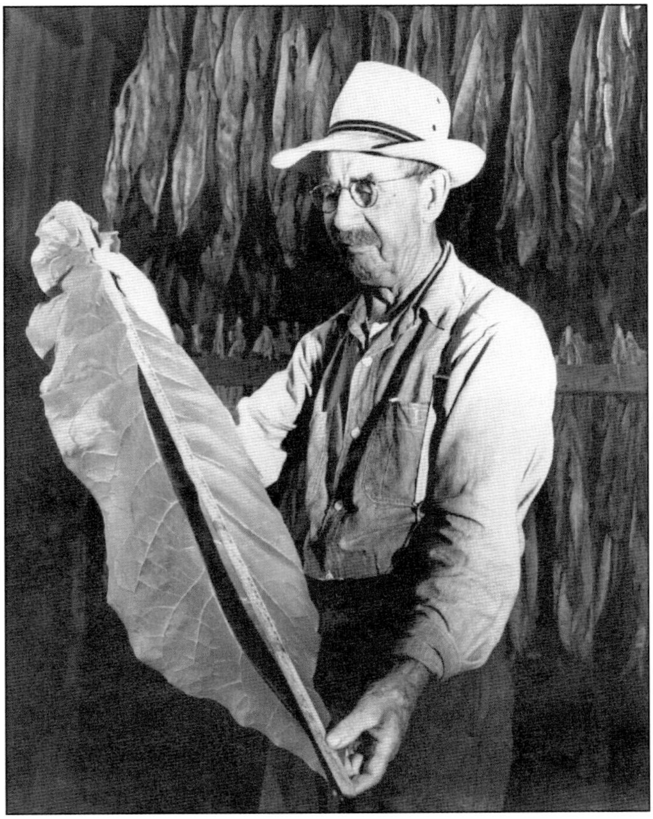

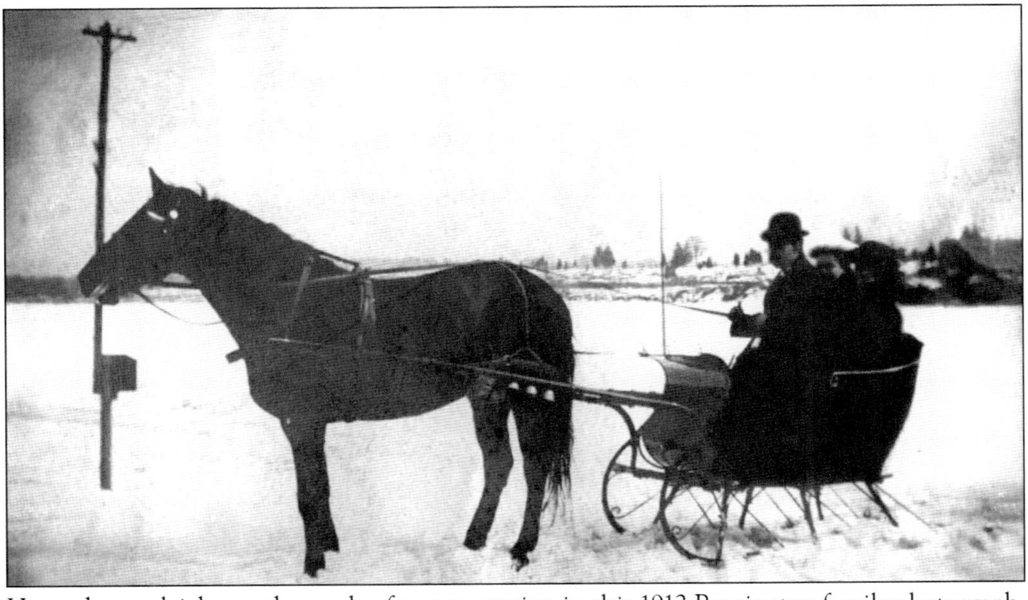

Horse-drawn sleigh was the mode of transportation in this 1912 Remington family photograph. From River Boulevard, the Thompsonville shoreline is visible. Harold Remington recalls his grandfather George Sr. speaking of the days when one could skate all the way to Springfield on the frozen river. The last time the river was solid enough for Harold to walk over to Thompsonville was Christmas of 1945. (Courtesy Remington family.)

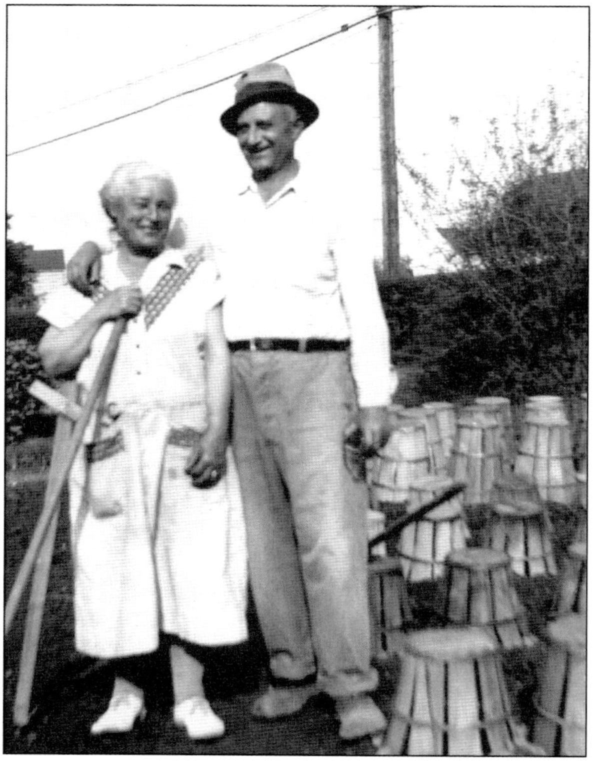

Raffaele Romano married Anna Cardorapoli in Bracigliano, Italy. He immigrated to the United States in 1920; eight years later, Anna and their son John joined him. They first lived in the Thompsonville neighborhood called Frenchtown, where Raffaele worked at the carpet mill. By 1941, the family moved to East Suffield. The Romanos enjoyed gardening, and their seasonal produce stand was patronized by commuters to and from Hamilton Standard in Windsor Locks. (Courtesy Louise Romano Sarno.)

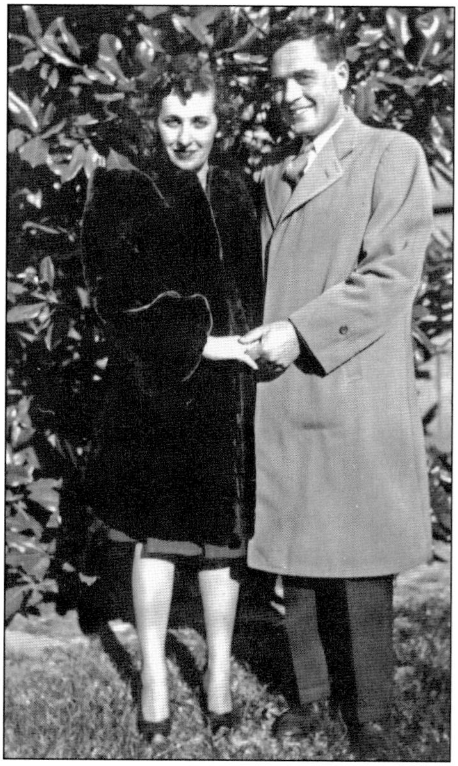

After serving in the Air Force Engineer Corps during World War II, John Romano married Theresa Tebaldi and started a cabinet-making business in his garage. Eventually he formed the John Romano Construction Company and was a successful contractor for 25 years. To his credit are Suffield Town Hall, Sacred Heart Church Hall, and numerous other municipal buildings and schools in the area. John and his wife, Theresa, are pictured here in the 1940s. (Courtesy Louise Romano Sarno.)

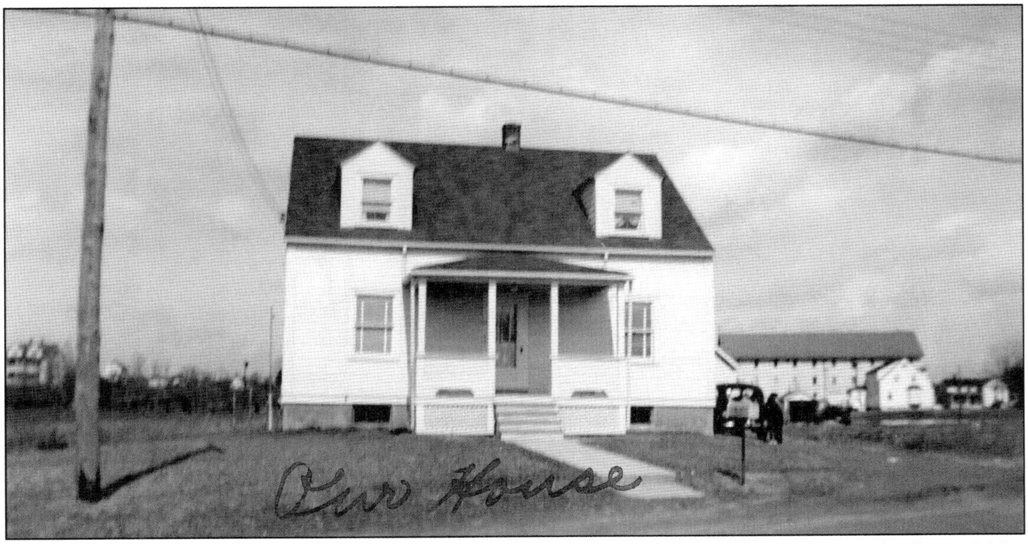

The Romanos' house on Thompsonville Road, built by their teenage son John in the late 1930s, is still home to his sister Louise and her husband, Mimi Sarno. On the far right is an almost unobstructed view of Sullivan's tobacco warehouse on Burbank Avenue. The open space was once known as "the Patch," which was comprised of parcels of land where people from both Suffield and Thompsonville kept gardens. (Courtesy Louise Romano Sarno.)

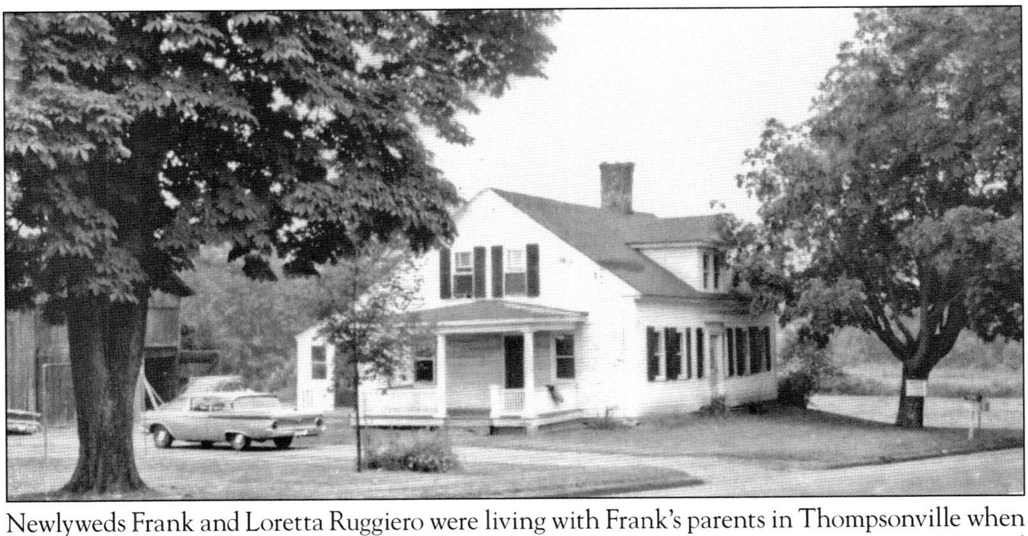

Newlyweds Frank and Loretta Ruggiero were living with Frank's parents in Thompsonville when they found their dream home on East Street in Suffield. It was built by Thomas King Sr. around 1805. During the renovation, they discovered a letter from that same period sharing the local news: "It is so cold that my husband walked across the Connecticut River" and "We appear to have a peeping Tom in town." (Courtesy Ruggiero family.)

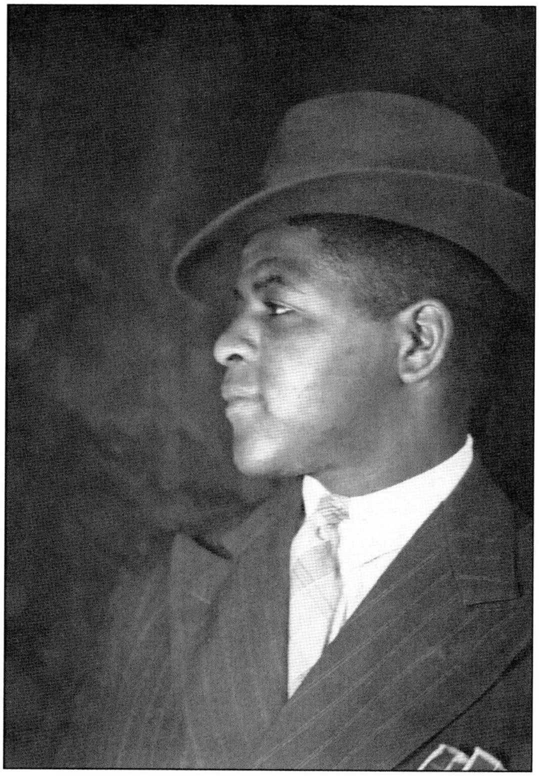

Herbert (Herbie) Scott, pictured here in 1942, was originally from Windsor. He served in the army during World War II and subsequently became very active in the VFW and AmVets veterans' groups. He and his wife, Lois Niles, were childhood friends, married, and moved to East Suffield in the 1950s. Herbie was employed at Krupa Oil Company for over 25 years. His son Brian also worked there as a mechanic and "Big Rig" driver for 26 years. (Courtesy Lois Niles Scott.)

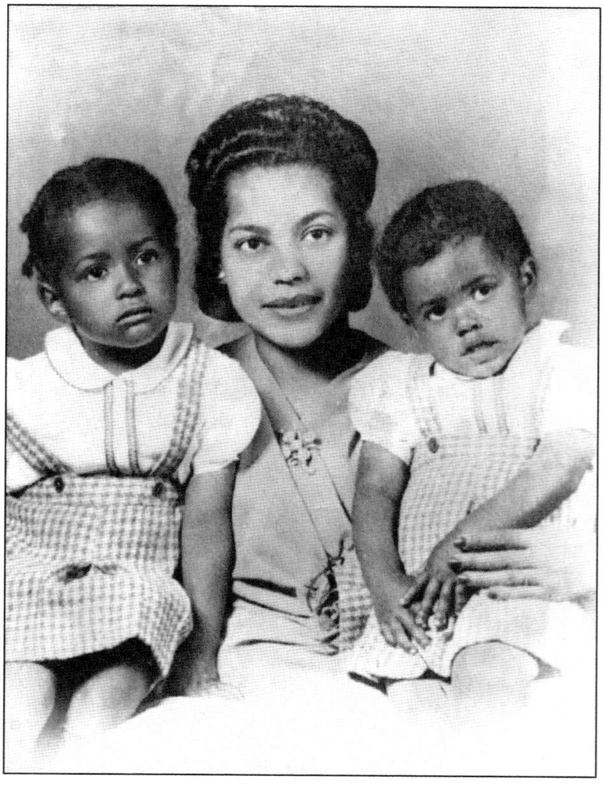

Lois Niles Scott sits with daughters Ethel (left) and Nancy. Both girls grew up, married, and raised their own families in this same neighborhood. Along with raising three children, Lois had a long career as a nurse's aide and cared for many of the elderly in the area. Proud of her work and her African and Native American ancestry, she has lived at the same Thompsonville Road address for 60 years. (Courtesy Lois Niles Scott.)

When the Giacomarra family emigrated from Sicily in 1901, their name was anglicized to Jackamore. Giuseppe plied his trade in the mines of Pennsylvania until a near fatal accident occurred. The prospect of employment in a carpet mill in Connecticut led the family to Thompsonville, where he worked as a weaver. In this 1908 photograph, Eugenia and Giuseppe pose with their daughters, from left to right, Elizabeth, Rose, and Ann. Of their 16 children, only 4 daughters survived into adulthood. (Courtesy Rose Vella Shelanskas.)

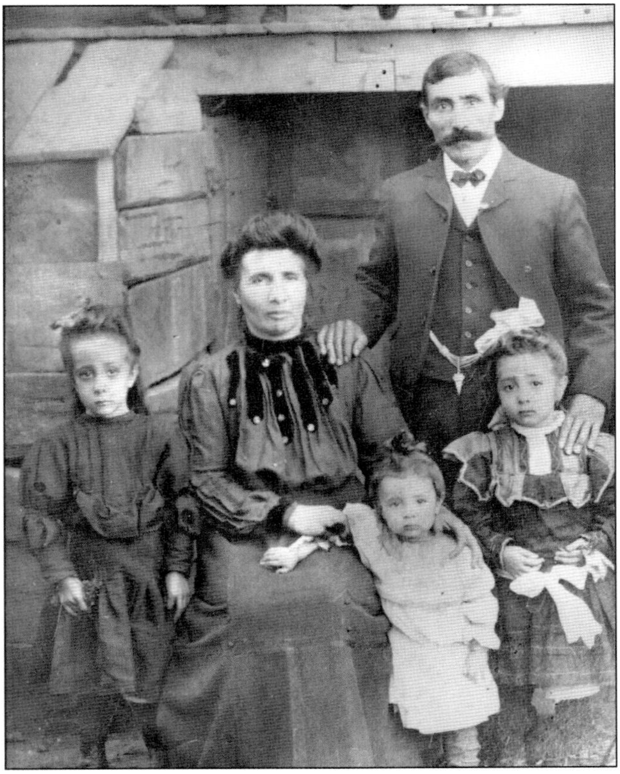

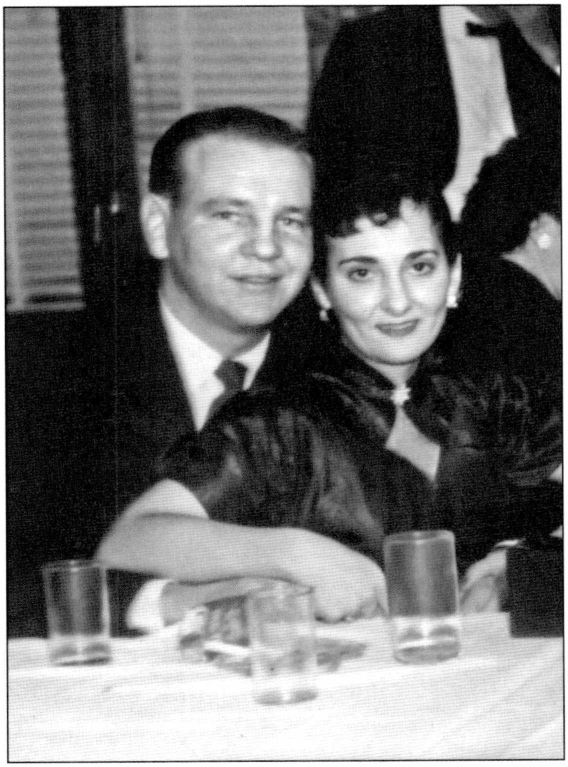

The Giacomarra grandparents of Rose Vella and the Lithuanian parents of her husband Raymond Shelanskas could not have imagined the unique American society that would emerge from the cultural mix of their descendants. Raymond and Rose, pictured here in the 1950s, followed the progression of prosperity that originated in the booming carpet mill town of Thompsonville and led to their home on River Boulevard Extension in East Suffield. (Courtesy Rose Vella Shelanskas.)

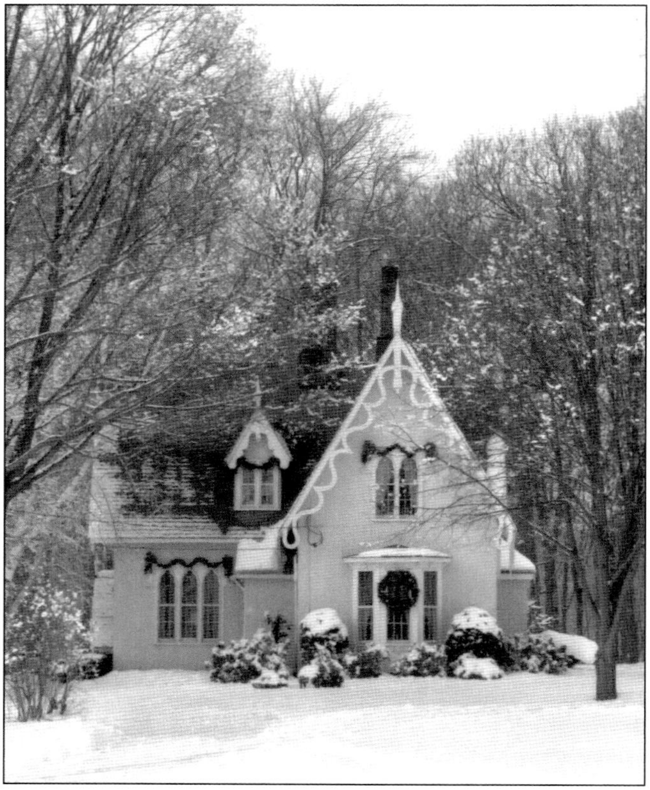

This picturesque Carpenter Gothic house on Mapleton Avenue was built by David Lyman Sikes in the mid- to late 1800s. He was the grandson of David Sikes, a Revolutionary War soldier. The Sikes family is among those that first settled Suffield, particularly in the northeast part of town. The original land grant was in 1680 to Victory Sikes, when Suffield was still part of Massachusetts. Victory was a carpenter, as all Suffield land grantees had to have a trade. (Photograph by Laurie Tavino.)

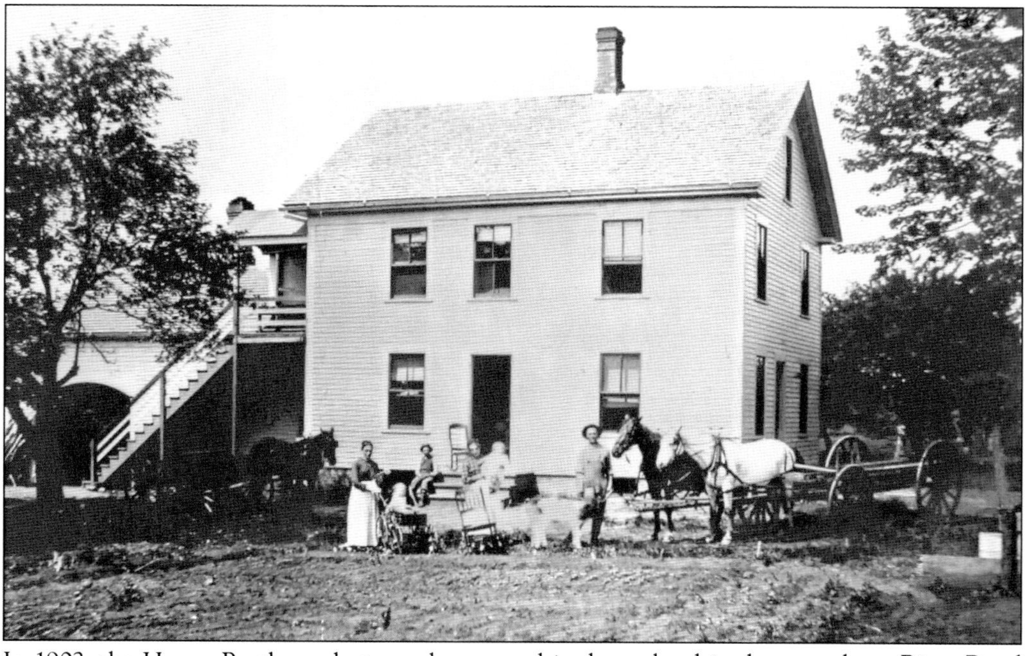

In 1902, the Howes Brothers photographers were hired to take this photograph on River Road (currently River Boulevard). It is most likely of Willard C. Sikes and family, who later built a new, Victorian-style house on the same street. The eight Sikes households in Suffield, now into their 12th generation, are all descended from Victory Sikes. (Courtesy KML.)

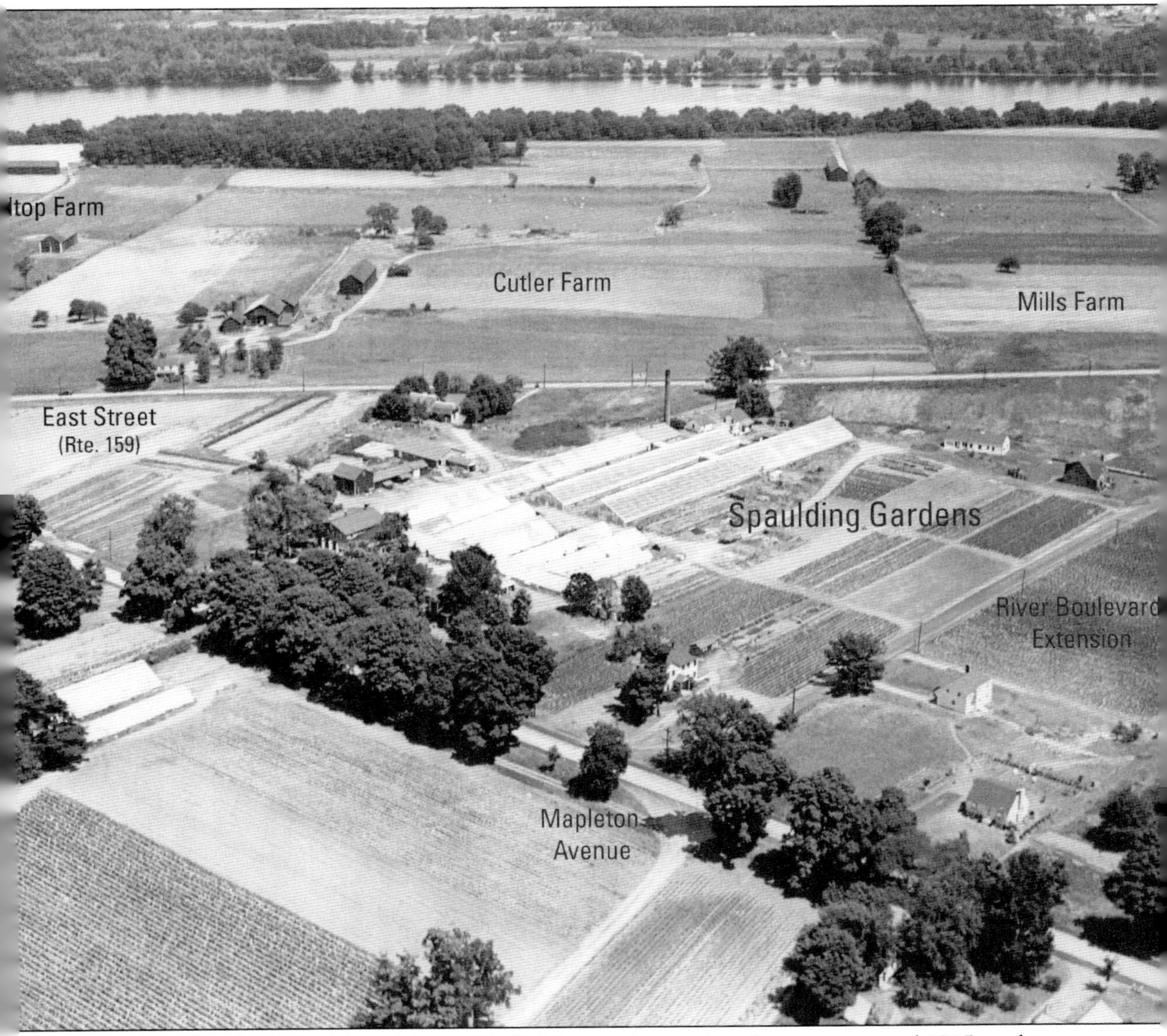

Brothers A. Ward and Earl Spaulding of Suffield started a produce business around 1915, making their first deliveries to Springfield Regional Market by horse and wagon. Learning that many other farms were also selling produce, they converted to a florist business that flourished for over 60 years. The brothers located Spaulding Gardens on a triangular parcel of land between River Boulevard Extension, Mapleton Avenue, and East Street. At its peak, the business employed dozens of workers in 18 greenhouses tending approximately 3 acres under glass and an additional 16 open acres, plus a cold storage cellar, barns, and a retail floral shop. They also staffed a retail shop in Thompsonville. In the early days of the year-round enterprise, heating oil for the greenhouses cost less than $5 a barrel. A sharp rise in fuel prices in the 1970s brought the business to a close in 1976. Meanwhile A. Ward served on the school board for many years, and the primary school in Suffield bears his name. This early-1950s photograph shows Spaulding Gardens in its Connecticut River valley setting. (Courtesy Glenn Spaulding.)

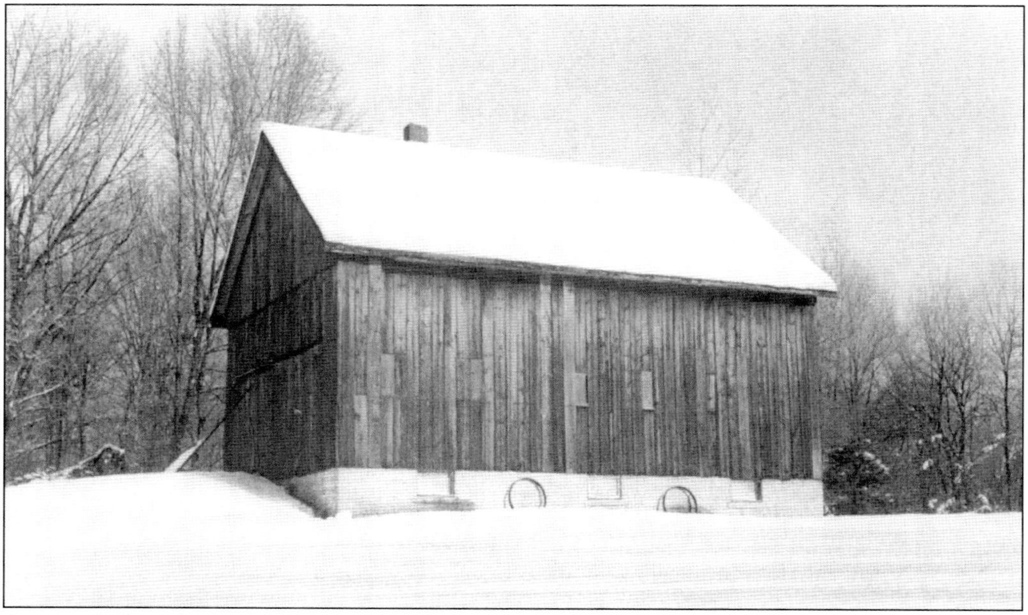

George Stelmack Sr., at age 19, immigrated to the United States from Poland. Over time he acquired farmland on River Boulevard and Thompsonville Road and leased land at various other locations. He was an ambitious tobacco farmer, and this well-kept barn on his farm was previously used as a warehouse for sorting and grading the cured leaves. (Courtesy Laurie Tavino.)

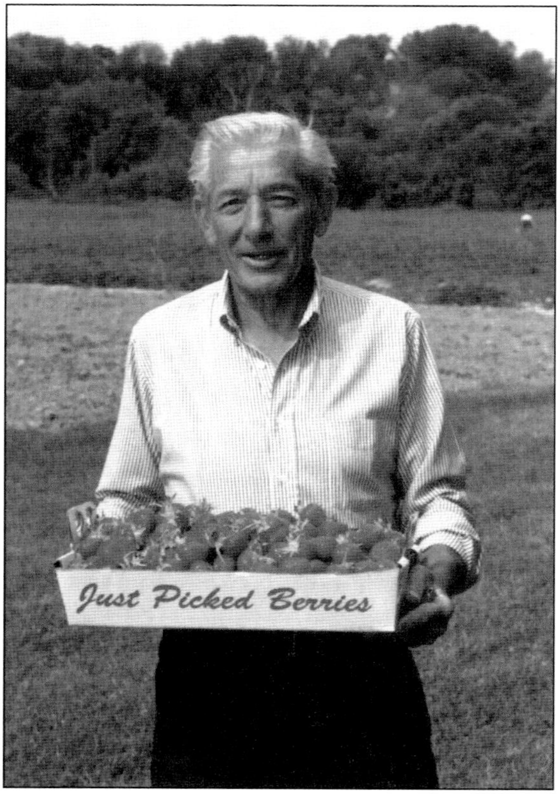

George Stelmack Jr., born in 1930, proudly displays a tray of his strawberries in this photograph. Although his trade was as a steamfitter, operating a tractor was his favorite pastime. Later in life, he and his wife, Esther Jachym, acquired their strawberry business when a local farmer renting property from them suddenly died and left them with acres of berries to harvest. Since their passing, the Stelmacks and their strawberry fields are sorely missed. (Courtesy Karl Stelmack.)

One of East Suffield's most prominent and influential tobacco men, John L. Sullivan rose from humble roots. His father, like millions of others, fled Ireland during the terrible potato famine of the 1840s. The family settled in Thompsonville, where John L. grew up. As a young man, he labored on the Windsor Locks Canal. The choice spread of land just north of the canal was to become his farm. Pictured here are his wife, Ellen, and nephew Edward Maher, tending chickens. (Courtesy Sullivan family.)

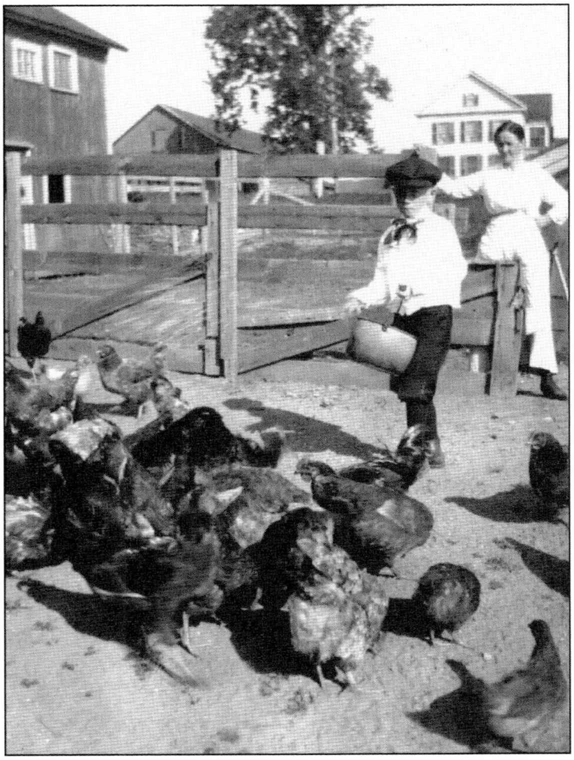

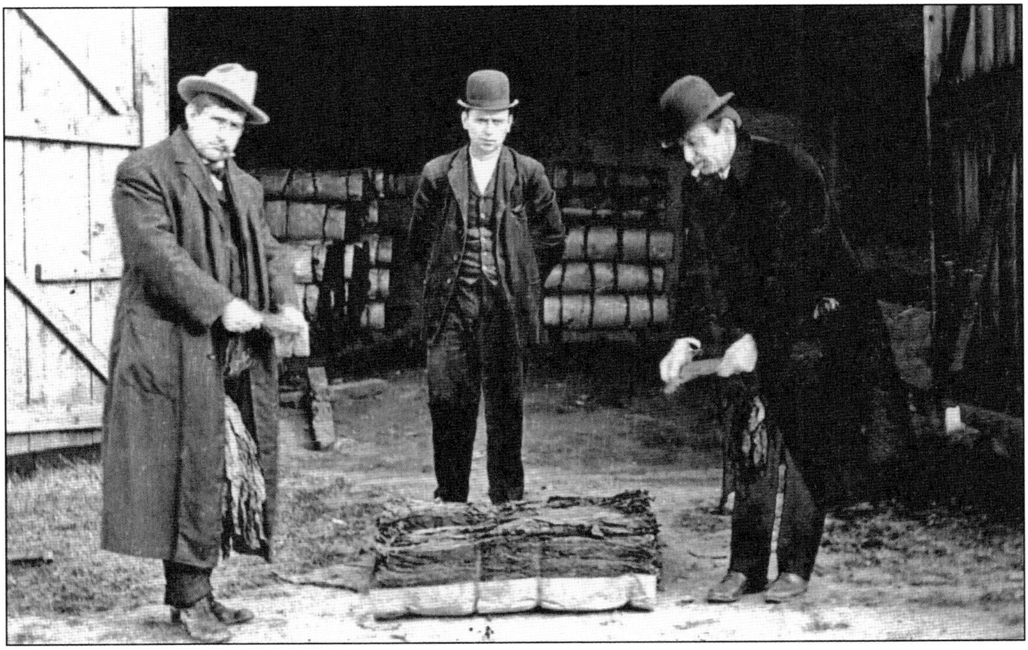

Seen here are, from left to right, John L., William Fleming (who later served as Enfield's chief of police from 1935 to 1951), and a prospective tobacco buyer (of the Schuster Brothers in Milwaukee) as they negotiate a sale. Traditionally the bunch or "hand" of tobacco is held with the legs so both hands are free to inspect the leaves. John L. not only raised tobacco but was engaged by several large firms as a buyer and procurer. (Courtesy Sullivan family.)

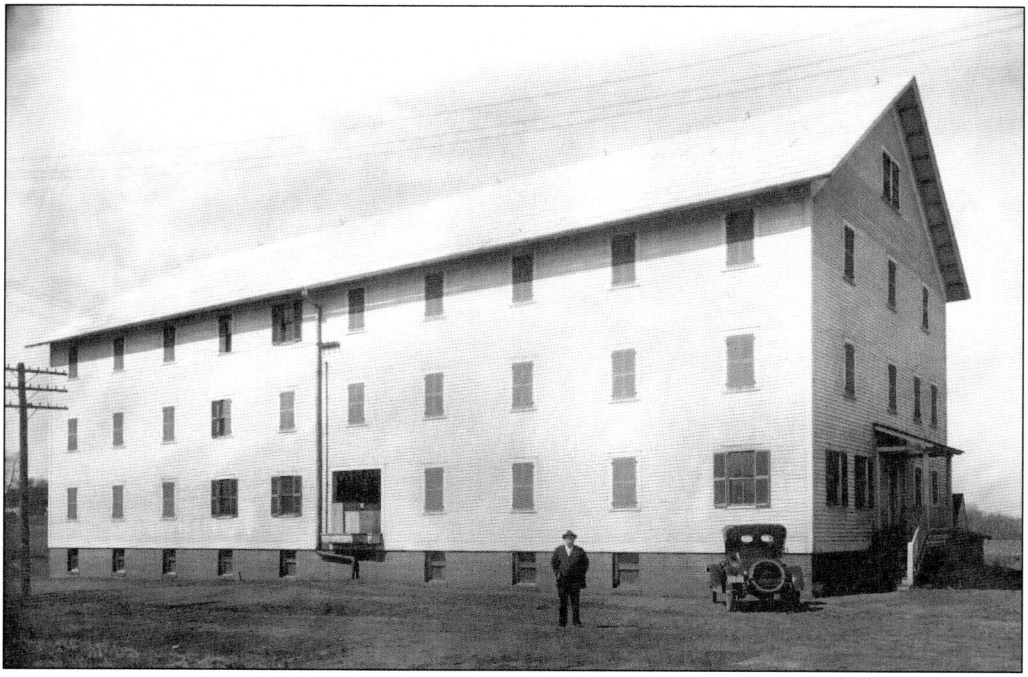

Originally a self-taught carpenter, John L. Sullivan stands proudly with his Pierce Arrow roadster before the tobacco warehouse he built on Burbank Avenue in 1910. Much of the lumber used for this building was harvested from trees along the nearby Connecticut River. John L.'s son James joined in the family tobacco business when he was 16 years old. The converted warehouse is currently home to the Burbank Shops. (Courtesy Sullivan family.)

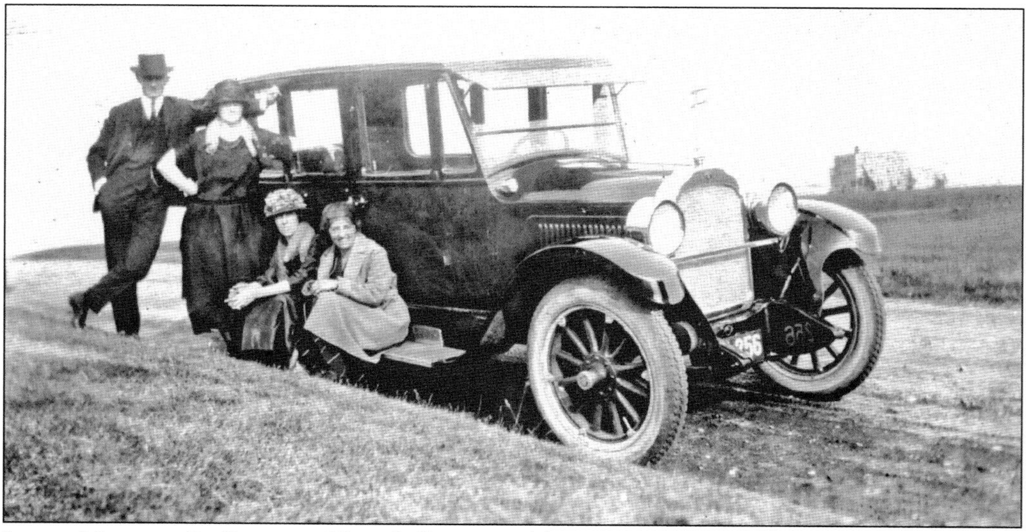

James, Margaret Baillargeon, Clara Sullivan, and her sister Linda Baillargeon pause along the roadside in the early 1920s. During the 14 years James served as Suffield's first selectmen, he was also constable and took part in forming the Suffield Police Department. Also to his credit were the positions of road foreman, director of the Suffield Savings Bank, vice president of the Northern Connecticut Bank, and grand knight of the Knights of Columbus. (Courtesy Sullivan family.)

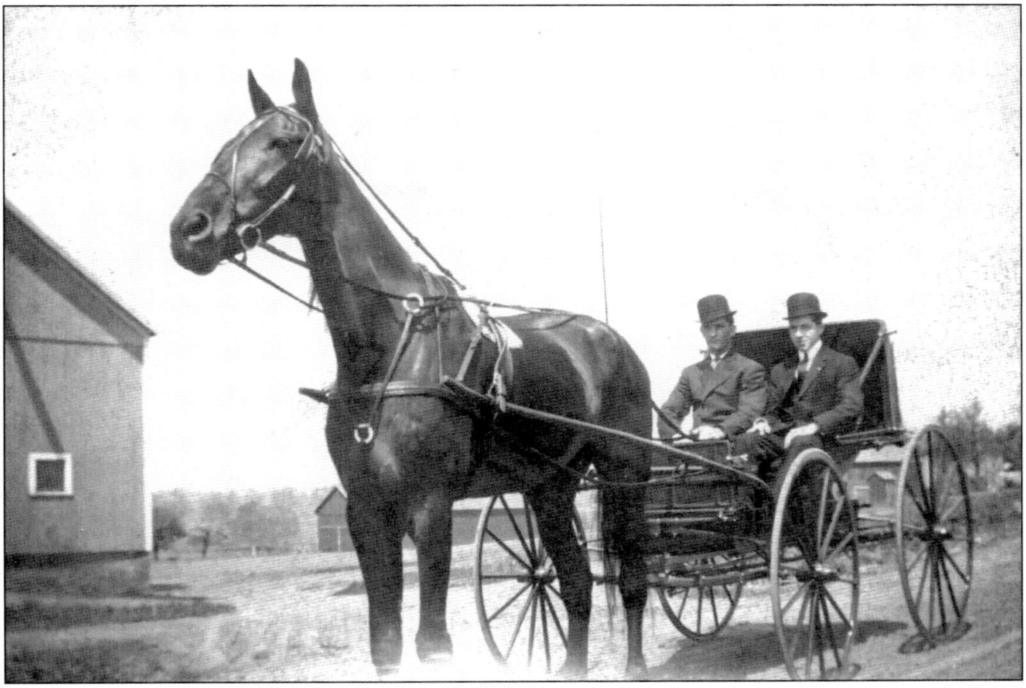

James Sullivan rose early every morning and cared for 14 horses before breakfast. One magnificent steed is depicted here with James (left) and an unidentified gentleman. Each week, one day was reserved for his hobby of horse racing. His Judson B was Champion on Ice, 1908–1909, at Malone, New York. James worked in the tobacco business until 1960. His son John H. continued until the farm was sold around 1968. (Courtesy Sullivan family.)

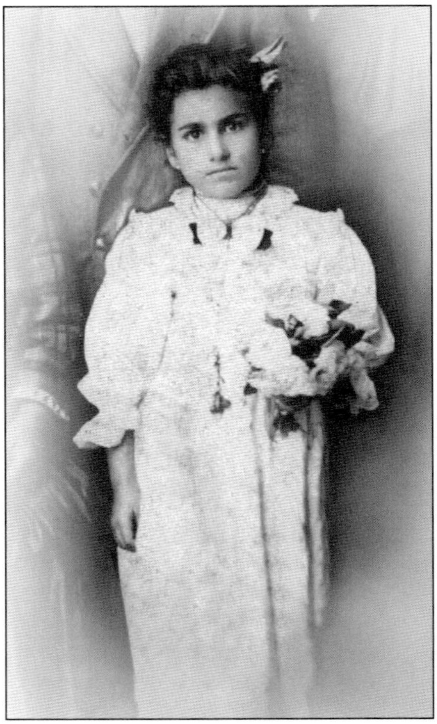

In 1906, Lorenzo Tavino married his true love, Teresa Del Monico, in a small hill town outside of Benevento, Italy. Lorenzo left for America, settled in Hazardville, a section of Enfield, and sent for his pregnant wife to join him. The required physical exam revealed tuberculosis, and she was not allowed to leave. Lorenzo never saw her again, as she died soon afterward. Some 16 years passed before his daughter Anna (pictured) arrived at Ellis Island, where they met for the first time. (Courtesy Tavino family.)

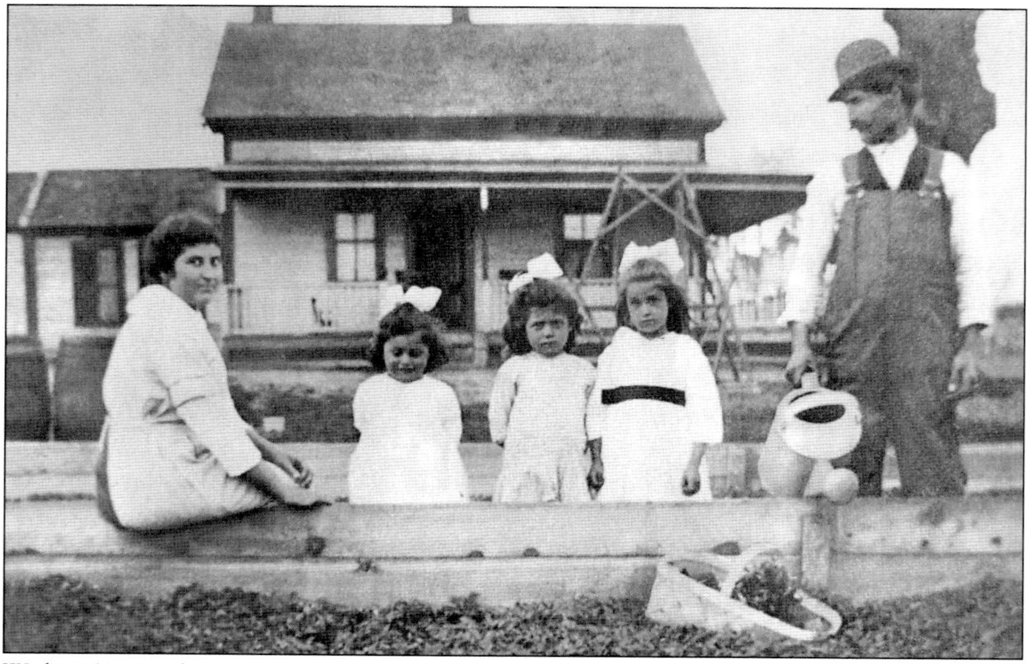

With a 60-acre farm to run, Lorenzo Tavino eventually sent inquiries to Italy about prospects for a wife. Luisa, a young woman from his home town of Montorso, learned of the opportunity to go to America and jumped at the chance. They married at St. Patrick's Catholic Church in 1913. Luisa and Lorenzo pose in 1920 with their three daughters, (from left to right) Jo, Romie, and Ida. (Courtesy Tavino family.)

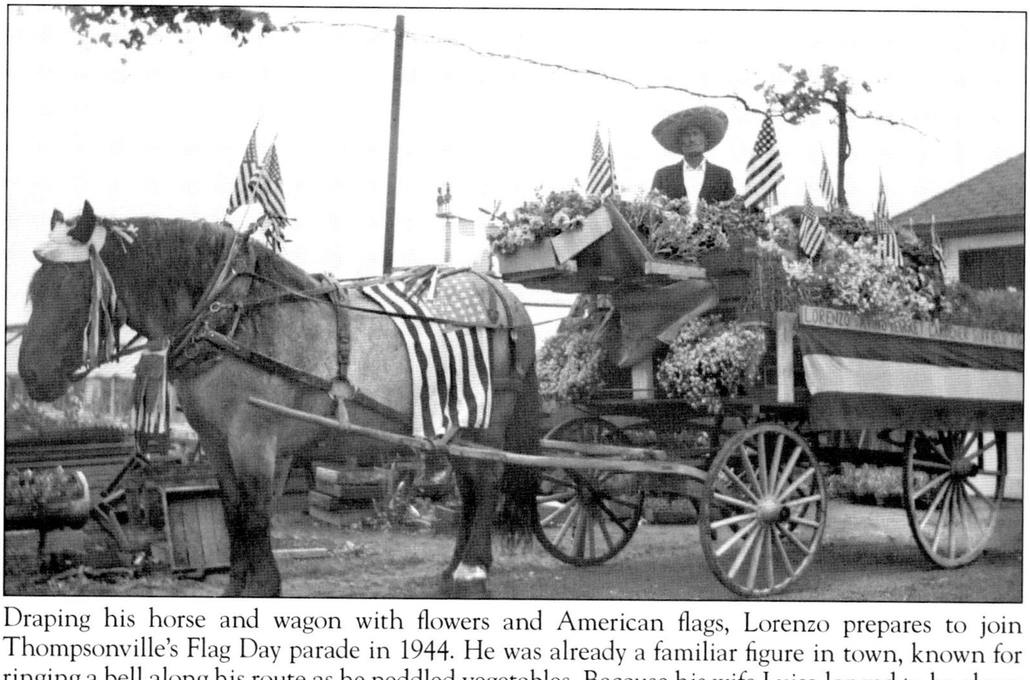

Draping his horse and wagon with flowers and American flags, Lorenzo prepares to join Thompsonville's Flag Day parade in 1944. He was already a familiar figure in town, known for ringing a bell along his route as he peddled vegetables. Because his wife Luisa longed to be closer to the Italian community in Thompsonville, the family moved from Hazardville to a small farm in East Suffield. (Courtesy Tavino family.)

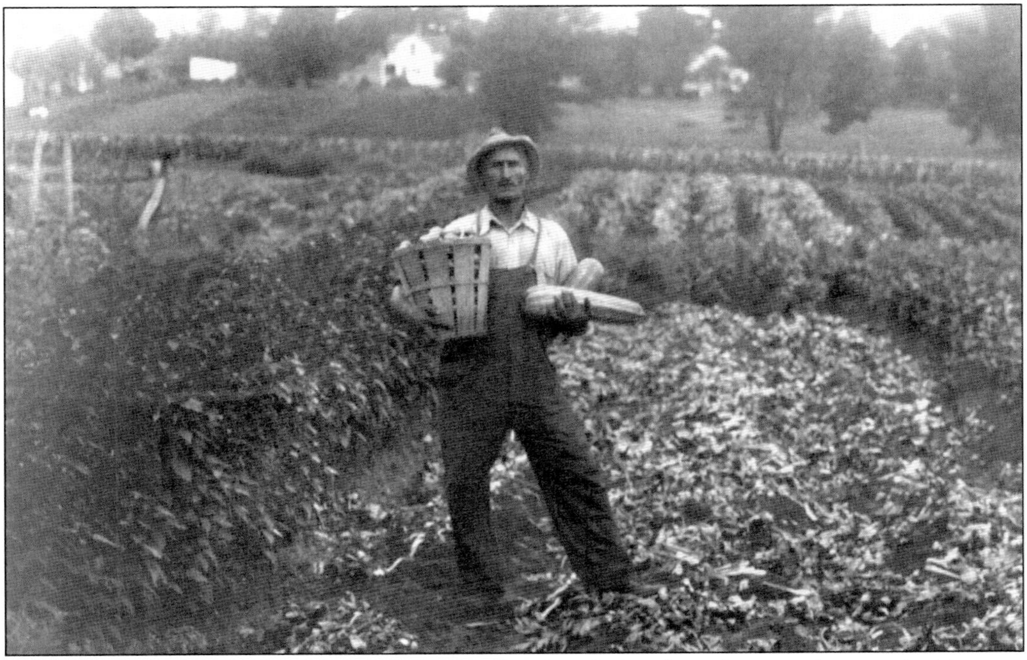

With 10 years having passed since the birth of his fourth daughter, Lorenzo (pictured with some of his produce) feared having no namesake. On a winter night in 1926, he rushed with horse and sleigh to fetch midwife Ersilia Daniele for his pregnant wife, Luisa. Ersilia assisted the delivery of a son, Lawrence. The ecstatic father gave bottles of homemade wine to neighbors and paid the midwife a generous $50. (Courtesy Tavino family.)

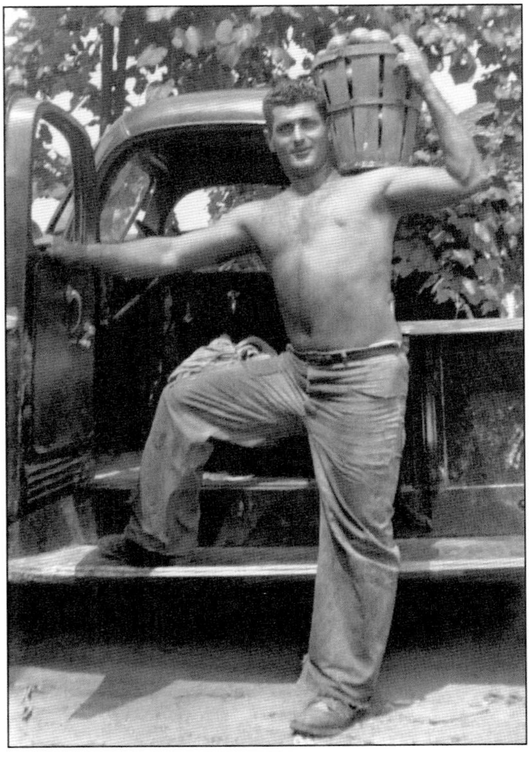

Lawrence shoulders a basket of his father's tomatoes to pose for a photograph before going to market around 1945. With heated greenhouses to extend the growing season, the Tavino farm was especially well known for flowers. The family operated a successful market garden business until the early 1960s. Presently the River Boulevard acreage is cultivated by neighboring Bielonko Farms but is still home to Lorenzo and Luisa's grandchildren and great-grandchildren. (Courtesy Tavino family.)

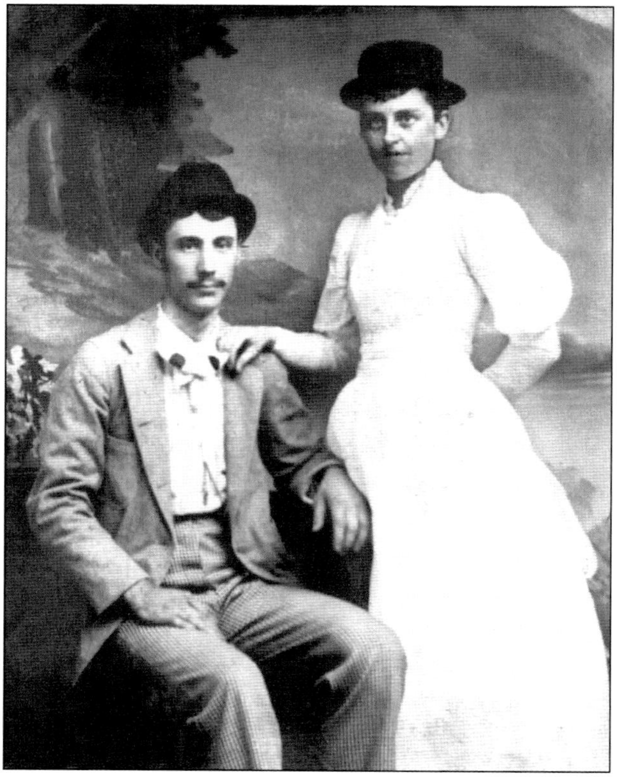

Researching the East Suffield Underwood family leads to Oscar Eastman, a Vermont Yankee, pictured here with his wife Harriet. Oscar joined his state militia during the Civil War but curiously transferred to a Connecticut regiment. After contracting tuberculosis he returned to Vermont, sold the family farm, and relocated to East Suffield with his mother Susan Thayer Eastman, son Samuel, but for unknown reasons without Harriet. Coincidentally, 200 years earlier, a landholder of this area was named Eastman. (Courtesy Underwood family.)

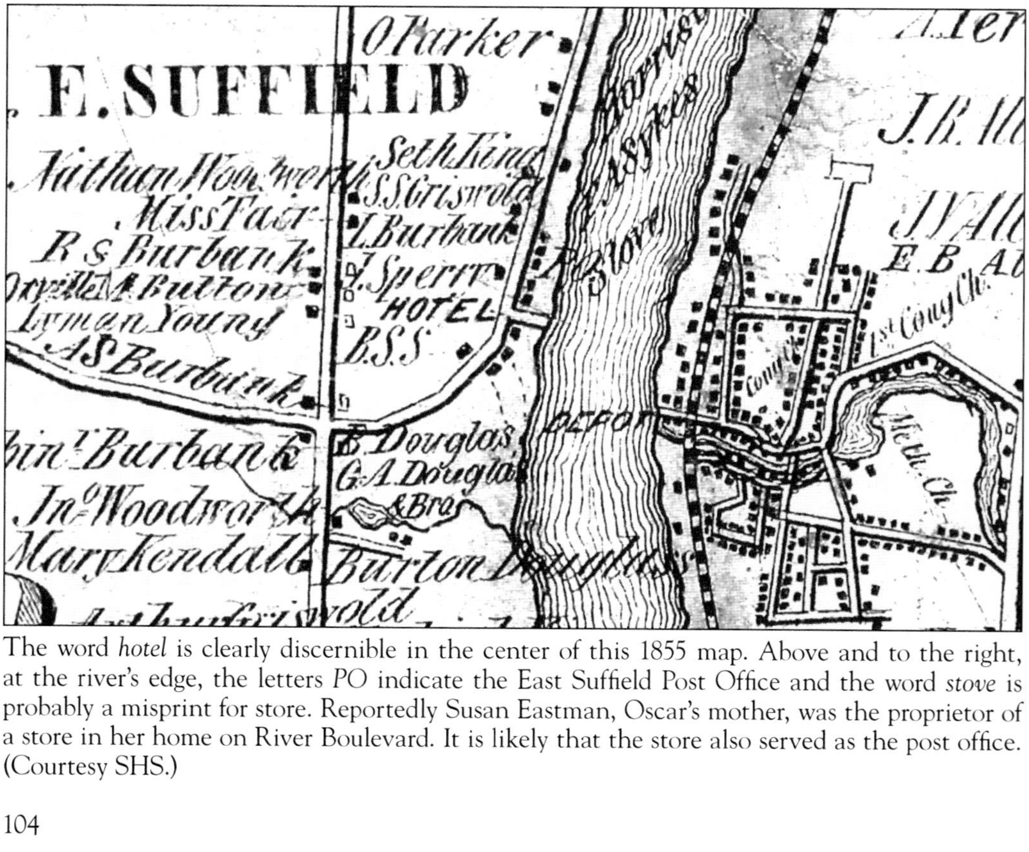

The word *hotel* is clearly discernible in the center of this 1855 map. Above and to the right, at the river's edge, the letters *PO* indicate the East Suffield Post Office and the word *stove* is probably a misprint for store. Reportedly Susan Eastman, Oscar's mother, was the proprietor of a store in her home on River Boulevard. It is likely that the store also served as the post office. (Courtesy SHS.)

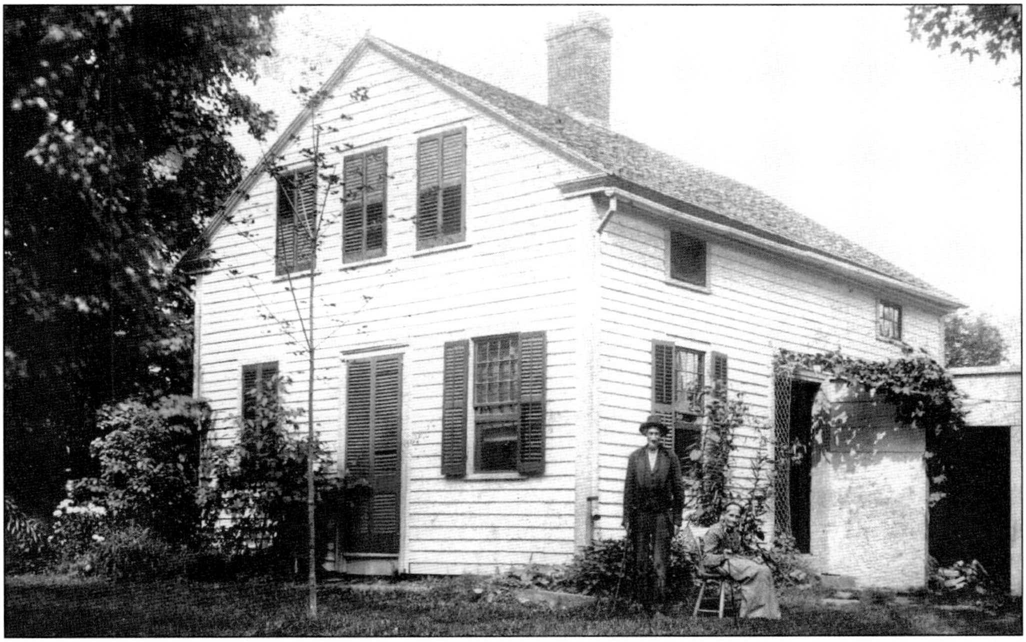

Oscar Eastman died of consumption soon after moving to Suffield but not before giving up his son Samuel to Hezden King for adoption. The Kings renamed their adopted son as Franklin King. For a time, Franklin was employed on *Cora*, the ferryboat that crossed between Suffield and Thompsonville. An elderly Susan Eastman and an unidentified gentleman pose before her River Boulevard home in 1891. (Courtesy Underwood family.)

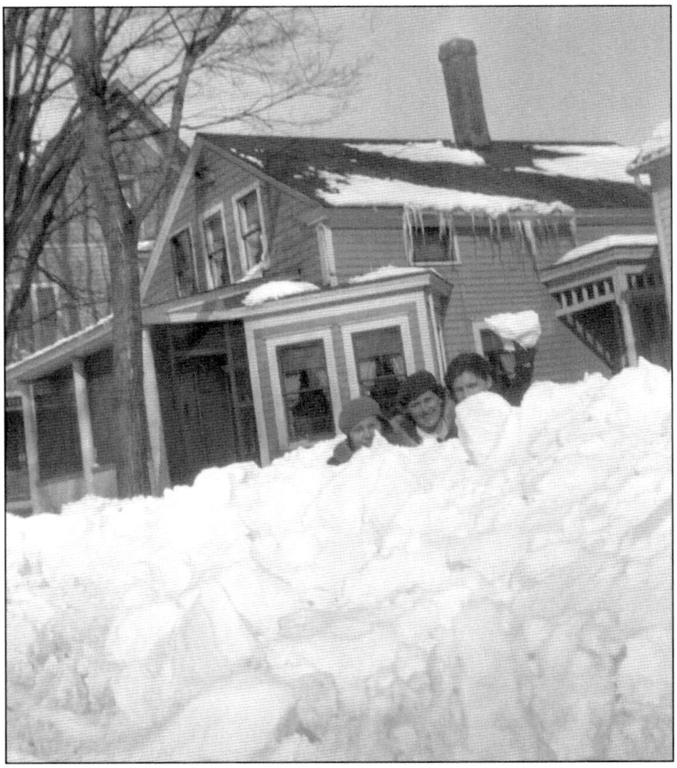

Pictured here is the same house as above, around 1930, with some distinctive added renovations. Records state that it was built as a store by John Brunson approximately 100 years earlier. A small village grew near the ferry crossing, and the store's convenient location saved local residents the toll to Thompsonville. The Martin family, descendants of Franklin King, lived here until the 1960s. (Courtesy Tavino family.)

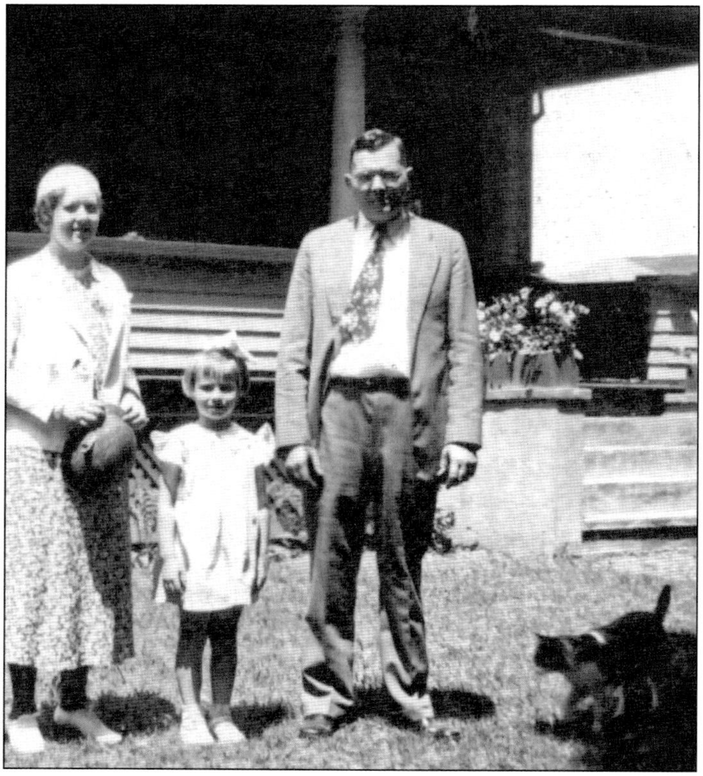

Helen King and Frederick Underwood, with daughter Betty, pose in front of their Thompsonville Road home. Helen was the daughter of Franklin King, descendant of the Eastman family from Vermont. She married Frederick in 1917. He held a position as athletic director while employed at the carpet mill, served as a constable in Suffield, and later worked for Kaman Corporation. The Underwood ancestors had emigrated from Kidderminster, England, coincidentally a carpet manufacturing center. (Courtesy Underwood family.)

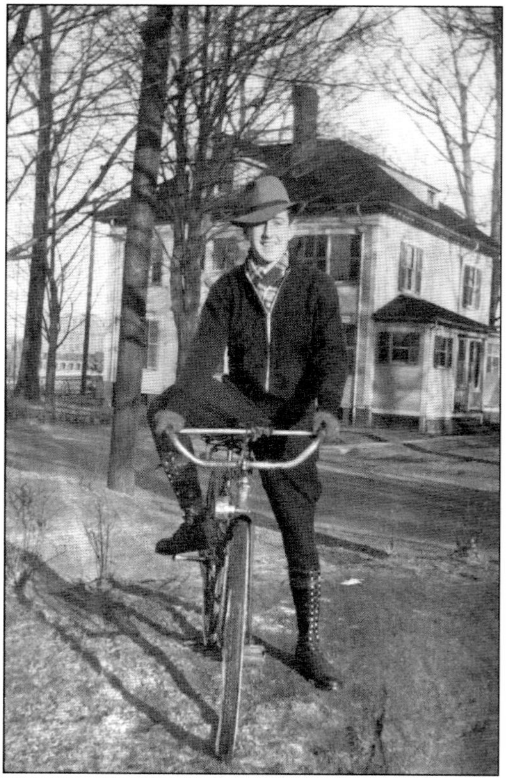

Robert F. Underwood, son of Helen and Frederick (above), is pictured opposite the intersection on the East Suffield side of the old bridge. Robert's various occupations were as a carpenter, carpet weaver, millwright, printer, and writer. In his time, he wrote numerous historical articles about Thompsonville and was a serious amateur photographer with an artistic approach. Many of his photographs are published for the first time in this book. (Courtesy Underwood family.)

This sign on Thompsonville Road marked the spot where customers from miles around picked up their holiday chickens and turkeys. James Vallides, a Greek immigrant, ran a shoe-shine and hat-blocking business across the river at the old Thompsonville Hotel. He bought Suffield land in the mid-1940s and started farming. His son Mike then turned an agricultural school project with chickens into the thriving Suffield Poultry Farm business. (Courtesy Vallides family.)

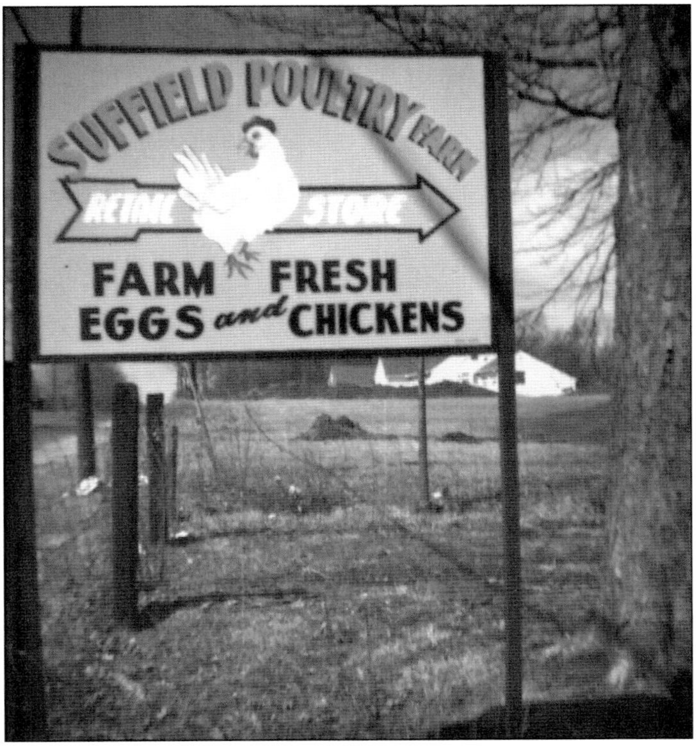

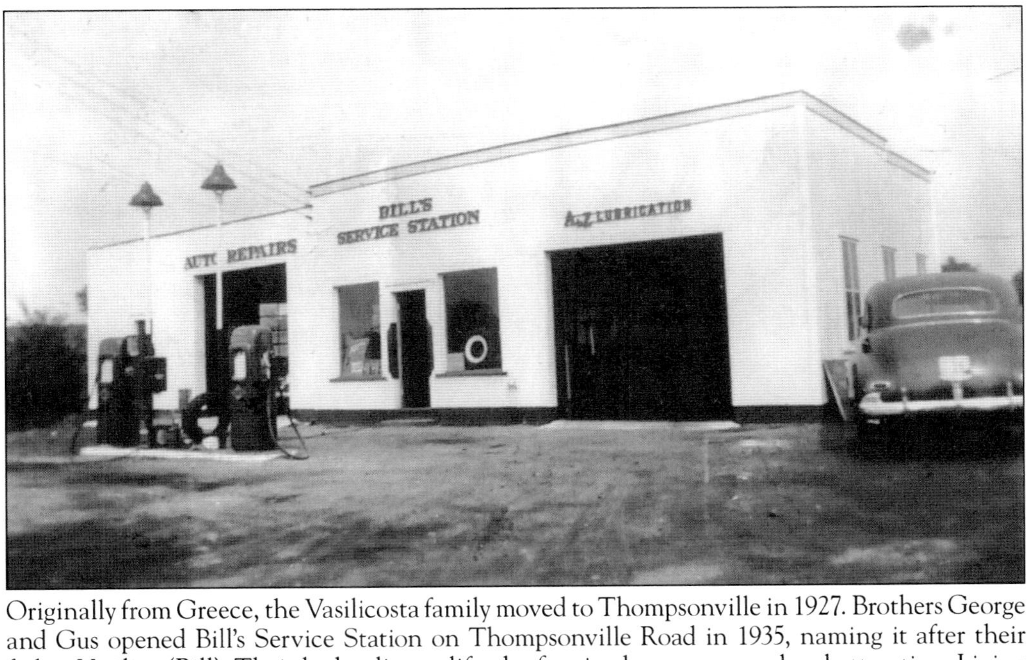

Originally from Greece, the Vasilicosta family moved to Thompsonville in 1927. Brothers George and Gus opened Bill's Service Station on Thompsonville Road in 1935, naming it after their father Vasilios (Bill). Their hydraulic car lift, the first in the area, was a local attraction. Living in Suffield with his wife Rosa and five daughters, George continued the business after Gus passed away until 1969, when the old bridge closed and traffic ceased. (Courtesy George Vasilicosta.)

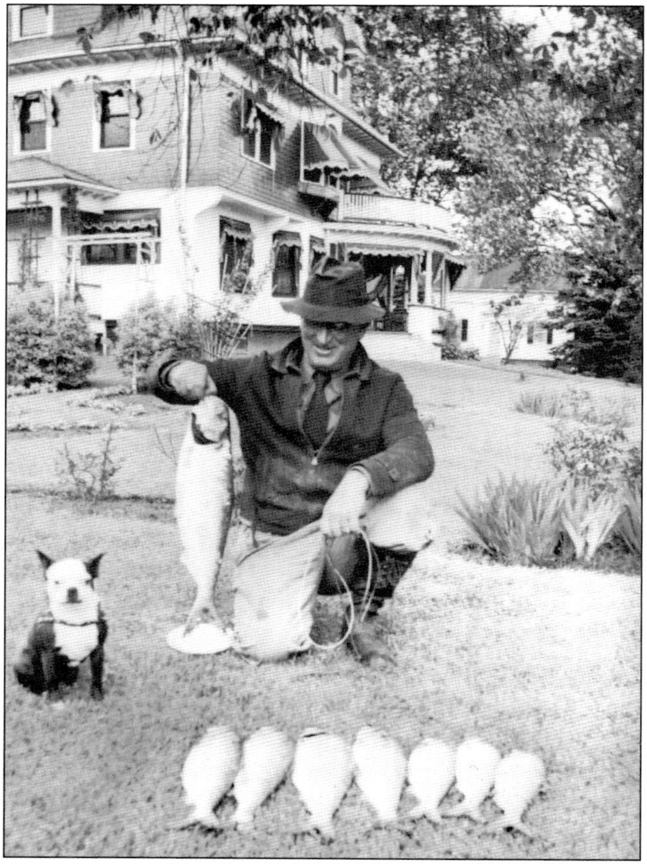

Born in 1881, Irving D. Woodworth, shown here with his catch of the day, was a prosperous tobacco grower. A side street in this neighborhood bears his family name. In preparation for building his grand, new home (pictured) on the corner of Burbank Avenue and River Boulevard, the existing Sperry house was moved up the street near Sullivan's warehouse. The new house had a third-floor ballroom where the Woodworths entertained, holding galas complete with hired bands and dancing. (Courtesy Elaine Alexopoulos Ford.)

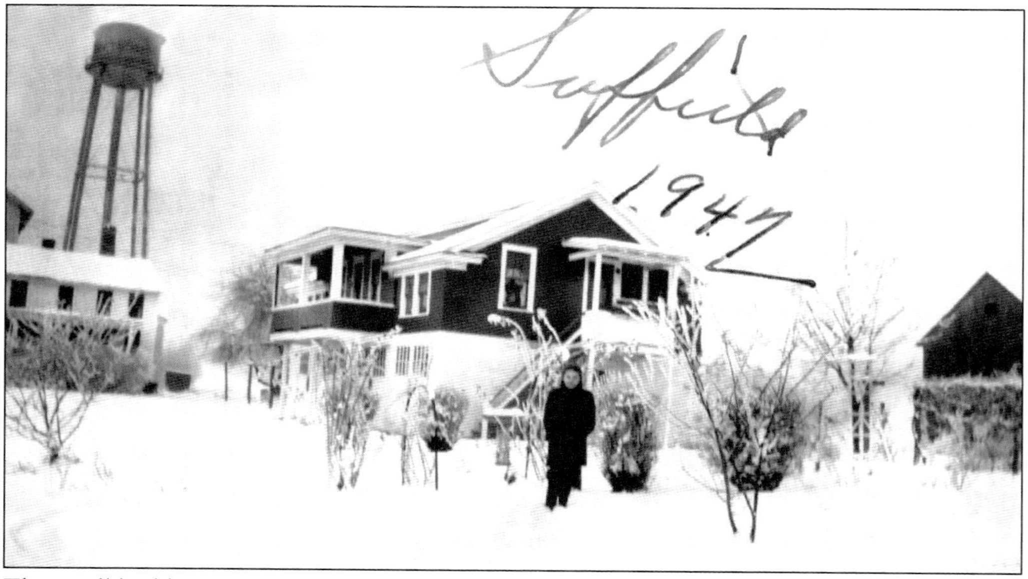

The small building at the far left is the old Sperry house (dated 1835), moved to make room for Irving Woodworth's mansion. His daughter Marlene stands before the family's carriage house, complete with chauffeur living-quarters upstairs. It was sold separately as a home to Hank and Doris Grabowski in 1955. (Courtesy Elaine Alexopoulos Ford.)

Five

CURIOSITIES

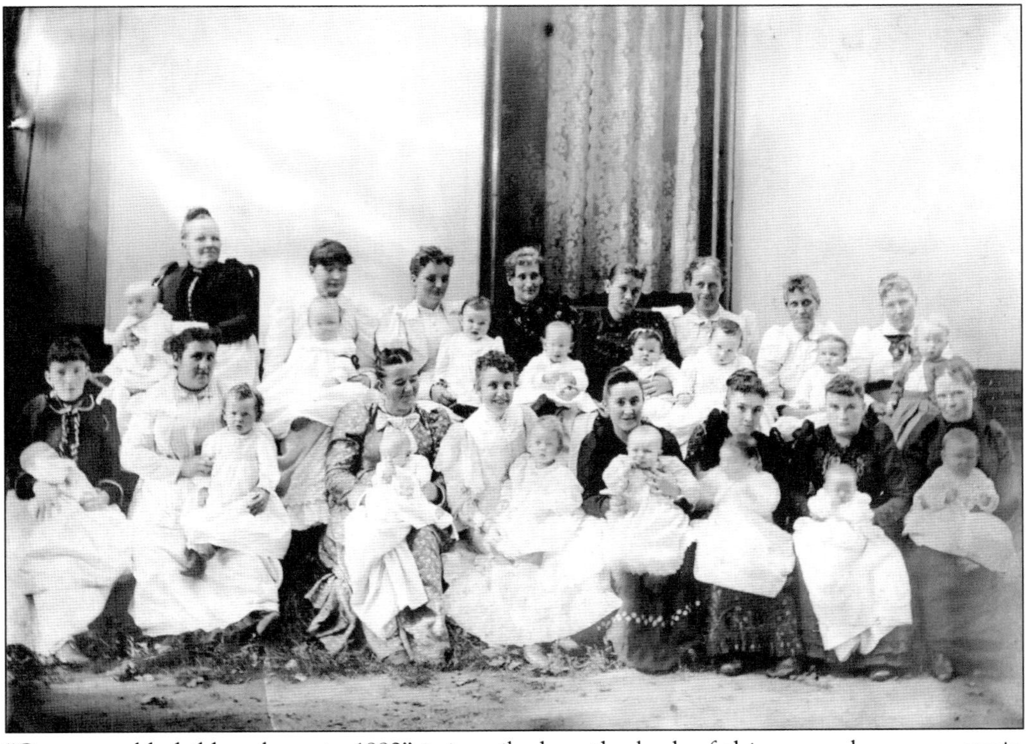

"One-year-old children born in 1892" is inscribed on the back of this unusual group portrait. The woman in white, seated front row center, is Eliza Maud Thrall, wife of Leroy Hamilton Sikes. She holds her baby Maynard Lyman Sikes. This birth year portrait is in the collection of the Sikes family, one of the first Suffield families that settled predominantly in the northeast part of Suffield. (Courtesy Art Sikes.)

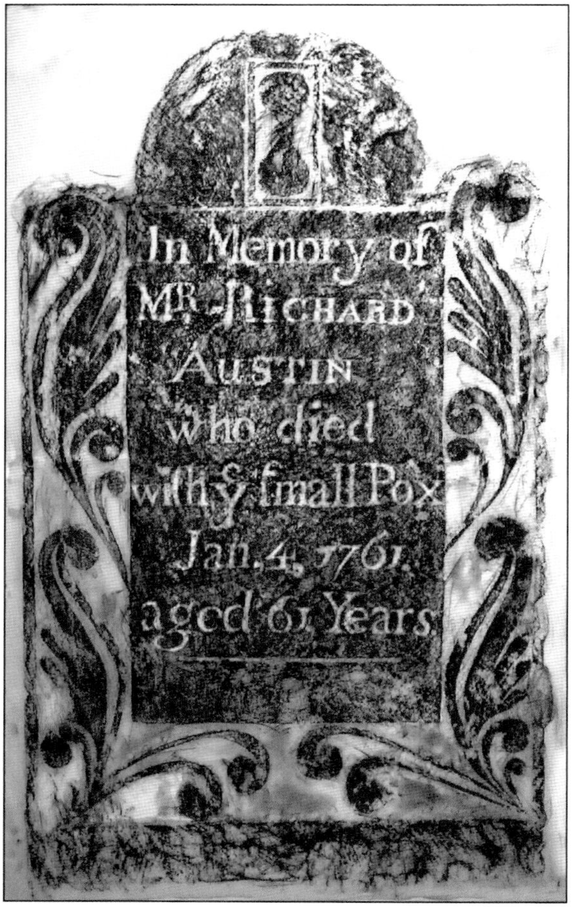

Atop the steep riverbank on River Boulevard is a brownstone marker illustrated in this stone rubbing. It marks the grave of Richard Austin, who died of small pox on January 4, 1761. In Colonial days, people with small pox were isolated in pesthouses and then buried nearby for fear of the disease spreading. Richard Austin's ancestry in New England began in 1638, when an English tailor named Richard immigrated to Massachusetts. His son Anthony settled in Suffield on Feather Street, later called East Street, and had seven children. He was the first town clerk, a schoolteacher, farmer, selectman, and captain in the foot company militia. This grave is of the fourth Richard Austin, a farmer, part-time carpenter, and the uncle and great-uncle of the most prominent Austin family members, Moses and his son Stephen. They were leading figures in the settlement of Texas. Austin, the capital of Texas, is named for Stephen. (Left, courtesy Laurie Tavino; below, courtesy Ray Pioggia.)

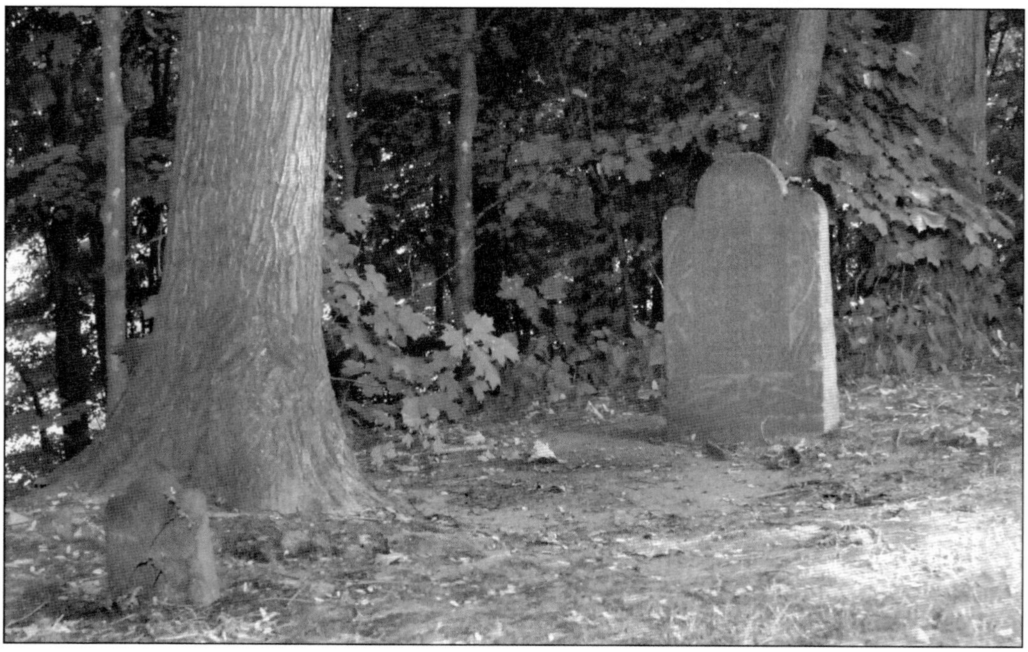

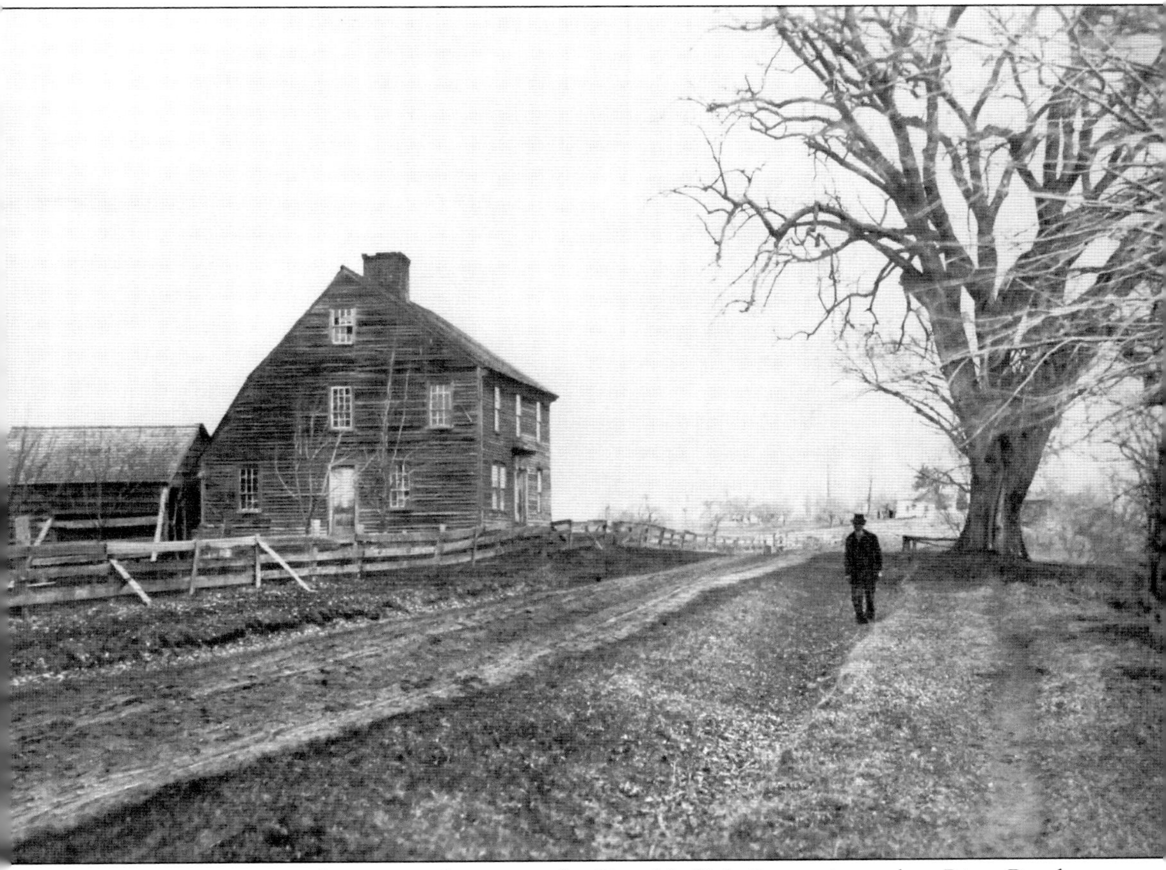

This enormous, noteworthy tree was known as the Trumble Oak. It was situated on River Road, currently called River Boulevard. The Suffield Trumble family was connected to Jonathan Trumbull (1710–1785), a Connecticut colony royal governor and first governor of the state, and reportedly the tree was planted by him. (The early spelling of the name was Trumble, which later changed to Trumbull.) Archival notes from Suffield's Kent Memorial Library identify it as "The Orrin Parker Place, possibly a very old house built by John Pengilley the ferryman—or perhaps built later by John Trumble. Shows the Trumble Oak stood on site of the erstwhile Dildilian place on River Road." The house in the photograph was built around 1776 on what is presently 1007 River Boulevard. Records state that the tree was cut down in 1910. Several neighbors have childhood recollections of a wooden sign that marked the site of the Pengilley Ferry at approximately this spot. On the 1882 map drawn by H. S. Sheldon of the first settlers house lots 1671–1684, there is written "Ferry 1691" across from John Pengilley's lot. Records show that John Pengilley was granted 60 acres in 1678. He died in 1735. (Courtesy KML.)

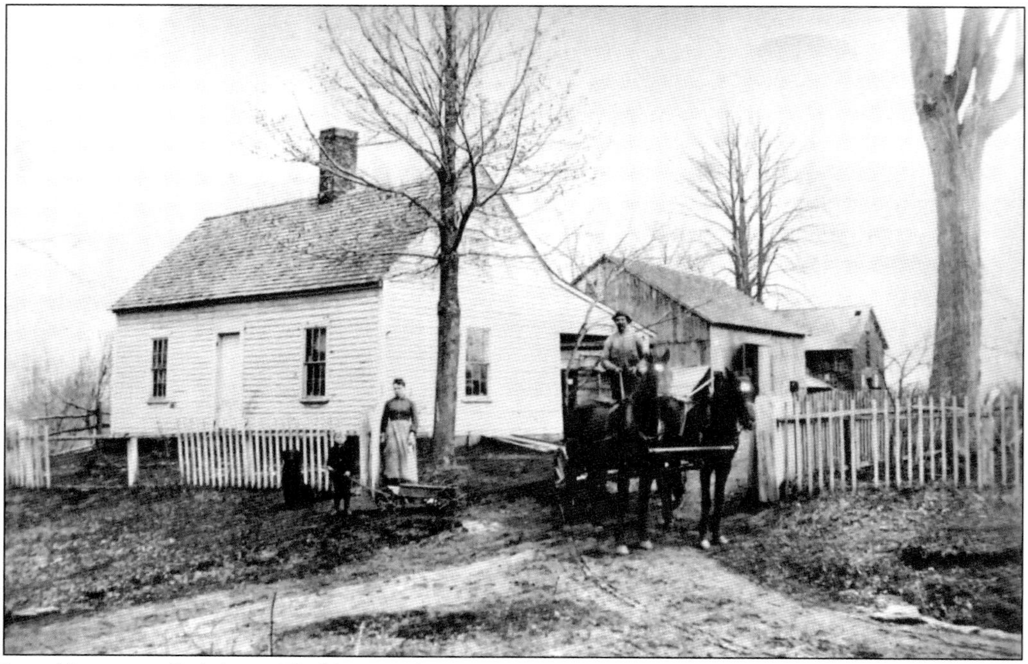

Local historian Delphina Clark's records state "Here Snow (Sephaniah) built the little house now standing on the bank of Deep Brook. It is a quaint little house but unfortunately is in a condition that will probably prevent its repair. It is now used for storage purposes. Fortunately we have a good picture of it taken some 75 or 80 years ago [about 1870]." It is gone now. (Courtesy KML.)

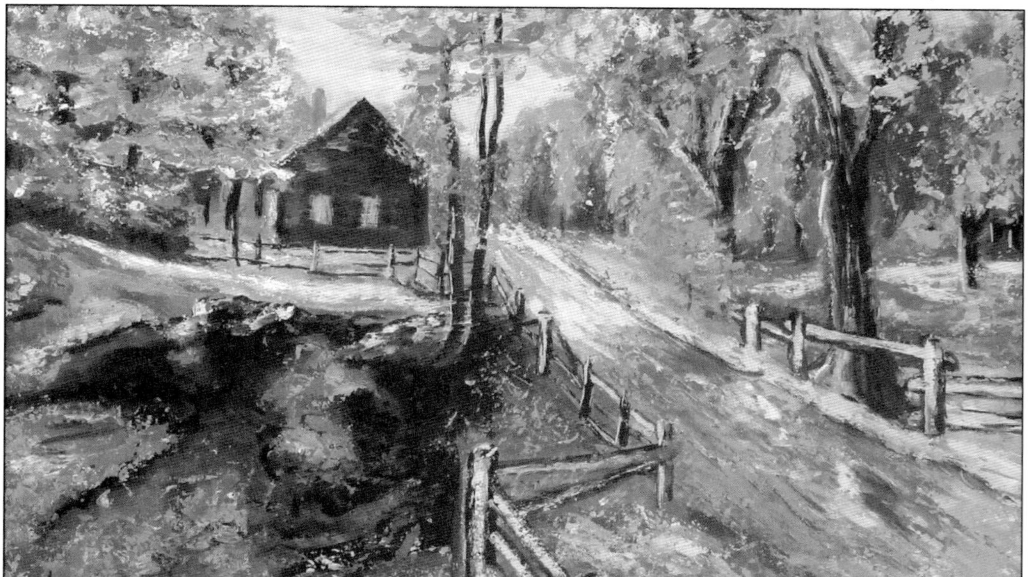

The deep curve in what was called River Road cradled several old Suffield homes over the ages. There is something appealing about these old, weathered buildings and shady brook that compels an artist to capture the scene. Availability of water is probably what encouraged early families to settle here. During the search for information, several artistic renderings surfaced of the setting of Sephaniah Snow's home. Artist Shirley Lane painted this scene around 1973. (Courtesy Pat Rippish.)

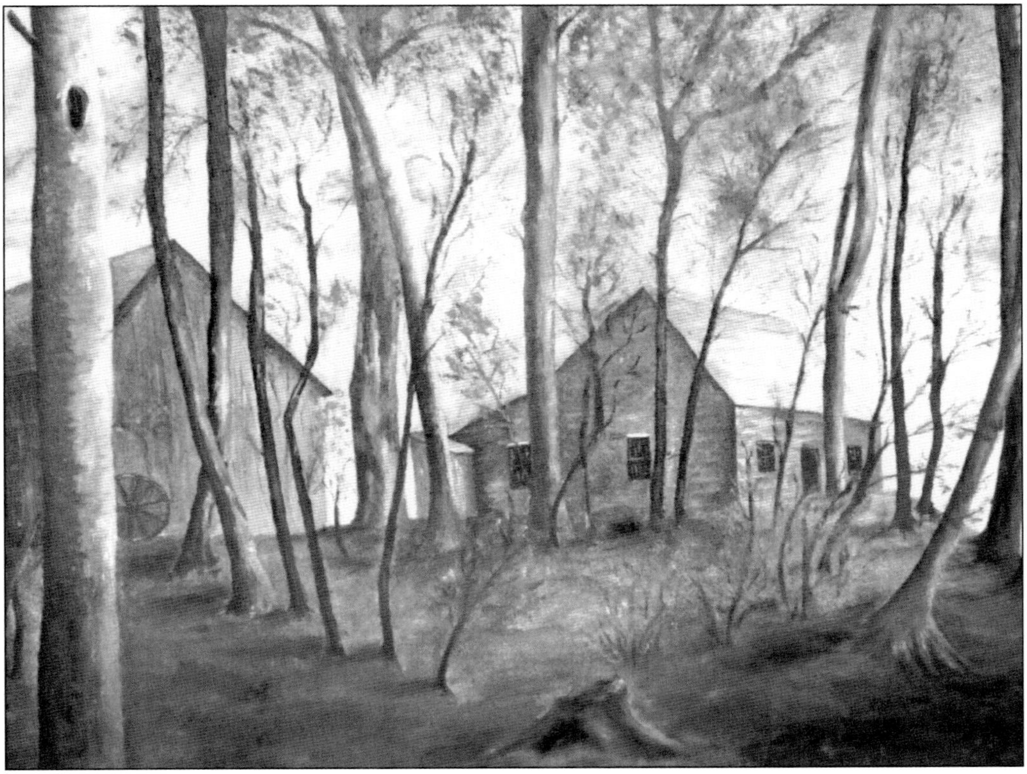

A 1960s painting of the same house depicts quaint details such as the small outhouse to the left of the home and a wagon wheel leaning against the barn. A covered well stood behind the house with a tin cup attached to its thin chain. The interior of the house was a single room with a large, open fireplace and one room above. All that remains now is the foundation. (Courtesy Jo Tavino Zajchowski.)

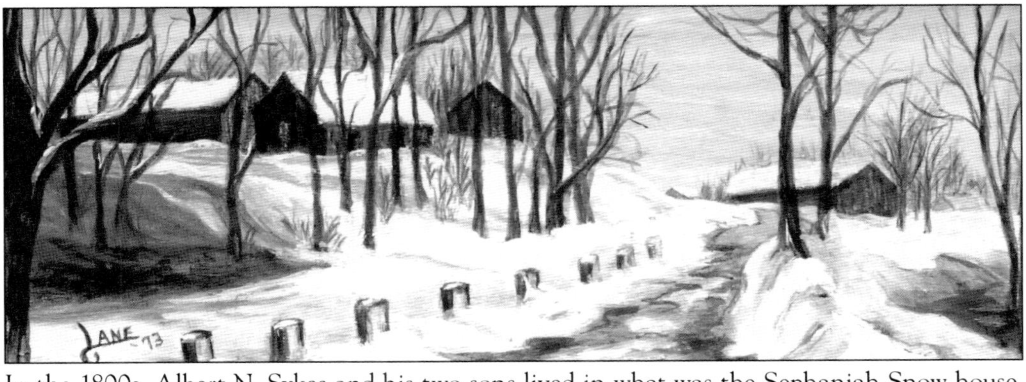

In the 1800s, Albert N. Sykes and his two sons lived in what was the Sephaniah Snow house. His occupation is listed as farmer, but on the 1860 census, he is listed as a "Box Maker." An 1869 map identifies the property of A. N. Sykes as a "shop." This was a water-powered cigar-box shop. It was later moved from its original site and used as a tobacco warehouse. Still standing today, it is visible at the far center in this 1973 oil painting by Shirley Lane. (Courtesy Pat Rippish.)

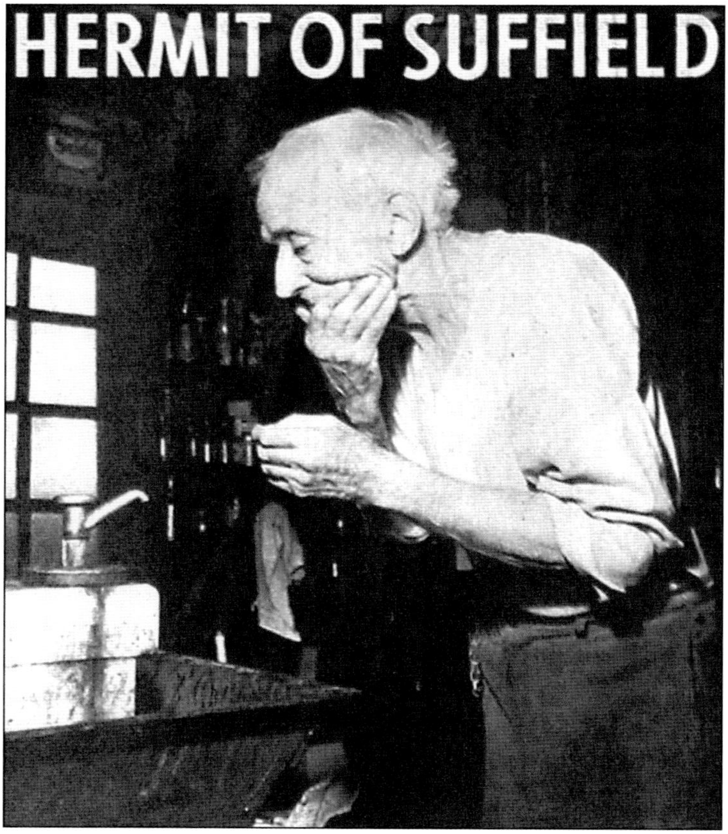

Leslie C. Adams was an "old Yankee genius," an inventor who could fix just about anything. He built a little house on River Road, furnished it with a hand-made lathe and some tools and earned a living by doing mechanical repairs. Leslie also worked at Indian Motocycle Company of Springfield and serviced the city's Campanile for years. Reportedly he was not recognized or compensated for contributing valuable mechanical innovations. For this reason, he became a recluse and was referred to by locals as "the Hermit." (Courtesy Springfield Republican.)

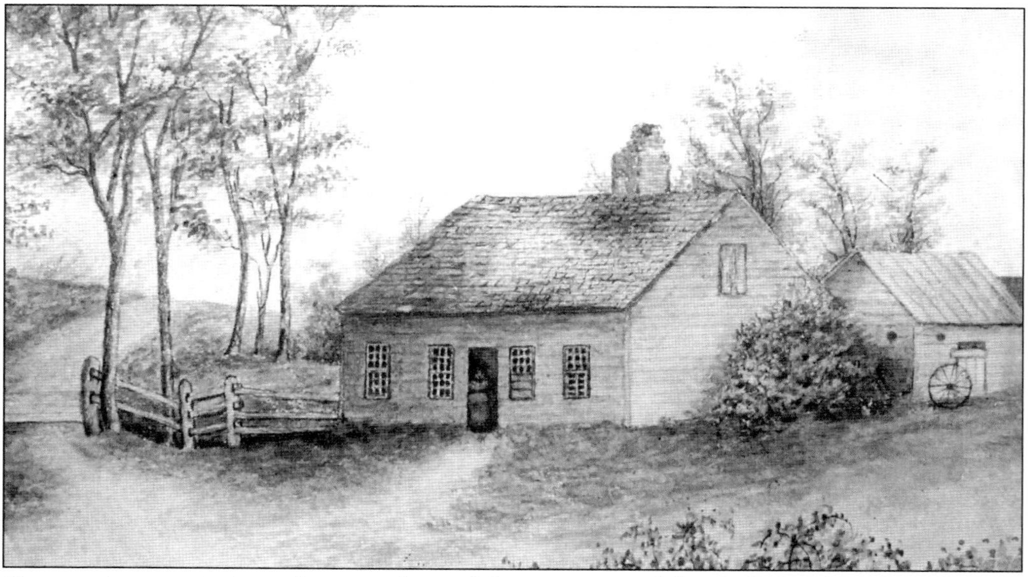

Once again, an artistic rendering surfaces of this same curved dip in the road near Deep Brook. Suffield archives have no photographs of this dwelling but historian Delphina Clark wrote "House which stood where Leslie Adams place is. Built by Silas Holcomb before 1815—Later home of Hiram K. Gambel. River Road." When Leslie built his humble abode he used a few things from the old house, such as windows. (Courtesy KML.)

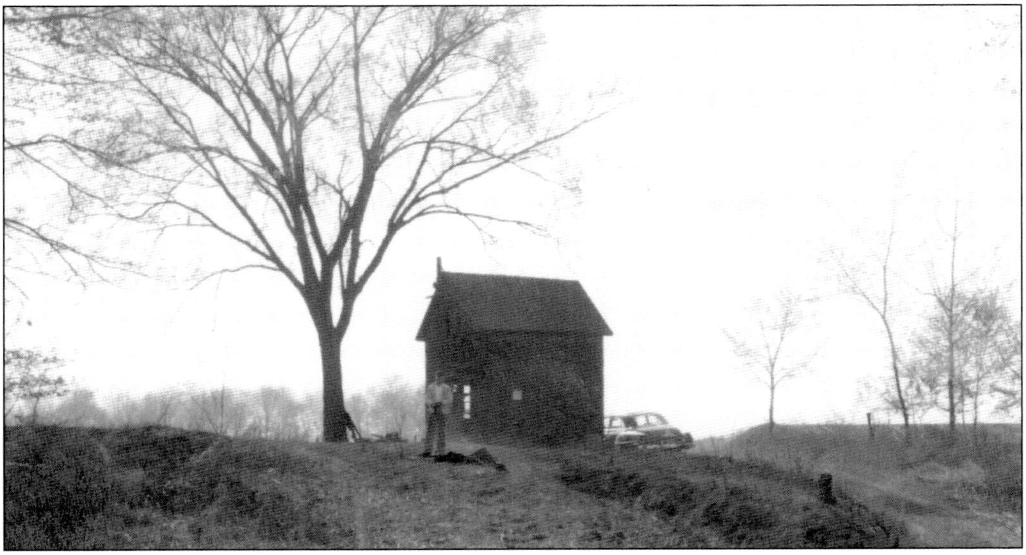

Sam and Elizabeth Frangiamore photographed the Hermit's tiny cabin after purchasing the property in the 1950s. Downstairs a single room served as Leslie's workshop. It contained an old sink and a soda dispenser holding two quarts of water, which he used daily for cooking and washing. Leslie used a rope and pulley to reach a small loft upstairs where he slept. The same rope dropped a blanket on him when he went to bed. (Courtesy Pat Rippish.)

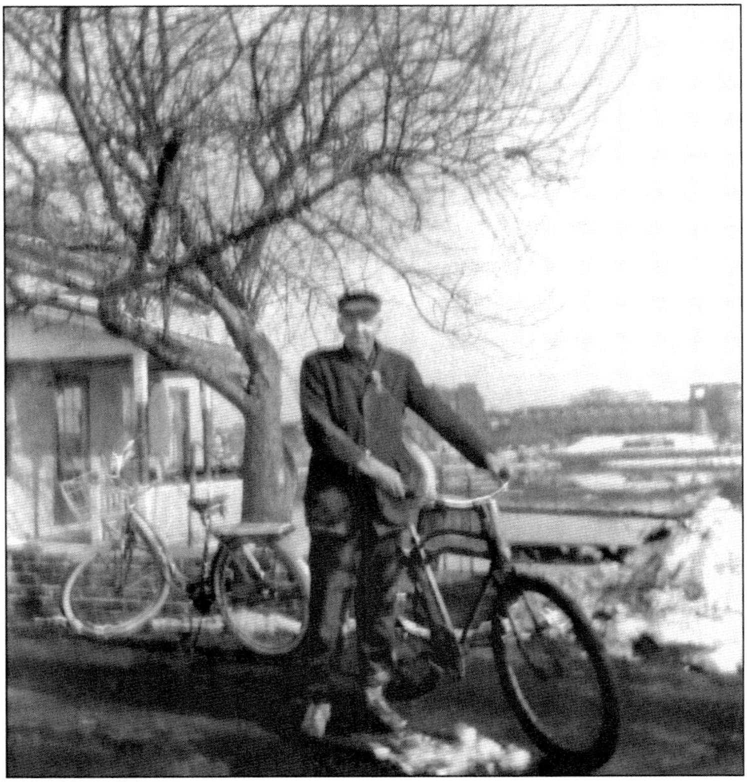

The Hermit is here with his bike in front of Gus Alexopoulos's house. A view of the Connecticut River and Thompsonville is in the background. Leslie always wore clips on his pants when riding his bike-combo-motorcycle for transportation. After World War II, servicemen gave him their heavy pants and uniforms to wear. (Courtesy Elaine Alexopoulos Ford.)

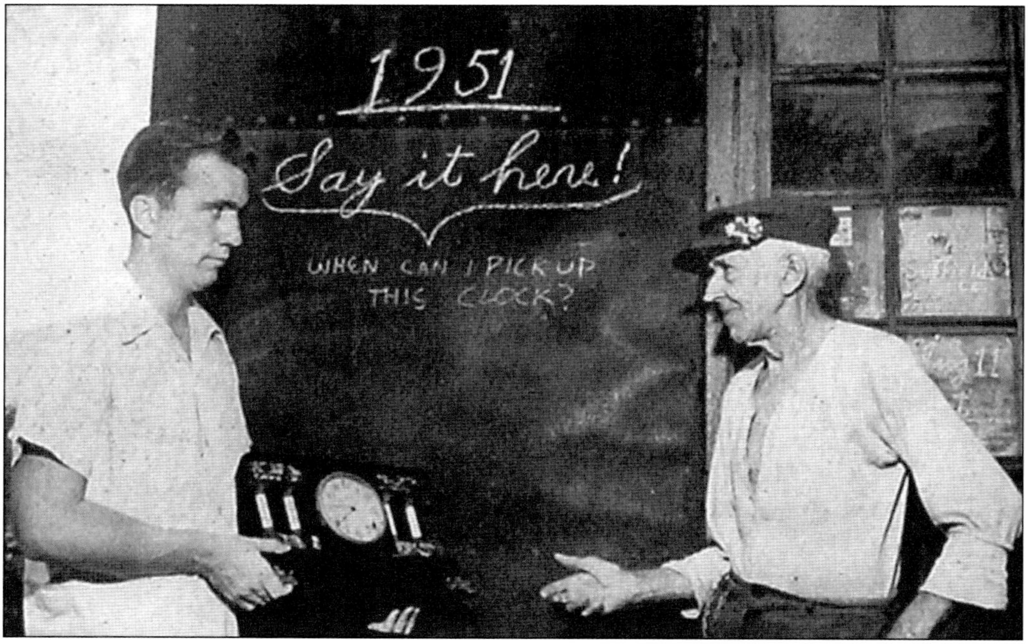

Being deaf, Leslie Adams arranged a light to alert him when someone was at the door. People dropped off assorted appliances for repair, writing instructions or questions on the wall of his workshop home. Leslie was an intelligent and ingenious man. The problem was that once he fixed something, the parts could not be replaced because he made his own. (Courtesy Springfield Republican.)

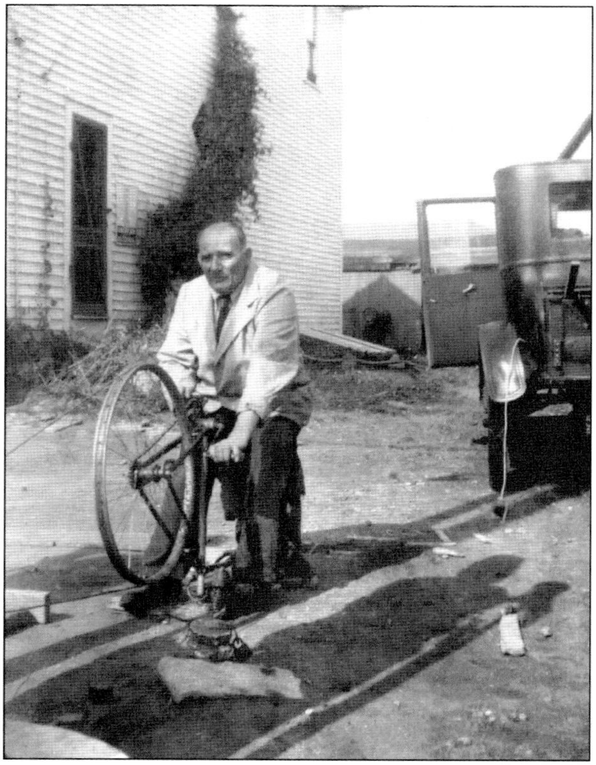

For two weeks after the Hurricane of 1938, Theodore Papafil, owner of Theodore's General Store on Thompsonville Road had no power to work his gasoline pumps. Leslie came by and after hearing what was wrong, said "We can fix that." Turning a bicycle upside down, he devised an arm-powered pump that dispensed gasoline when the pedals were turned. This photograph shows Theodore seated on Leslie's invention. (Courtesy Rookey family.)

Another of Leslie Adams's neighborhood inventions includes a foot-powered sewing machine rigged up to wind wire from large spools onto smaller ones. It did the job in seconds for the Suffield Evergreen Company, owned by Gus Alexopoulos. This invention saved time and money and was used continually for years. Leslie is pictured here with a hand truck behind the Alexopoulos home along the Connecticut River bank. (Courtesy Alexopoulos family.)

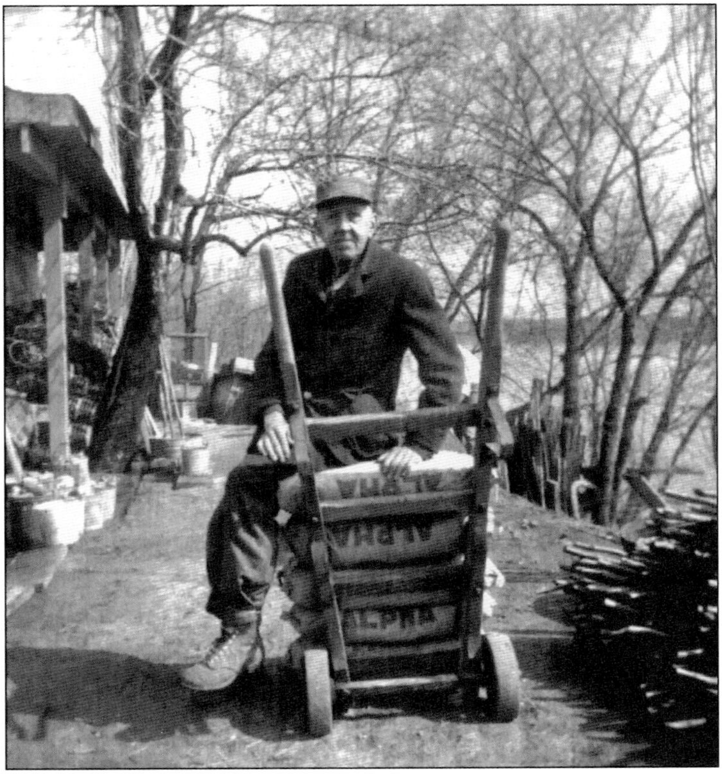

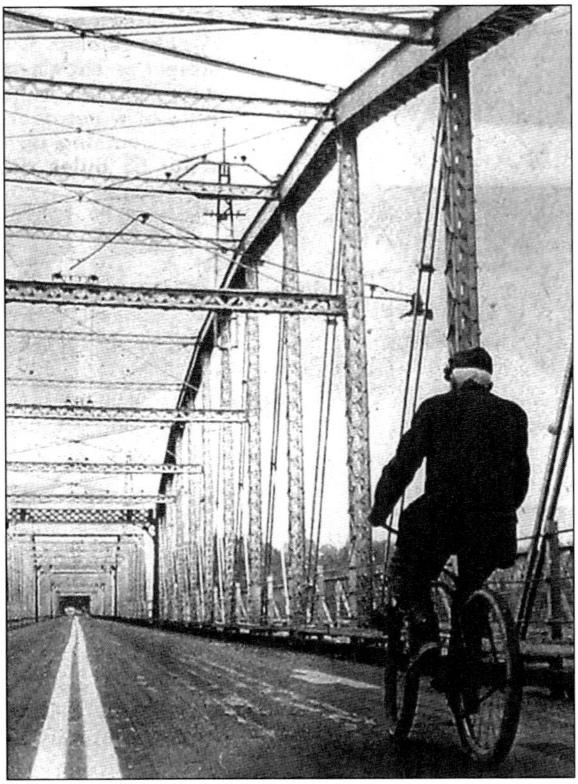

Although a loner, Leslie was often friendly if one dropped by to see him, and he was always kind to children. Found ailing in his little cabin in 1957, he was brought to a hospital but soon passed away. A stone marks his grave behind the First Congregational Church in Suffield. A descendant of a long line of American Yankees, Leslie Adams once said "I'm a genuine American, nothing else." (Courtesy Springfield Republican.)

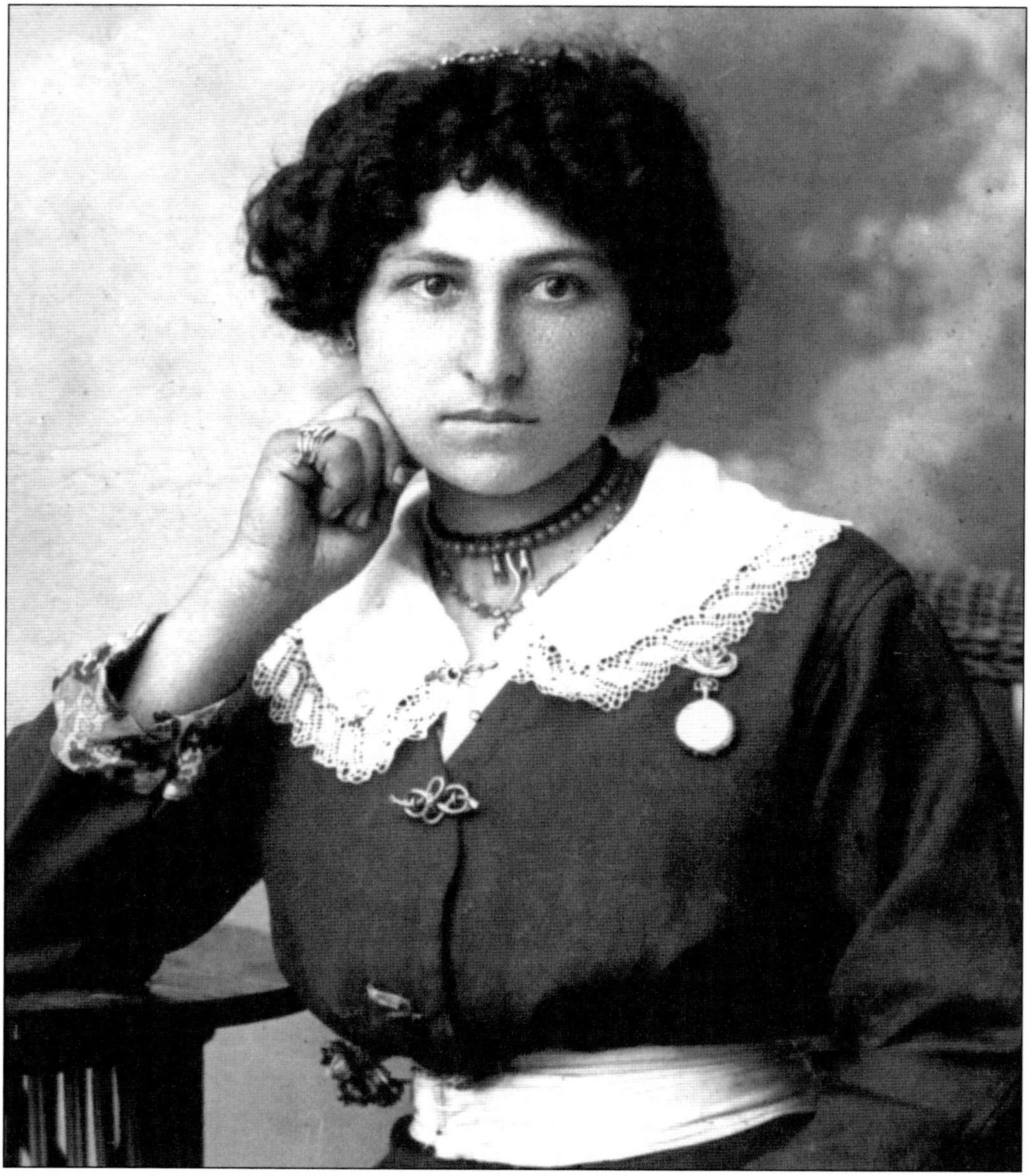

Newly arrived immigrants brought not only their religions and recipes across the Atlantic but their folklore and superstitions as well. Interpretations of symbolic dreams and omens, handed down from ancient times, were a reality to many. Belief in the evil eye is a long-standing one in many parts of the world. Basically it is believed to be caused by envy. Expelling the evil eye is still a common practice in small towns of the Mediterranean region of Europe. One should remember that many of these uprooted immigrant families were from isolated towns with sparse communication with the outside world, and they had little formal education. Note the gold hands and horn on the necklace in the photograph of Matilda Conte. These charms were worn for protection. Thompsonville's abundance of jobs lured Matilda and her husband, Lorenzo, from southern Italy in the early 1900s. They both found employment at the carpet mill. Missing their homeland, the Contes returned to Italy. Later their two children immigrated back to the United States and raised their families here, leaving all of Matilda and Lorenzo's descendants living in America and none in Italy. (Courtesy Tavino family.)

Some people guided their lives and activities, be it planting seeds or making wine, by the phases of the moon. Gus Alexopoulos, in this 1945 photograph, had his own remedies for skin ailments. At a certain phase of the moon he would softly recite in Greek while rubbing the afflicted area with soil. Those who had this done claim their ailments disappeared. In the photograph, Gus is returning from Thompsonville to his home on River Boulevard. (Courtesy Elaine Alexopoulos Ford.)

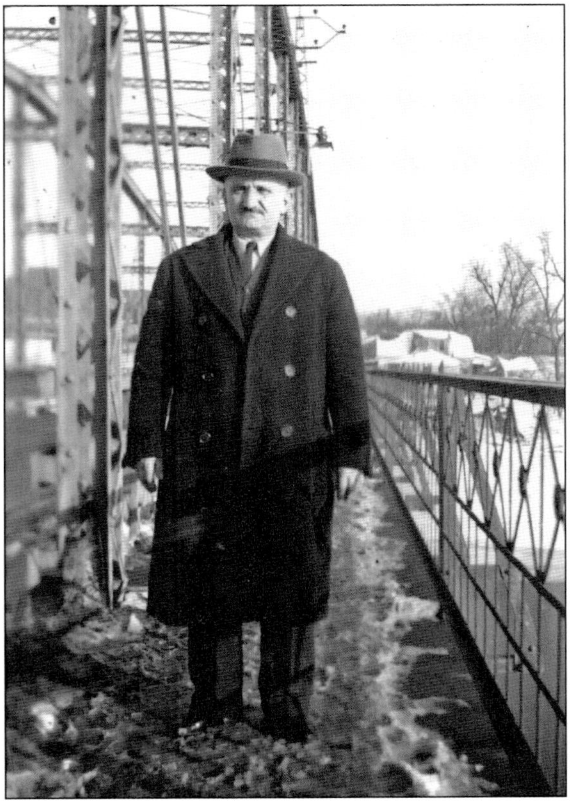

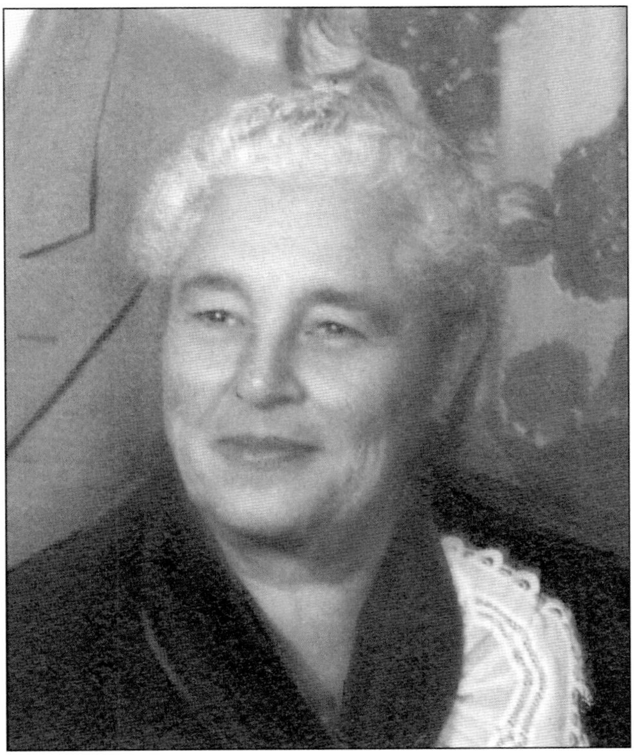

Anna Cardorapoli Romano, born in Italy, brought a wealth of medicinal, herbal folklore to her adopted country. People called on her for a variety of ailments. Some of Anna's most commonly sought-after treatments were poultices and compresses to prevent or cure infections. The remedies that she prepared were from old-world herbal recipes and practices. Unfortunately her knowledge, never documented, has been lost. (Courtesy Louise Romano Sarno.)

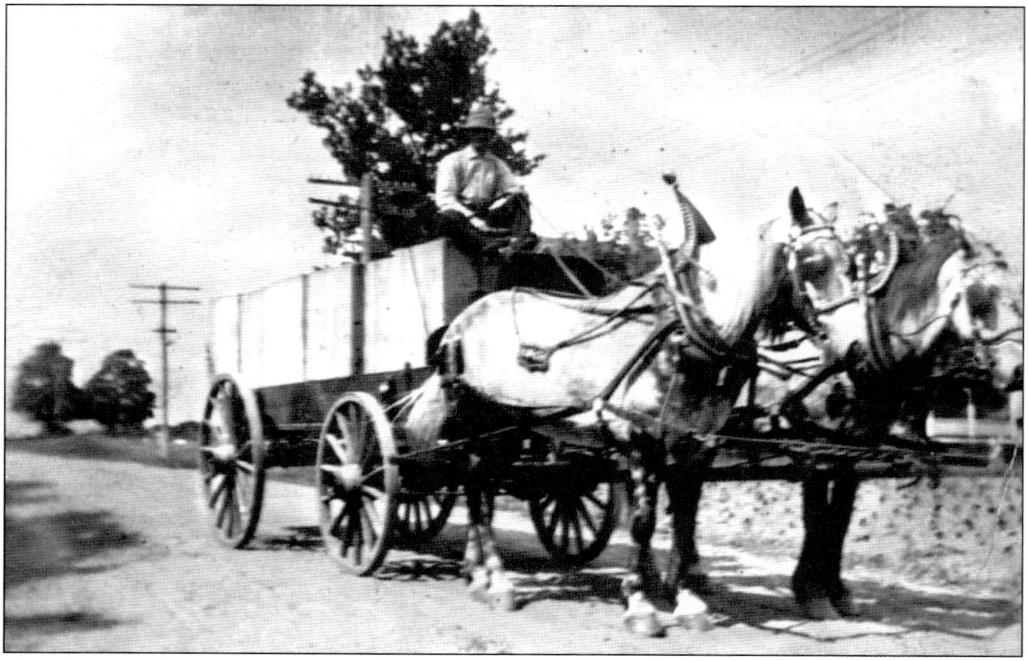

East Street, a dirt road once called Feather Street, rose steeply just north of the present access road to the Suffield-Enfield Bridge. Locals called it Mile Hill. In the 1920s when the road was paved, the hill was leveled substantially. It also became known as Sullivan's Hill because it ran adjacent to Sullivan's tobacco farm. This photograph shows John Conley driving a team and wagon on the hill's peak. (Courtesy Sullivan family.)

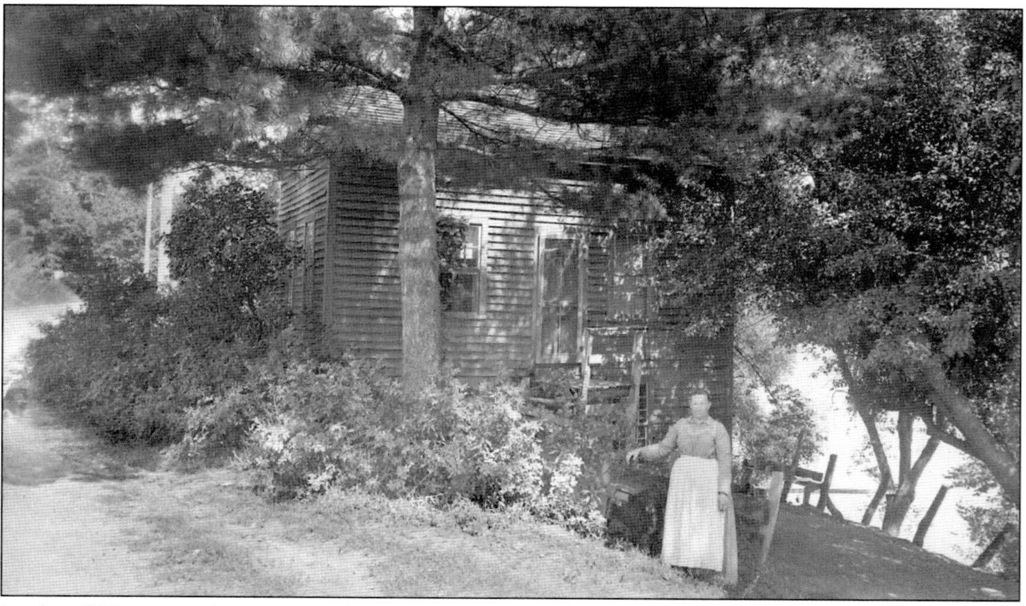

In the 1990s, a gentleman visited 1060 River Boulevard and told the owners, the Flasinskis, that as a child he visited Woodworth family relatives here. He gave the Flasinskis photographs of their home. Town hall records show that Lyman Woodworth owned this house at the beginning of the 19th century. Civil War military records document his son Milton's service in the 6th Regiment of the Connecticut Infantry. (Courtesy Ashfield Historical Society.)

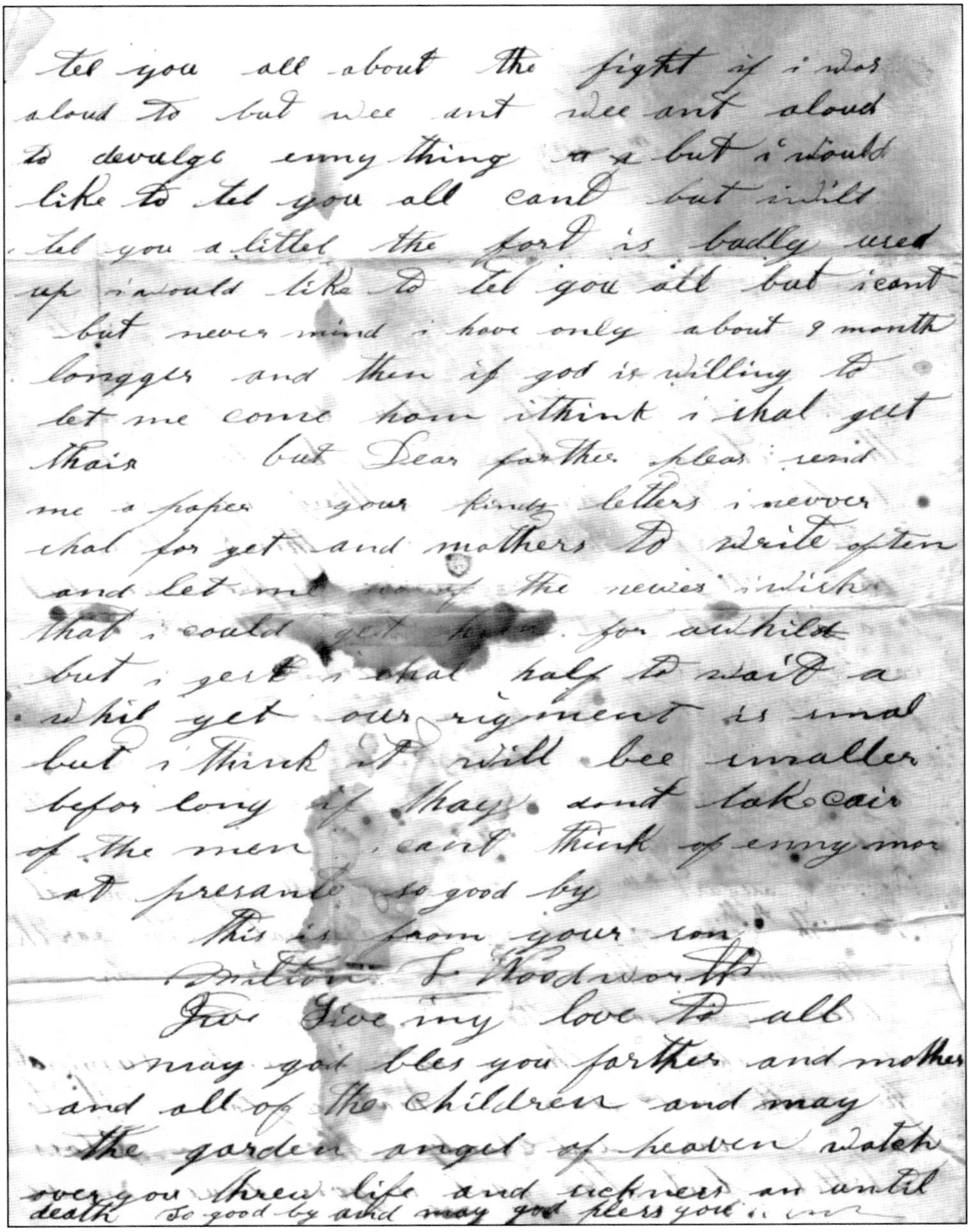
tel you all about the fight if i was
aloud to but wee ant wee ant aloud
to develge enny thing but i would
like to tel you all cant but i will
tel you a littel the fort is badly used
up i would like to tel you all but icant
but never mind i have only about 9 month
longger and then if god is willing to
let me come hom ithink i shal get
thair but Dear farther pleas send
me a paper your kindy letters i never
shal for get and mothers to write often
and let me [illegible] the newes i wish
that i could get [illegible]. for awhilst
but i get i shal half to wait a
whil yet our rigement is smal
but i think it will bee smaller
befor long if thay dont take cair
of the men i cant think of enny mor
at presance so good by
This is from your son
Milton L Woodworth
[illegible] Give my love to all
may god bles you farther and mother
and all of the children and may
the garden angel of heaven watch
over you threw life and sickness an until
death So good by and may god bless you [illegible]

During renovations the Flasinskis found this Civil War letter behind a wall. Portions read "General Hospital Hilton Head August 25, 1863 Dear father and mother . . . I thought I would rite and let you now how i am geting along i begin to feal a littel bettar now the weather is a littel coller . . . it is vary unhealthy hear at presance for the yaler fever . . . it wil take the men off like a whirlwine . . . it is a bad deases down in this part of the country . . . it raind all night mingal it with the voice of god and iluminated the earth with the fire of heaven [thunder and lightning] and the wind blew in a gail the rain calm down in a drivin heat . . . tel you all about the fight if i was aloud to but wee ant . . . aloud to devulge ennything . . . our rigement is smal but i think it will bee smaller . . . if thay dont take cair of the men . . . this is from your son Milton L. Woodworth . . . may god bles you . . . and all of the children and may the garden angel of heaven watch over you." (Courtesy Alice Flasinski.)

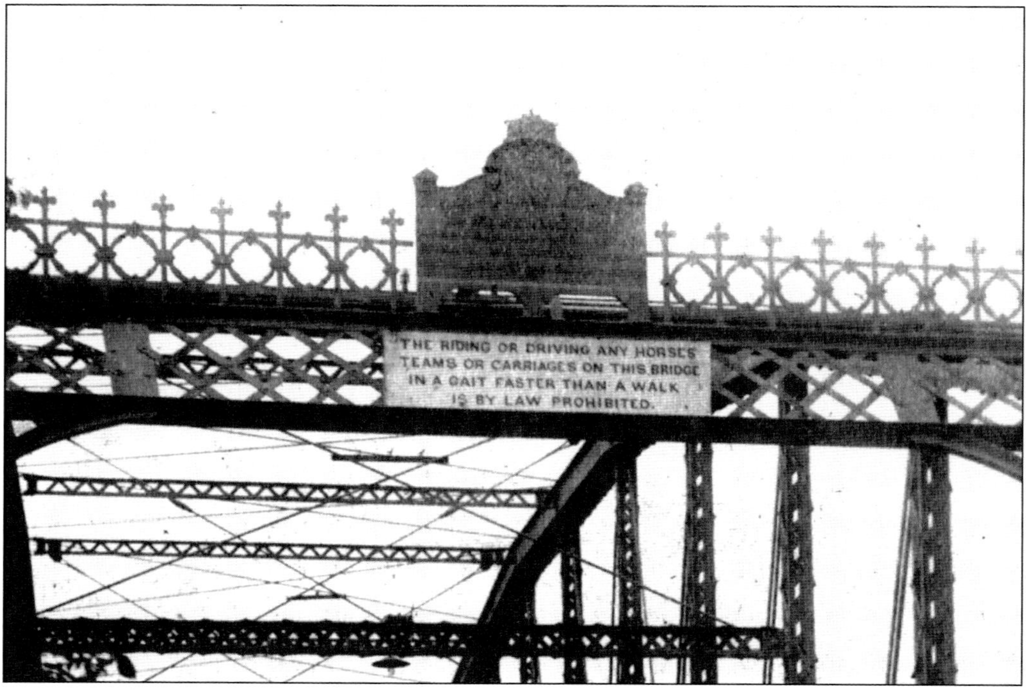

Crowning the east entrance of the Thompsonville-Suffield Bridge was an iron sign that read "1892, Built by the Berlin Iron Bridge Co., East Berlin, Conn., The Suffield & Thompsonville Bridge Co., Edward S. Shaw, Consulting Engineer, O.M. Weand, Contractor For Substructure." When the bridge was demolished in 1971, the Enfield Historical Society recovered their plaque but the Suffield sign went missing. (Courtesy Bob Sullivan.)

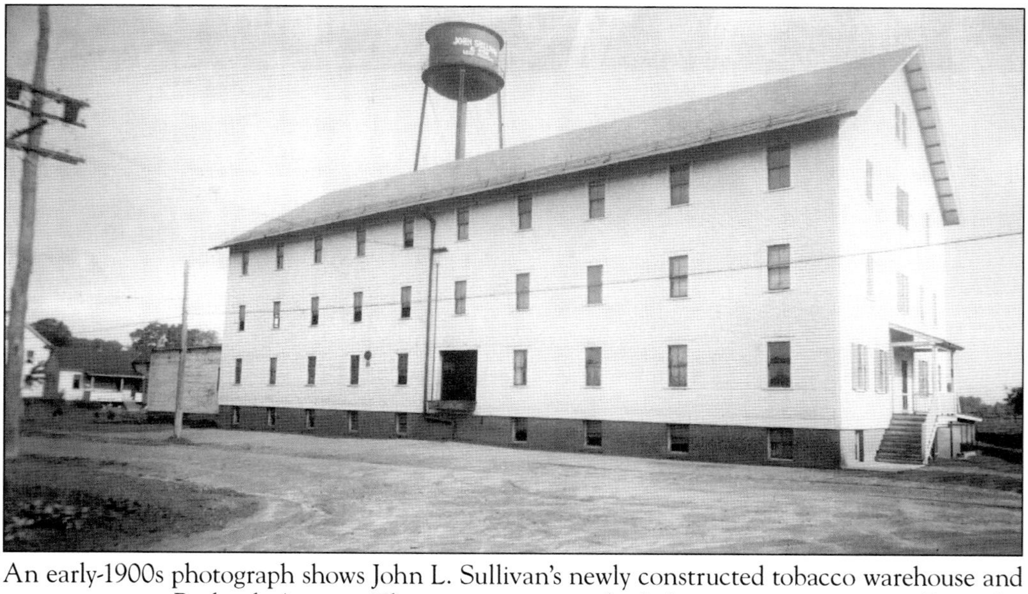

An early-1900s photograph shows John L. Sullivan's newly constructed tobacco warehouse and water tower on Burbank Avenue. The water tower was built for insurance purposes. From the beginning, the storage tank leaked. A crew of men was needed to burn coal beneath it to keep it from freezing in the winter. It was not used for long but served as a local landmark for close to 70 years. (Courtesy Bob Sullivan.)

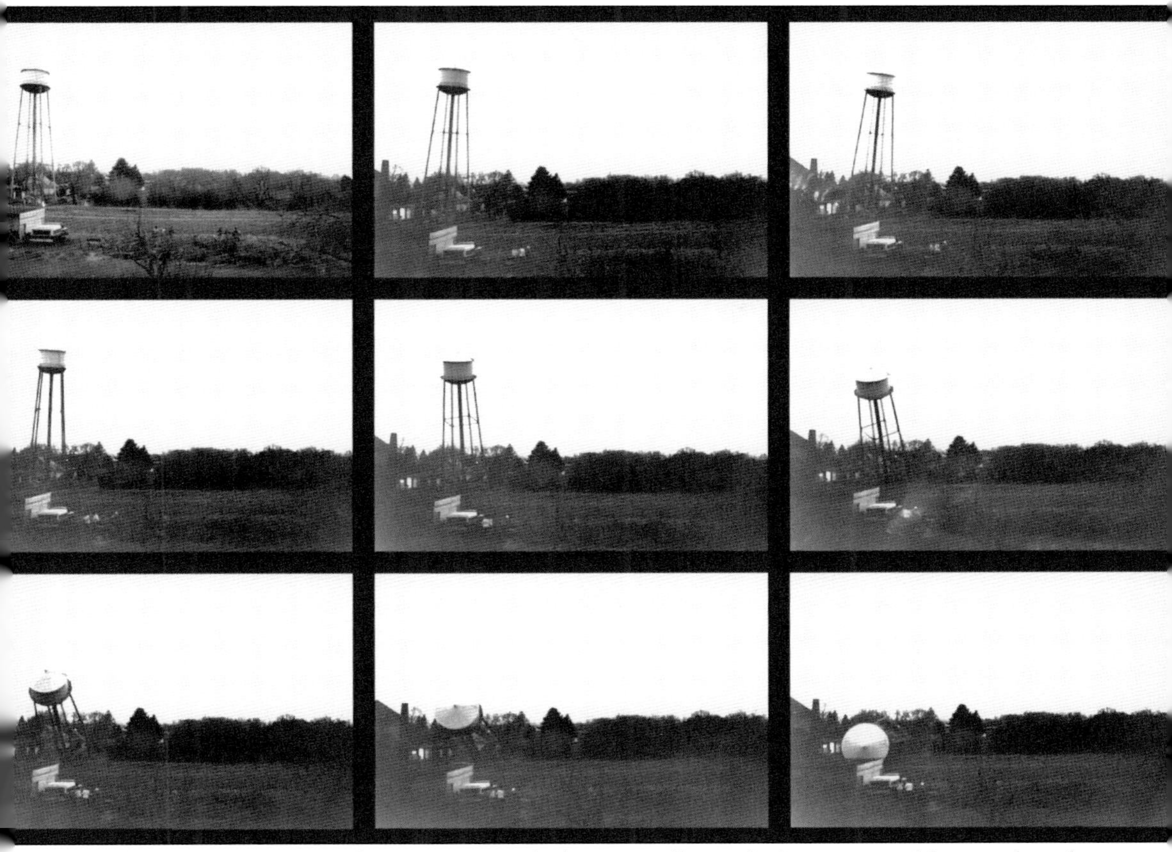

The old water tower comes down. It was 1985 when a small crowd of curious neighbors gathered and kept their distance as workers used blowtorches to cut supports out from under the structure. But the tower did not give way easily. By the time it finally began to weaken, it was nearly dusk. The plan was to have the tower fall directly to the north, away from the warehouse. At first the tower tilted north but then suddenly twisted and fell due east, much to the surprise of all present. Fortunately the building was spared. There were some cheers and applause then a gathering around the wreck with stories and recollections abounding. A favorite was of a group of teenagers back in the early 1970s that dared each other to climb all the way up the tower and touch the pinnacle. Imagine their terror when they reached the top and began sliding on the coating that had been applied to resist rain. (Courtesy Ray Pioggia.)

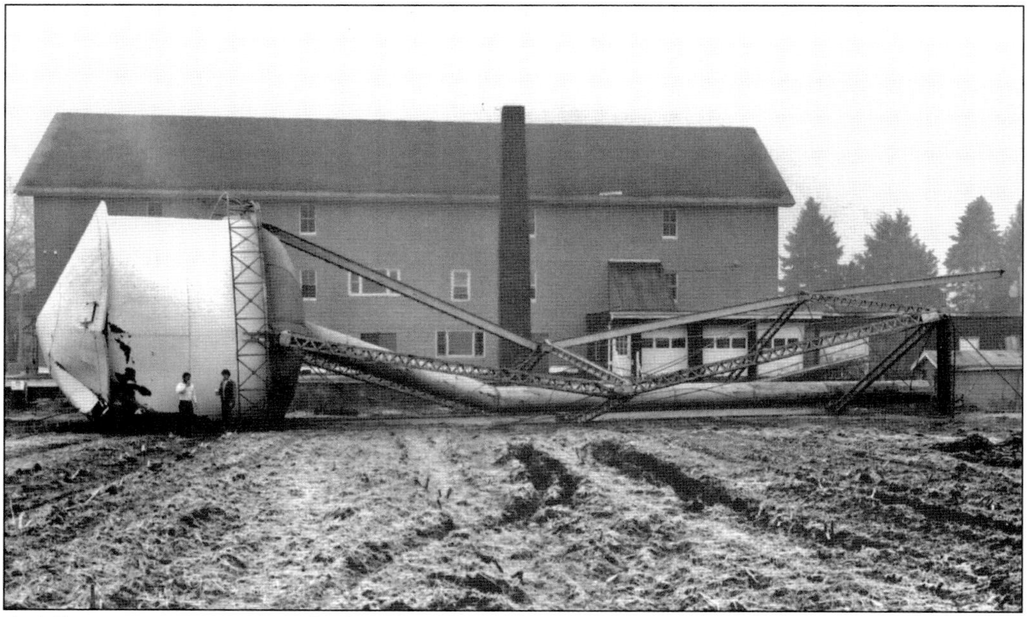

A fallen giant came to mind when neighbors surveyed the scene the following morning. The tower lay crumpled in a bare corn field where a cold mist hung over the frost-covered autumn ground. Both photographs on this page were taken with an old press view camera—the same vintage as the tower. The figures in the photograph give a reference in scale to the size of the tower. (Courtesy Ray Pioggia.)

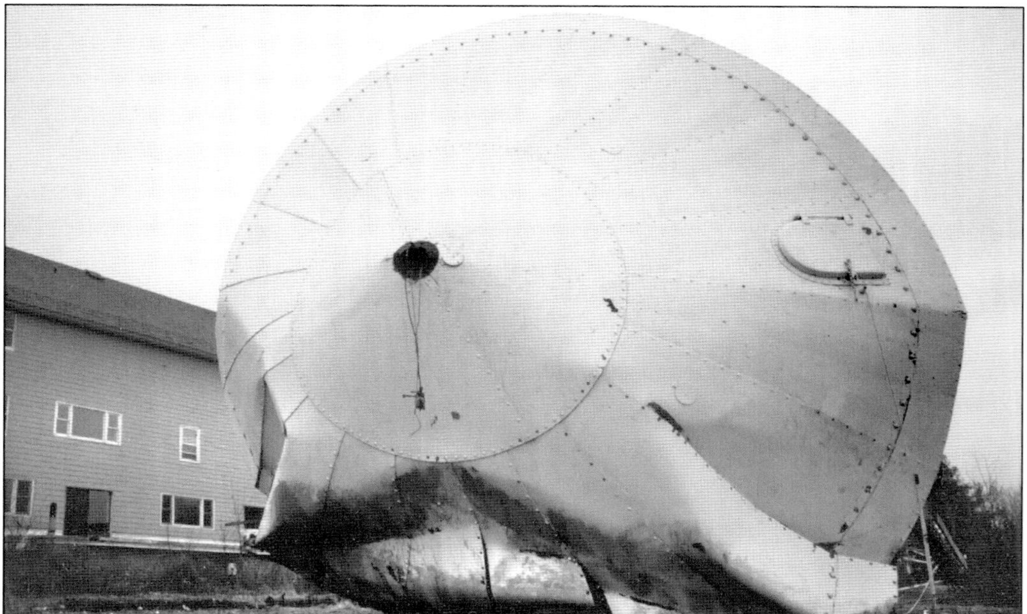

The impact with the partially frozen ground crunched the quarter-inch boilerplate steel like aluminum foil. Its interior condition was remarkably good, as the walls had been protected with a thick, waxy coating. The steel was hauled away and recycled. The pinnacle of the tower, however, found its way to West Suffield and the home of Bob Sullivan, great-grandson of the tower's builder, John L. Sullivan. (Courtesy Ray Pioggia.)

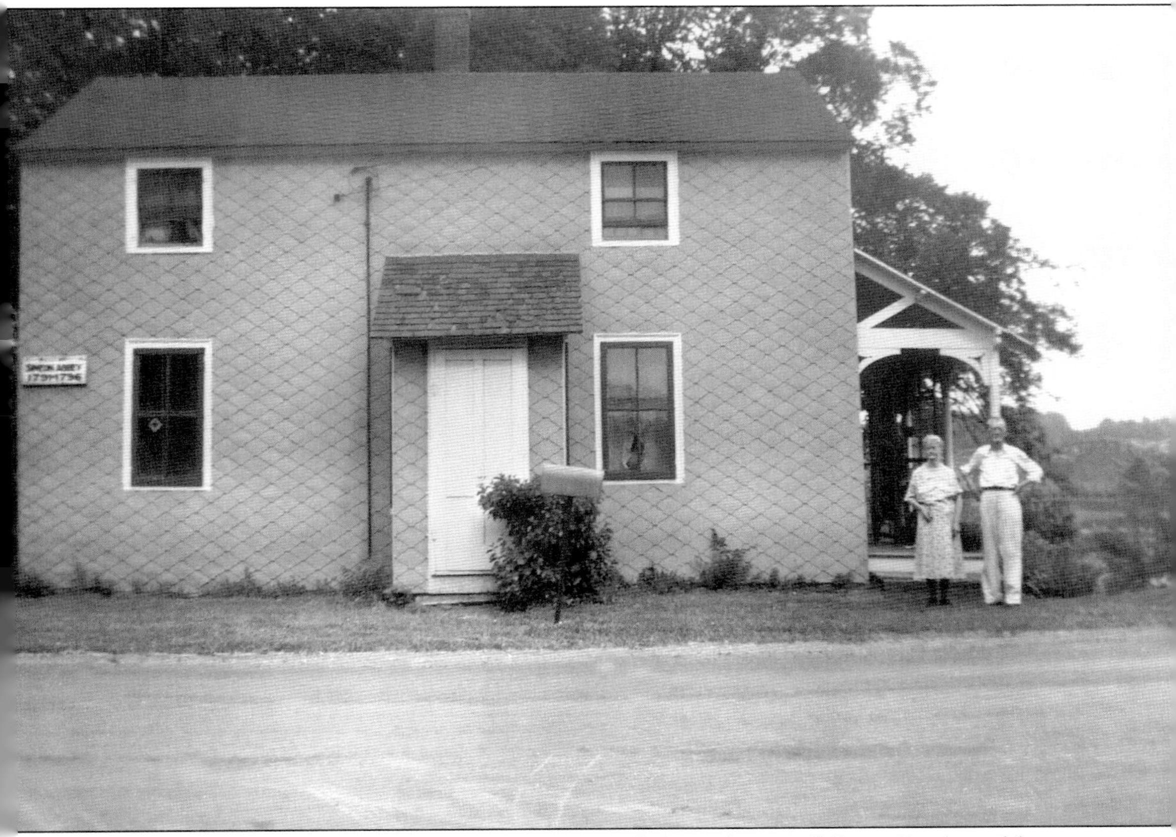

The discovery of an obscure 1930s photograph reveals how this small River Boulevard home looked when the McArtheys owned it. Judging by its present-day appearance with aluminum siding, one would never know that it is one of the oldest continuously used structures in the neighborhood. The sign reads "Simeon Abbey 1791–1796," indicating some uncertainty in the date. In 1791, this quarter-acre property on the riverbank changed hands from Ebenezer King to Simeon Abbey. Simeon was the youngest son of Capt. Thomas Abbey (1731–1811), a prominent Revolutionary War figure in Enfield, known for, among other things, alerting people of the Battle of Lexington and Concord. There is evidence that Simeon used the building as a blacksmith shop. The construction is primitive, consisting of a stone foundation, with sills and floor joists made from hand-hewn timber. (Courtesy Tavino family.)

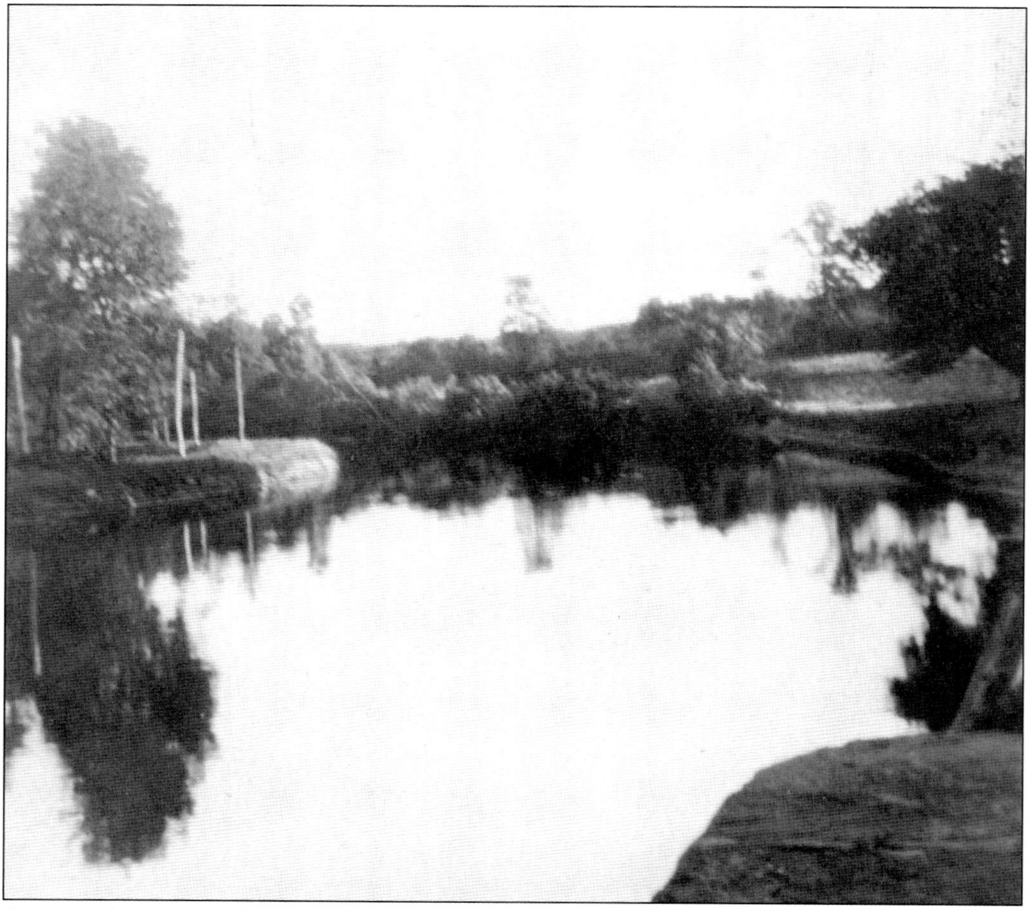

A tranquil view near Stony Brook and the Windsor Locks Canal does not reveal the sweat and blood that went into its construction. In 1827, one of the first Catholic masses was celebrated near the canal for an injured Irish worker named Timothy McMahon. The canal workers' camp was in Pine Meadows (now Windsor Locks), but when Timothy died later that year, he was buried in Suffield, becoming the first Catholic to be documented in Suffield's history. Below in a diary from 1892, John L. Sullivan wrote "coald and windy worck down to foot of the cannal putting in gates to fil the locks with." John L. worked on the canal in his early days and knew almost every inch of it, from the lower locks in Windsor Locks to the head of the canal in Suffield. (Courtesy Sullivan family.)

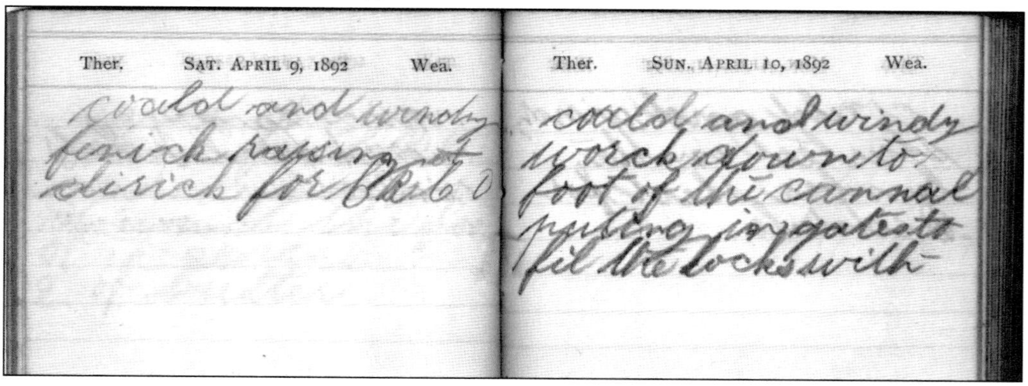

Ther. SAT. APRIL 9, 1892 Wea.

coald and windy

Ther. SUN. APRIL 10, 1892 Wea.

coald and windy
worck down to
foot of the cannal
putting in gates to
fil the locks with

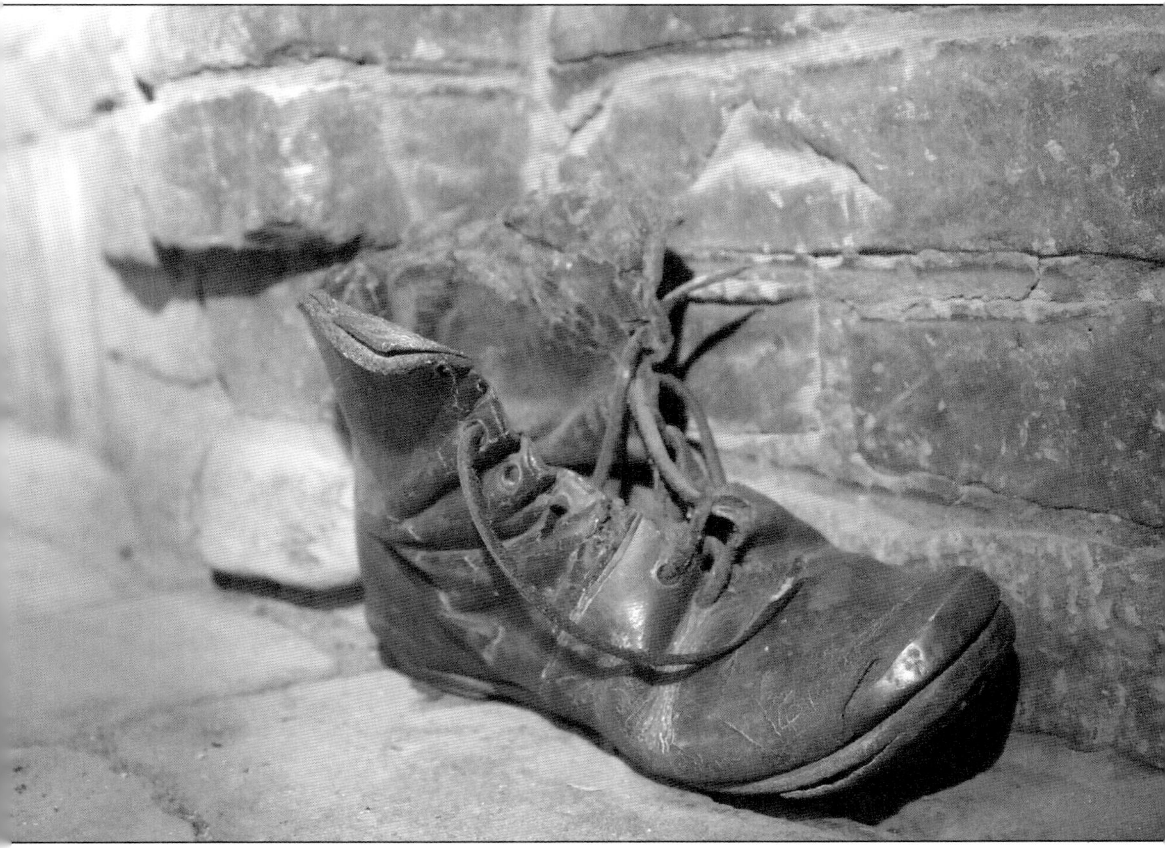

While Frank and Loretta Ruggiero restored their early-1800s East Street home, many collectibles were found behind the lime-and-cattle hair plaster walls, including a baby cradle and a tiger maple chair, along with a sack of antique whiskey bottles. Written in chalk on an attic rafter was "February 3rd 1830, very cold." Most interesting, though, the Ruggieros discovered a "concealment" shoe. This was the antiquated custom of hiding a shoe in a house to ward off harmful spirits. Early European settlers brought the custom to America in the 1600s, yet knowledge of this old tradition is vague. The Northampton Museum in England keeps a catalogue of over 2,000 concealment shoes. It is unknown why almost half of these hidden shoes belonged to children. Most concealment shoes are found hidden around chimneys, walls, and windows and are well worn. Seldom found in pairs, these shoes were often accompanied by other articles, such as toys, spoons, food, coins, old sleigh bells, and even cat bones. This metal-tipped child's boot found by the Ruggieros was hidden in their brick oven. (Courtesy Ruggiero family.)